More Lost Loot

Ghostly New England
Treasure Tales

by Patricia Hughes

Schiffer Publishing

4880 Lower Valley Road, Atgle

Schiffer Books are available at special discounts for bulk purchases for sales promotions or premiums. Special editions, including personalized covers, corporate imprints, and excerpts can be created in large quantities for special needs. For more information contact the publisher:

Published by Schiffer Publishing Ltd.
4880 Lower Valley Road, Atglen, PA 19310
Phone: (610) 593-1777; Fax: (610) 593-2002
E-mail: Info@schifferbooks.com

For the largest selection of fine reference books on this and related subjects, please visit our web site at www.schifferbooks.com
We are always looking for people to write books on new and related subjects. If you have an idea for a book please contact us at the above address.

This book may be purchased from the publisher.
Include $5.00 for shipping.
Please try your bookstore first.
You may write for a free catalog.

In Europe, Schiffer books are distributed by
Bushwood Books
6 Marksbury Ave.
Kew Gardens
Surrey TW9 4JF England
Phone: 44 (0) 20 8392-8585; Fax: 44 (0) 20 8392-9876
E-mail: info@bushwoodbooks.co.uk
Website: www.bushwoodbooks.co.uk

Designed by Danielle D. Farmer
Cover Design by Bruce Waters
Type set in Zapfino Forte LT Pro/!Sketchy Times/New Baskerville BT

ISBN: 978-0-7643-3627-0
Printed in The United States of America

Dedication

This book is dedicated in memory of Richard "Rick" Alvin Hughes. He is a hero in every sense of the word. He is and always will be loved. We miss you.

Acknowledgments

A Special thanks to:

Barbara L. Narendra, Peabody Museum of National History, Yale University, for the tour of the meteorite collection.

Neal J. Kirk for being "a pirate" in the book (Free Men Of the Sea – Pirates/Privateers for hire – contact fmos@comcast.net or phone 860-267-8447).

Jay Manewitz, Bristol Public Library Historian, for his help in starting me on the magical historical journey through southern New England.

The Connecticut River Museum for their historical knowledge of this area (Steamboat Dock, 67 Main Street, Essex, Connecticut www.ctrivermuseum.org).

Contents

Chapter One: In the Beginning... 6
Chapter Two: Rhode Island 18
Chapter Three: Massachusetts 56
Chapter Four: Connecticut 135
Conclusion 237
Bibliography 238
Index 253

In The Beginning...

The line from Christopher Columbus' journal of the fourth voyage in 1503, "Gold is most excellent. Gold constitutes treasure, and he who possesses it may do what he will in the world, and may so attain as to bring souls to paradise" best explains what the mind set was when America was first discovered. It was the search for this precious item that enticed the explorers to go west toward the setting sun. There is an old saying that "Gold follows the sun," so it is no surprise that the first explorers would head over the dark, unknown Atlantic Ocean toward the west searching for the yellow ore. This is where the story begins for the search for haunted lost treasure in Connecticut, Rhode Island, and Massachusetts.

Gold is the first metal known to man. Columbus believed that when he came to America he would find the place where "gold grew." At least, that was what he hoped. So much gold and silver was pouring out of South America, it was logical that these precious commodities could be found in abundance in North America. Even when told by the Native Americans that there was no such field or mountain of gold, they were not believed. Gold was such a powerful symbol that it could actually alleviate superstitious beliefs, even in the Puritans. For example, it was believed to be unlucky to buy or sell bees. However, you could be safe from bad luck, if the payment was made in gold.

No one is really sure what the origin of gold is. Astronomers have suggested that neutron-rich heavy elements like gold might be created in the rare neutron-rich explosions of the universe, such as the collision of neutron stars.

Gold follows the sun. That is why the Europeans sailed west, searching for gold. A beautiful sunset in Rhode Island.

Those neutron star collisions are also the suggested origin of short duration gamma-ray bursts. So, gold may actually be formed in one of the most powerful explosions in the universe. No wonder it is so valued.

The story of lost and haunted treasure sites are usually intermingled through all three states in southern New England. There is no one story that belongs to only one state, as the people, treasure, and ghosts traveled throughout the area, so did each of the stories. For example, a lone mariner named William Blackstone lived with the Shawmut Native American tribe on Beacon Hill in Massachusetts in the 1620s. When the English settlers came to Boston in 1630, he felt crowded and left for the wild outback of Rhode Island, for whom the Blackstone River was named. He was thought to be a zealous cleric, at that time. He was however the first lighthouse keeper in Massachusetts. He would keep a fire burning on Beacon Hill as an aid to the men out in the sea. Hence, the story of Rhode Island and Massachusetts are forever connected.

There are certain places that are truly magical or enchanted in New England. Why events happen in these areas over and over again is amazing and truly unexplainable. Is it because these are the first places populated; or is there some lure to these areas that people are drawn to that creates these circumstances and situations to occur? Block Island, just thirteen miles off the coast of Rhode Island is one of those magical and mysterious places. Not only does it have numerous lost treasure stories and most of them with a haunted tale connection, but even the name has such a bond to what is unknown and different in the world that it is even mentioned when astronomers speak about outer space. Block Island is the name planetary scientists have given to the largest meteorite ever found on the surface of Mars. The NASA Mars Rover, *Opportunity*, took a photo of a watermelon-sized, nickel-iron meteorite in July 2009. What still intrigues the scientists is that this rock should have disintegrated when it entered Mars atmosphere. The fact that it was not destroyed may

The treasure and supernatural history of New England is not limited to one state. All share in the wealth of dark history. Fort Shantok Pond in Connecticut.

mean that it landed when Mars' atmosphere was still thick and may tell us much about Mars' history. The name of this unique object is Block Island.

There are four geologic terranes found in New England, which include, Newark, Proto-North America, Iapetus, and Avalonian. The Downeast coast of Maine, coast of New Hampshire, coast of Massachusetts, coast of Connecticut, and coast of Rhode Island all are Avalonian, which was once the west coast of Africa. The western parts of Vermont, Massachusetts, and Connecticut is Proto-North America.

The Central part of Connecticut is Newark. The rest of New England is Iapetos. Connecticut's Marble Valley was created by the collision of Proto-North America, the Iapetus Ocean, and Avalonia. The ocean slipped under the two land masses. It is one of the more unique terranes found in New England. This is the reason for the amazing natural gems found in the region.

This deer was feeding near the underground river in the center of Hartford, Connecticut.

Fort Shantok is a state park in Montville, Connecticut. It is also the Mohegan burial grounds.

New England people held many superstitions to explain their new world. This was an unknown and very scary place to the people who first settled here. Nothing and nowhere felt safe to them. The places that are called "Devil" something comes directly from the Puritan days, when that was the only way to explain what was happening in this strange land. These were the places where the settlers saw or thought that the work of the Devil existed. Even the kelp found on the sea-washed rocks on the shore are called, "the Devil's apron." The residents of Martha's Vineyard sometimes called Nantucket Island, the "Devil's Ash Heap." There are places all through the book with the word "Devil" attached to them – usually because of something unknown seen or experienced. Again, is it no wonder that these places were considered supernatural somehow? And what better place to hide treasure, in a place where no one wanted to venture in the first place? It is why ghost and treasure tales are forever continued.

There were six major tribes living in southern New England when the settlers first arrived. There were also many sub-tribes, extinct tribes, and merged tribes. The tribes battled amongst themselves years before the settlers arrived. Where they lived and where they fought are the places where most of the Native American artifacts have been and can be found. More information is given about these tribes in various sections of this book, depending on where they lived. The six tribes were: Pawtucket, Massachusetts, Pokanoket, Narragansett, Pequot, and Mohegan.

This book will describe old foot paths, where Native Amer-

Treasure Hunting Tip

When seeking Native American artifacts, always check what the tribe called an area. The roots of words can be the same and will explain what a site is.

ican villages once existed, where old battle sites are located, and where old ferry and stagecoach stops were. All these places, once known, may lead the treasure searcher to find items left behind and/or forgotten by those who once passed that way. Many people had critical traumatizing times while living in these places; it should not be forgotten that some of that misery or hardship may have stained the land.

There were three major Native American paths that were used by all the tribes in New England. U.S. Route #1, called the Pequot Path in Connecticut; the Boston Post Road; and the King's Highway. Boston Post Road was called Mishimayagat by the Connecticut tribes. This was the great path from New York to Boston. The first Native American route used extensively by settlers from Massachusetts Bay to Hartford is still known as "The Old Connecticut Path" or the Nipmuck Path.

Another tradition and common artifact, other than the arrowhead, that is found throughout the area is the pipe. All the Algonquin tribes in New England used the Calumet or peace pipe filled with tobacco. The stem was decorated with feathers and the bowl was made of stone. It was the emblem of peace and hospitality. To refuse the pipe meant war, to accept the pipe meant peace and friendship. The villages of the various tribes were filled with dwellings called the wigwam. This was place covered with bark, hide, or thatch, not gold and silver as many of the European tales state.

Pirates in New England were numerous. Piracy is the third oldest profession in the world, following prostitution and medicine. This entire region was the bank for the pirate treasure stolen from the rich Spanish treasure fleet, and the numerous French and British ships that roamed in the Atlantic. Why are there so many tales of ghosts and treasure? One main reason is that pirates really did believe the saying, "Dead men tell no tales." No one would tell where the loot was buried, because they did not usually survive after the treasure was put into the ground. Also, remember that the settlers were very superstitious during this time. Who would want to search for a treasure being guarded by the dead?

Pirates had an especially hard time on the New England coastline in the winters of the eighteenth century. These winters are considered some of the worst winters ever known. The *Boston Newsletter* reported that in January 1712 that "our rivers are all frozen up, so that we have no vessels entering the area for at least a week." In 1720, the Charles River in Massachusetts froze so deep that men and horses could cross on the ice. It comes as no surprise that the pirates would spend winters in the warmer Caribbean climates!

The first references to a black flag were recorded in ship logs in 1697. Pirates would often use symbols found in graveyards to strike the most fear in victims. Most pirates were considered masters with firearms. Pirate weapons were: boarding axes, cannons, and glass grenades, which were a glass bottles with fuses and gun powder inside. Their ships carried grog to drink. This was a mixture of water and rum. Rum was added to the water to make it safer to drink. Safe drinking water did not last too long on a pirate vessel.

In 1698, a blanket royal pardon was issued for all pirates, except Captain Kidd. Though the pirates had to give all their loot to the Crown to receive the pardon, the question still remains as to why Kidd was excluded. No explanation is ever given. September 5, 1718 was the last day for pirates to

Neal J. Kirk – Free Men Of the Sea, with authentic pirate attire
at the Essex Connecticut River Museum.

surrender and receive full pardon for all crimes committed.

As a side note, a doubloon was a rare fifteenth century Spanish gold coin. Pirates really stole gold escudos, but called them doubloons. Escudos were a common sixteenth to nineteenth century Spanish gold coins. That is the coin most buried in pirate lore. Many did not give up their ill-gotten gains, however.

Following are a few basic biographies of some of the pirates who are in this book. There will be more details of each treasure and pirate in the different state chapters.

Thomas Tew

Thomas Tew was a Rhode Island pirate who was described by Governor Thomas Fletcher of New York as "a very pleasant man who tells wonderful stories." He was well liked in the area and was often greeted at port as a hero. Tew was shot and killed while boarding a Great Mogul of India ship that he was trying to steal.

William or Robert Kidd

William or Robert Kidd is the man that is usually responsible for burying any pirate treasure in New England and was hanged in London. He was really a privateer and this marque has been discovered.

William Fly

William Fly was known for his raging temper and brutality. He would often whip his captives, even after he got everything he wanted. He was finally captured off the coast of Newburyport, Massachusetts, and hanged. He was only a pirate for one month.

Joe Brodish

Joe Brodish escaped from a Boston jail twice before he was shipped to London and hanged.

Blackbeard

Blackbeard lived up to his gruesome description and reputation. His head was cut off during a battle with the British forces.

John or Jack Quelch

Quelch dumped the Captain of the ship *Charles,* overboard at Half Way Rock outside Salem, Massachusets. He was hanged in Boston in 1704.

Thomas Veal or Veale

Thomas Veal or Veale was one of the four pirates to seek escape in Lynn, Massachusetts. He supposedly died in a cave during an earthquake with his treasure.

Charles Harris

Charles Harris was one of the twenty-six pirates that was hanged in Newport, Rhode Island, in the 1720s.

Thomas Pound

Thomas Pound was a pirate from 1689 to 1703, and commanded a small ship in the Massachusetts area.

Not many pirates lived to enjoy any loot they managed to steal and bury. It is not surprising that there may be many pirate treasures still hidden beneath the earth to this day.

Silversmith shops in New England were places where the precious silver metal was shaped into useful items. This metal was considered hammered white gold. In the eighteenth century, the silversmith had to do everything in the shop At this time, many items were made of silver. Some of the items of that time do not even exist today. Wills of that era talk about a silver retort, or silver cucurbit, which is thought to be a species of retort, shaped like a gourd, and may have been used to distill perfume. These shops made silver medals, buttons, jewelry, rings, bookplates, watches, coins, platters, punch bowls, whistles, hairpins, seals, bodkins, thimbles, clasps, chains, shoe and knee buckles, hat bands, pots, cups, snuff boxes, teapots, gravy boats, spoons and dram cups, which were miniature bowls that held a dram or spoonful of medicine. Who knows what can be found in old silversmith areas, so it is worth knowing where they once existed. This book will explore some of the areas where known Silversmiths once worked.

Throughout the book there are places where precious metals, minerals, and out-of-this-world stones are found. The word *mineral* comes from the Latin *minare*, meaning "to mine." The word, *crystal* comes from the Greek *Krystallos*, meaning "ice." It was thought by the Greeks that the minerals had frozen so solidly that they would never melt. The word *copper*, comes from the Latin *Cuprum* or "Cyprus Ore," due to the early discovery of this metal in Cyprus. Minerals are really created and destroyed at a fairly regular rate in the earth, so what we discover today are just moments in geologic time. The precious minerals would change, if found eons from the present.

A question often asked is what process creates the gold, silver, tin, or platinum deposits to begin with? It is thought that running water, ocean currents, and wind may be responsible for the concentration of heavy metals in one place. In these same places, the gemstones are also found. The gems that can be found in this area include: diamonds, zircon, sapphire, ruby, topaz, tourmaline, and garnet.

As an interesting side note, though diamond is the hardest substance known, it can not cut through wood, but can cut concrete. Legends state that if a person is born on a certain day, certain gems worn or owned will bring good fortune. It is one of those superstitions of our ancestors. Those born on Sunday should wear gold and sapphire; on Monday, silver and crystal; on Tuesday, iron and diamonds; on Wednesday, mercury and bloodstone; on Thursday, tin and Carnelian; on Friday, copper and emerald; and on Saturday, lead and onyx.

An unusual gem find here would come from a meteorite. These stones from outer space can fall anywhere and have fallen in southern New England. The book tells the area where documented falls were noted. There are basically two types of meteorites, iron and stone. Around eighty-seven percent of all meteorites are stone. Iron is a rare material, and the stony-iron is the rarest of all falls.

After a meteorite falls to earth, it may be possible to discover minerals that are not usually found on earth. Moldavite is a volcanic glass of extraterrestrial origin. It was first discovered near the River Vltava (Moldau) in Bohemia. A meteor shower once dropped hazel nut-sized glass droplets here and the glass was found soon after.

Another mineral would be Olivine, which is a gem from a stony and pallisite meteorite. This substance is only found in space, not on earth. This yellowish-grey substance called schreibersite was found in the Springwater meteorite in Sakatchewan, Canada in 1931. Meteorites are always named where they fall.

Many meteorites are worth as much as gold. To illustrate this point, Steve Arnold in Brenham Township, Kansas, found a meteorite that weighed just under a ton. It is worth over one million dollars. The very first meteorite ever seen and found by the Europeans was in Weston, Connecticut, in 1807. Amazingly, it is also one of the rarest types that fall; a stony-iron meteorite. The fireball was seen over Massachusetts and Vermont, and fragments fell in at least six places throughout the region. One of the largest pieces can be viewed at the Peabody Museum in New Haven, Connecticut, as part of the Yale University mineral collection. It is worth the trip to view this and other meteorites. The United States President at that time, Thomas Jefferson, stated, "I would rather believe that those two Yankee professors would lie than to believe that stones fell from heaven." He was mistaken, of course; stones falling from the sky is an uncommon event, but does occur. The real question is why more meteorites are not found? The answer is that over seventy percent land in the ocean. Actually, the Chesapeake Bay was created by a meteor impact.

The beginning is just the first stop on this journey. Now, on to the details of where the haunted treasure sites are located. Good luck, but beware what you may find in your search!

Chapter Two

Rhode Island

GENERAL

Amor Vincit omnia, meaning, "Love conquers all," is the motto for Aquidneck Island, as this small state was called by the Native Americans. This name was changed to Rhode Island by Giovanni da Verrazano who discovered it in 1524. He named it in honor of the Greek Island of Rhodes. The official name of Rhode Island is the State of Rhode Island and Providence Plantations. It was once lush with strawberries. Rhode Island is almost split in two by the ocean and the Seekonk River. Rhode Island residents are known as Rhode Islanders.

This fifteen-mile-long and three-and-a-half-miles-wide region is a glacial moraine and has two unique, but distinct environments: salt ponds and true estuaries. The Blackstone River runs through the northern part of the state. It is known as the hardest working river in America and was named for William Blackstone, a renegade cleric who is said to have rode into the area on the back of a bull in 1630 after leaving a crowded Massachusetts. The 1872 Mariville Mill ruins can still be seen on the Blackstone River, but to see them, the visitor will have to canoe through the class 1 and 3 rapids. These ruins are not accessible by car. All rapids are rated 1 through 5, the more difficult being a class 5, and class 1 is the easiest (less fast).

The journey to searching for any haunted treasure starts with the first step down a long road.

Verrazano found Native Americans living here when he first arrived. A large amount of Native American petroglyphs and artifacts have been found in Rhode Island. There was an ancient Native American trail from Fall River, Massachusetts to Little Compton, Rhode Island, called the Pequot Trail. The most powerful and largest tribe living here were the Narragansetts, a Native American word, meaning "at the small narrow point" or "at the island."

When the Europeans came, the Sachem or Chief of the tribe was named Canonicus. He is the Sachem who sent the famous war challenge to the Pilgrims. This challenge came in the form of arrows wrapped in snakeskin. When the Pilgrims returned the snakeskin wrapped with musket balls and powder, the message apparently satisfied him. No aggression followed this challenge. This tribe practiced little writing, which is why the numerous petroglyphs that have been found are in question as to who really them. There is much more about the strange carvings found all through New England in later chapters.

The Narragansetts were friends of the fearless and warring Mohawks from New York. Some sub-divisions of this nation were: Coweset, Sakonnet, Manissean, Pawtuxet, Sauk, Sogkonates, and Quinebaug. Native American meanings are important to know. They often suggest treasure areas to seek artifacts. Some Native American word meanings: Sauk means "yellow earth people;" Coweset means "place of black rocks" or "black cliff place."

Coweset shore in Kent County, was an ancient Coweset village site. When the Europeans came, the plagues that followed killed seventy-five percent of the Native Americans there.

The Narragansett tribe believe that the spruce tree is sacred. It is believed that the red-hearted spruce tree grew on the spot where every drop of blood shed by an innocent Narragansett fell to the ground. The tale goes that sometime after King Philip's War, a colonist settled on 500 acres of land that once belonged to the Narragansett tribe. There were many spruce trees, and he decided he would cut them down. He told others that the trees made him uncomfortable and he felt haunted by them. He started to cut them down, and did not cut very many, before one of them fell on him, killing him instantly. Another legend is that Sakonnet Rock found on the island state is the stone wife of the giant hero Wetucks or Maushop, or Native American god.

The Narragansetts had one of the only female sachem named Quaiapen in the 1670s. Awashonks Park and Swamp in Newport County was the area called Suncksqua, meaning "woman who rules" of the Sogkonate tribe. She aided the English during King Philip's War.

King Philip's War destroyed the Narragansett rule of Rhode Island, because they aided King Philip against the English and the British won that war. There were many dreams and prophecies of the coming of the Europeans many years before they came and what would happen to the Native Americans when they did show up. The Narragansett have a legend that says they heard a strange tune all around them one day. They had no idea where it came from or what it was. Years later, they heard that same tune in a European Church and amazed the settlers when they were able to sing the tune with them. It is perhaps no wonder that the Native

Americans were fearful at times of the changes occurring in their world.

The Niantic tribe lived on the west coast of Rhode Island. Their name describes where they once inhabited. Niantic means "at the point of land on a tidal river or estuary." Originally this was thought to be one tribe, but were split in two by the Pequots, into the east and west Niantic tribes. They refused to join the Narragansetts in King Philip's War. The Polanaukets lived on the east side of Rhode Island.

On May 19, 1780, there was a slight thunder shower and suddenly candles were needed at noon. What caused this sudden darkness over Rhode Island is not known. However, it was reported that days before, a dry smoky vapor hung in the air. The sun could actually be looked at with the naked eye. Perhaps it was caused by a volcanic explosion somewhere in the world, but the darkness was only reported in Rhode Island.

There was a tragic train accident at Richmond Switch in 1873. The dam gave way and the water from Meadow Brook washed the train bridge away. The train from Stonington, Connecticut, called the "Steamboat Train," making an early morning run from Boston to Providence, came rushing down the track and could not see the chasm before them. The train crashed into the river bank below. The flames and water killed many of the passengers that day. Rescue trains were quickly dispatched from Providence and Westerly, but many passengers were not identified and some say ghosts remain guarding their belongings.

New England is famous for the stone walls found all through the area. In 1802, Silas Clapp was largely responsible for many of the stone walls built in Rhode Island and Connecticut. He started building walls for money, and he was considered the best in either state. Ironically, he died because a strap holding stones broke and the cart tipped. His head was crushed under the stones. He is buried on the brow of a slope overlooking the New London Turnpike. At one time, one could see his grave from the highway. Stone walls are one place where home owners would bury the family treasure. Numerous treasures have been found near stone walls. They are found all through New England.

As an interesting side note, the word Turnpike was created in the early 1800s. The term comes from "whether its surface was hard enough to turn the point of a pike or not."

Islands, lighthouses, and pirates are forever linked in treasure and ghost lore. This statement is true for the islands off the Rhode Island coast. The Newport Islands found in the Bay are: Prudence, Patience, Hope, Despair, and Hog. There is more about the haunted treasure of this area in the Newport section of this book. Hope Island found in Narragansett Bay was a lucky place for a fisherman in 1923. During a winter storm, he found several gold and silver Spanish coins dating from the eighteenth century.

Captain Kidd is also said to have buried treasure on Hog Island, Patience Island, Pirates Cove on Conanicut, Skakonet Island, and on Watch Hill. Patience Island was also known as Chibacoweda, a Narragansett word that means "separated by a passage." Patience Island is separated by a waterway from Prudence Island. Prudence Island is the site of an abandoned naval base found at South Prudence State Park. Gould's Island was once called Gold's Island, though the reason remains unclear. There is even a story that pirate treasure may be found on Providence Island. It is said that the pirate William Rous used to hide in this area.

Rhode Island was proud of the privateers who roamed the shores. Over eighty commissions or letters of Marque to capture vessels of the enemy of England were issued by Rhode Island in King George's War. Over sixty letters were issued in the French and Indian War. It is said that agents warned the French that "this colony was extremely obnoxious to the French, and much an object of their resentment, on account of the great mischief done to their trade during the last war by Rhode Island privateers." One French pamphlet stated that Newport should be destroyed as it was a menace to French commerce. There was a price to pay for being considered against the more powerful European powers, however. In the summer 1778, the southern part of the state was destroyed by the British. Warren was raided by the Hessians, and Bristol was attacked twice.

The protection of the important Narragansett Bay was vital to the economic health of the nation. This is considered

one of the best natural harbors in the world. Over twenty forts were built in here, and many have been lost through the passage of time. Nine of the forts were destroyed in the Revolutionary War along the Providence River. Many artifacts can be found where battles and/or forts once stood. Following are some of the forts, what part they played in history, and where they may have been located.

Small islands abound in Narragansett Bay of the larger Rhode Island.

Butts Hill Fort

This fort, located in Portsmouth on the Sakonnet River, was built by the British in 1777. It played a major role in the Battle of Rhode Island and is now considered a ghost fort because its exact location is unknown.

Green End Fort

This ghost fort was located between Middletown and Newport, and built in 1743. The Battle of Rhode Island raged in this area, and was the last stand of the Americans. Though ultimately defeated, the Americans held strong here, while the British destroyed the town (Newport) on August 10, 1778.

Fort George

This fort was built on Goat Island in 1778 by the British. No trace of it remains today.

Fort Greene

The Patriots were at this fort in 1776. It is said to be located somewhere between Washington Street and the harbor and is perhaps now under Battery Park.

Fort Varnum

Beryl was found at this fort site, but the actual location is vague.

The gemstone Beryl was found in Bonnet Point in Washington County. In Kent County, Bloodstone, red-orange Chalcedony, or Carnelian was found. This is a clear quartz gemstone that looks like pieces of broken china. It was believed that this gem would make the wearer never separate from God. It is said to stop nose bleeds and make the wearer slow to anger.

The lost Durfee Hill Gold Mine is said to be located on Durfee Hill Road, north of Ponaganset Reservoir, and four miles southeast of West Gloucester. The lost Foster Gold Mine is said to be found on Harrington Road, just north of the Moosup Valley, southwest of Foster Center. There was a mini gold rush in Foster when the gold was found.

Treasure found on the shore from shipwrecks is a very real possibility. Below is a partial list of all the known shipwrecks that occurred near the Rhode Island shore: *Addie M. Anderson, Belleville, Blackpoint, Cape Fear, Empire State, G-1,* schooner – *Harry Knowlton* in 1907 on Quonochontaug Beach, *L-8, Lake Crystal, Llewellyn Howland, Lydia Skolfield, Mary Arnold, Progress, Onondaga, Rhode Island,* Brig – *Waterwitch* in 1896, *Norness, Spikefish, and* Schooner – *Granville R. Bacon* at Weekapaug Point in 1933 *Suffolk.*

Brenton Reef is also known as Graves Point. There are so many shipwrecks here that sometimes the ships lay on top of each other. There are many bodies still on these submerged ships. The worse wreck was the Spanish Brig, *Minerva,* on Christmas Eve 1810. Gold and silver coins, as well as artifacts, are still wedged between the rocks. The *George W. Humphreys* was wrecked here on July 6, 1904. People who visit here say they hear strange grinding noises, cries, and gunfire. In 1957, the freighter, *Belleville* was wrecked at this location.

In 1864, forty miles southeast of Rhode Island, it is said that a Russian steamer, *Spasskaya,* wrecked while transporting South American emeralds worth $3 million. It has never been found. It sank in a violent gale and a large wave capsized the ship with the entire crew and cargo plunging to the bottom.

The reason the above locations are given to the reader is to show that there are many places to search for treasure, but just remember that these were places of history, and today, they may be owned by others. The treasure seeker must always seek

permission to search at these places or pay the consequences for trespassing on private or state property.

BLOCK ISLAND AND WATCH HILL

The legal name for this island is New Shoreham and it is located thirteen miles off the coast of Rhode Island. There are 365 fresh-water ponds and it is the location of the United States Weather Bureau Station. Europeans first settled on this seven-mile-long and three-and-a-half-mile-wide island in 1661. The explorer Verrazano visited in 1524 and mentioned it in his logs, but it was named after the Dutch explorer, Adrian Block, in 1644. He called it "Adriaen's Eyland."

The oldest rocks found here come from the Cretaceaus Era. There is constant erosion occurring, especially on the northern side. Geologically speaking, this place will someday completely disappear under the ocean.

The Narragansett Tribe considered this island sacred and it was a burial ground for the tribe. As early as 1642, the Narragansett Sachem, Miantonomo wanted to rally all the New England tribes to resist the English rule. The Block Island tribe was a sub-division of the Narragansett nation called Manissean, and they called their island, Manisses, meaning "little island" or "island of the Little God." The 200-foot Mohegan Bluffs, also known as Bloody Bluffs, holds the legend that the Mohegans set up a last defense there, but were wiped out and thrown over the cliffs to their deaths.

Whale Rock Lighthouse could be found north of Point Judith Lighthouse on Block Island in the mouth of Narragansett Bay. It was built in 1882 and completely destroyed in a hurricane in 1938. The assistant keeper lost his life during the destruction. The remains of this four story lighthouse can still be seen today at low tide. Look west toward the Narragansett shoreline for something that looks like a submarine tower. The Native American name for this place was Weynanitoke, an eastern Niantic word meaning, "a sweep-around a high point" or "winding river." The area is also known as Mattoonuc Neck, which means "place at the lookout hill."

The ocean constantly pounds at the shore in Rhode Island, causing some parts to disappear, and other parts to be born.

Point Judith Lighthouse, also found at the mouth of Narragansett Bay, guards the east entrance to Block Island and has the distinction of being the first documented wooden lighthouse destroyed by a hurricane in 1815 – but it was re-built. The lighthouse was built in 1810 for $5000. Many coins and artifacts are found here. The coins could come from the over sixteen wrecks which occurred in one year, 1855. There were two British Warships wrecked here during a gale in 1777; the *HMS Syren* and *HMS Triton*. In 1778, this is the site of the wreck of the sixteen-gun, *US Columbus* lost during a battle with the *HMS Maidstone*. Artifacts abound in this haunted area.

Captain Kidd is said to have buried coins at the northern tip of Sandy Point. Coins from his era have been found. The pirate Joe Bradish or Braddish (the name is spelled differently) roamed the area and a treasure of his is said to be buried here. Bradish and his crew, on the ship *Adventure*, raided several Spanish ships in the Caribbean Sea and was loaded with gold and jewels when he came to unload his ship on the island. It was damaged and he came here to regroup and repair the ship. He decided to bury some of his treasure to make the ship less heavy, and hopefully, easier to escape pursuers. The details of exactly where the loot was buried is unclear.

This island was the scene of numerous pirate landings and gold doubloons or really escudos are often found. During

the French and Indian War, it was used as a pirate base of operations. It is no wonder that in 1705 the Governor of Massachusetts charged Rhode Island with consorting with pirates.

Sandy Point is located in this state for now, but for centuries the wind and tide have been moving it toward Stonington, Connecticut. Sandy Point was once part of Napatree point off Watch Hill. During a hurricane in 1938, a split occurred and Sandy Point became detached. In 1997, the point split into two islands, moving about two and a half yards per year. One will eventually hit the Connecticut coast.

In 1738, the German ship, *Princess Augusta*, was destroyed with a great loss of life and property. The treasure lost from this ship is said to be over $100,000. In the same year, the German ship, *The Palatine*, was wrecked. This ship was bringing wealthy German Palatines from Rotterdam and wrecked during a snow storm. It has been suggested that perhaps this ship was actually wrecked by the wreckers who resided here at the time. A small child survived the wreck and told authorities that there were other survivors and they buried what gold and silver treasure they could take with them on the island, but died later, though the cause of death remains a mystery.

There are stories of how the wrecker's dead victims would come ashore as people were burying and/or digging up their treasure and drag the wreckers to the sea, never to be seen again. It probably would be considered a form of justice for some of the wreckers who killed the survivors. Old Chrissy was a Dutch woman who built a shack on the beach where her ship was wrecked, but for some reason the wreckers spared her life. She, however, was not so generous to the survivors of the ships that she wrecked. She was finally turned in to the authorities by other islanders when it is said that she killed her eldest son, Edward, when his ship was wrecked and he survived, though not for too long after Old Chrissy found him.

Many unexplained voices have been heard all around the island, but one of the most-heard voices says, "Let me out of here." The ghostly ship called the Palatine Light will burst into flames as a woman appears screaming, then the ship disappears off shore. It heralds an impending storm. It is said that the woman is looking for Block Island pirates

and wreckers that supposedly lured the ship to its doom, or even perhaps their descendants.

What is a fascinating story about Block Island is that the clergy became vested in wrecking, though it was through force. According to William Blindloss, the person who built South East Lighthouse at Block Island, in the late 1600s, a preacher named Seth Baldwin came to the island to preach against the practice of wrecking. No one on the island listened, and no one would help the preacher survive. It is said that he was almost dead with starvation, so when the islanders gave him a special hook to survive. The hooks were a pole with a bent nail on the end of it. These were used to fish items out of the water from shipwrecks. It had been agreed that everyone's hook would be the same length, so no one had an advantage in gathering ship wreckage. The islanders decided that the preacher could have a hook one inch longer than the rest to help him survive. That is where the story ends.

On Southwest Point, coins have been discovered. The Irish Merchantman, *Golden Grove*, wrecked here during a gale in 1765. The Navy Collier, *U.S.S. Nero* wrecked in 1907. The steamer, *Larchmont*, sank in twelve minutes in 1907 in high winds. Just a few more of the island shipwrecks, sunk either by natural or man-made wrecking are: *Achilles, Bass, Essex, Grecian, Jennie R. Dubois, Leyden, Meteor, Montana, Puszta, and Spartan*. In 1939, the Texaco Tanker, *Lightburne*, was wrecked. In 1941, the steamer, *Essex*, sank and the visitor could still see the tanker years after it sank.

It is a fact that the Gulf Stream does transport tropical fish to New England. The Block Ness Monster, a sea serpent, was seen here in June 1996 by fishermen. This was a dead monster when it was discovered, but its carcass has since mysteriously disappeared. It was said to have been a fourteen-foot serpentine skeleton with a narrow head and whiskers.

Watch Hill was home to the Niantic tribe in the 1600s. The Chief was called Ninigret. Fort Ninigret is thought to once be a place of prehistoric mounds, but now it is thought of as a Dutch Trading Post, probably found somewhere on the Old Post Road. Native American artifacts have been discovered all over the island.

This was a great place to watch for enemy troops, hence the name. It was used throughout its history as a look out. There are remains of a Spanish-American War fort here. There is also an overgrown Naval Base on Ninigret Point. In 1806, the lighthouse was built to help with the shipwrecks that were constantly occurring in the area, but the number of ships that sank around this island remain almost too high to count.

BRISTOL/MOUNT HOPE

There is a claim in the Mount Hope area that the Norseman, Leif Erikson, landed here in the year 1000 and built a home on the Sakonnet River. It is even said that the name "Mount Hope" finds its origin from the Norse. The word is said to come from the Native American pronunciation of *Montop* or *Monthaup*. However, it is the word "hop" that is said to be the name that Thorfinn Erikson, brother to Leif, gave to this region in 1008. Tradition states that a rock was once found on the shores of the Bay. That proves this point. There was a carving of a figure in a boat that may be runic in origin. It is interesting to note that the Native Americans had no written language, so any carvings in the area may be from elsewhere. There is also a legend that this is the site of "singing rocks," which is where the Norse Sagas' said the Vikings landed. Many towns in Rhode Island claim to be the landing site. But what is known is that Giovanni da Verrazano landed here on July 8, 1524.

Today, the Bay is located in southeastern Massachusetts and Rhode Island. It is a 112 square mile estuary of National Significance ordered by the Environmental Protection Agency in 1987. This area is home to the Kemp's Ridley Sea Turtle, a federally endangered species of sea turtle.

The traumatic tale of King Philip and his war will unfold in the book where significant events occurred. This entire area was the seat of power for King Philip in 1600s. It was the main village of the Wampanoags, a sub-tribe of the Pokanoket Confederation. In 1662, King Philip wanted to push the English settlers back into the sea where they came from.

At this time, there were about 36,000 Native Americans and 60,000 settlers, with more coming all the time. The Native American name for this area was Montaup, which meant "this island is sufficiently fortified." It is obvious that a Native American fort was once located here. On June 26, 1675, there is a story foretelling the start of King Philip's War to the British in the region. Soldiers were marching out of Bolton toward Mount Hope when they saw an eclipse of the moon. That was considered an ominous sign, with bad things happening that would deal with Mount Hope area, but there were more bad omens to come. Another omen would be seen in Warren.

King Philip was not happy with how the settlers were destroying his land and educating his people in their ways. The war started because the settlers took land in Rhode Island and did not pay King Philip for it in 1675. There were ninety towns that existed in New England during that time, and forty were damaged or destroyed by King Philip or his alliances. This war cost was immense. One out of every sixteen British military age men were killed. The war destroyed any and all the power of the New England tribes. Things would never be the same for the Native American or the settler again living in the new world. King Philip's War was a major turning point in New England history.

It was once called the Mount Hope Lands, which included all the land between Narragansett Bay east to Massachusetts Bay. This town was settled in 1699 and named after Bristol, England.

The town was also the actual site of the first battle of King Philip's War that began in 1675 at Pokanoket Neck. This place was attacked twice by the Mohegans during the war. The idea of King Philip's War started at Mount Hope, also known as Pawkunnawkutt, Rhode Island, where King Philip lived. King Philip's War last only one year, 1675-1676. Though this was not a long, drawn-out war, it was bloody, and King Philip lost his life during the war by the knife of a Native American called, Alderman. It was a war of extermination and the battle sites are found throughout southern New England. Sites will be revealed in all three states, but what the war was about is found here. Another name for King Philip was Wonkees-ohke – meaning "fox county." King Philip is the English name for

the Sachem Metacom of the Wampanoag Tribe. His father, Massasott, sold the area (Rhode Island), except for Mount Hope to the Europeans. When he died, Metacom started to destroy the settlements in the area. He did not want the Europeans to be here. He felt the Europeans stole the land.

There were shipwrecks in the bay, the Steamer, *Empire State*, sank at the pier in 1887. There are remains of an earthwork fort that was destroyed during the Revolutionary War. The British raided this town in 1777. Perhaps it is Arnolds Point Fort, located at Lehigh Hill, about one mile south of the Bristol Ferry site that failed to protect the region. This is considered a ghost fort, because it no longer exists, but was once there. The Bristol Ferry site is also considered a ghost town or site. It was located at the west of the Mount Hope Bridge, south of Bristol. Knowing where places and structures used to be is one way to find relics of that era.

Jasper and Amethysts have been found in the region and there are local claims that the Norsemen or Vikings landed as well as the other places in Rhode Island. There are over 1,000 structures found that predate the year 1800. Artifacts are discovered here quite often.

CENTRAL FALLS/BARRINGTON

Barrington is found along the Barrington River. This town claims to be an ancient Native American village site of the Wampanoag tribe in 1670. In Central Falls, a place called Dexter's Ledge, there was a battle site, fought one year after King Philip's War ended, near the Blackstone River. This battle was fought by the Narragansett's, who were led by the great Sachem, Canonchet. The attack was revenge for the Great Swamp Fight, the last battle in King Philip's War. After that war ended, the Narragansett's, who fought with King Philip, were headed to attack Plymouth, Massachusetts. Captain Michael Pierce was sent to stop them and they met in battle at Central Falls on the banks of the Blackstone River. It is said that you can still hear the screams of the dying when you put your ear to the stones here. There have

been arrowheads found, as there are in numerous Native American battle sites.

COVENTRY/CHARLESTOWN

In Charlestown, there is a Narragansett legend of the Crying Rock or Bastard Rocks area. Unwed mothers would abandoned their children here to die. This is also the site of Coronation Rock, near King Tom Pond, where the Narragansett would crown their Sachem or chief.

This town was the site of a Native American village. There are ruins still seen. The tribe still meets each August for ceremonial purposes. From 1709-1880, there was continual tribe occupation here. That 200-year span of Native American occupation in one area is unique in New England. The narrow lane off Route 2 and Route 112 is a Royal Narragansett Burial site.

The 1898 ruins of Fort Mansfield can be found in town and was built during the Spanish-American War. This ghost fort was located on the beach of Napatree Point. However, most of the fort was washed into the ocean in the 1939 hurricane. After storms, pieces and items from this era may wash onshore. The west top of Napatree Point no longer exists due to the hurricane.

Coventry is the site of the George B. Parke Woodland area, which is an Audubon Society Nature Preserve, found off Route 102N. In the 1700s, this was the town center complete with a sawmill on Turkey Meadow Brook. The town was abandoned, but the visitor can still see the cellar holes, remains of the mill, and rock walls. Stone and rock walls were the places where many people buried their precious items during a time of crisis. Also, there is a mysterious series of stone cairns in this town that may have been built by the Native Americans, the Narragansett tribe, or it has even been theorized that perhaps the ancient Celtic people built them. However, why they were built is still unknown.

A large sea serpent was once found here before the Europeans arrived. The story is that the serpent lived on a ridge known as Carbuncle Hill. It was said to have a bright

red gem glowing in the center of its head and was greatly feared by the Narragansett Tribe. The creature would attack the village near the Pawtuxet River. Finally, the tribe sent a war party to invade the Hill, and after a long and bloody battle, killed the creature. The gem was taken as a prize. This gem possessed unusual powers. If danger approached, it would glow brilliantly. When the Europeans came, they heard about the gem, and wanted it. During another battle with the Native Americans, the Sachem, who was carrying the gem, was fatally wounded. He flung the gem into a nearby pond, and died while the gem sank. It was never seen again.

CUMBERLAND

This town is a very haunted area in Rhode Island, so it should come as no surprise that a variety of gemstones can be found here. On the very narrow, twisting, and dark Tower Hill Road, children ghosts are seen. There is a place called the deadliest curve and there the ghost of a little boy can be found running with his dog. There is also the ghost of a toddler on his bike. People feel watched here all the time.

Rhode Island is also known as the vampire capital of America. There are twenty documented vampire legends through America and six are from Rhode Island. The first vampire case was in Cumberland in 1796. Rhode Island vampires were all young women in their late teens. The story of the 1796 first vampire is that a town council member reported that he was going to "try an experiment" to save his daughter's life. He was going to dig up his recently deceased daughter and stop her from killing his still-alive daughter. There are no more details, but usually it meant doing horrible things to the dead.

To this day, some of the supposed vampire graves are places where nothing ever grows and are considered cursed. Perhaps these women are still around hoping someone will tell their story. The grave writing on Nelly Vaughn's tombstone (an alleged vampire) states, "I am waiting and watching for you."

Like in the 1690s Salem, Massachusetts, witch trials, the Rhode Island vampires were a supernatural cure for the real mysteries of death for very scared people.

If one dares to come to this place, milky quartz has been found in the Calument Hill Quarry. Smoky quartz, Jasper, and Amethyst have been found at Diamond Hill Quarry. "Thetis" Hairstone, a transparent quartz, has been found near Sneatch Pond, and Rhodorite has been found on Beacon Hill. Smoky quartz has also been found on McLaughlin Ledge. It is a mineralogical heaven.

With a name like Diamond Hill, there must be diamonds to be found. That is not true, however. Diamond Hill State Park was created millions of years ago. There was mineral-rich hot water flowing along a fracture for about one mile. Quartz was deposited here and can still be viewed. The quartz sparkles in the sun like diamonds, hence the name. Diamond Hill Beacon Light was used by the Patriots during the Revolutionary War to alert movement of the British.

This place is also haunted by the monk ghost at the Cumberland Monastery, now the Cumberland Public Library. He is known to move or close books on people. The monks of the Our Lady of the Valley Monastery quarried all the granite to build this place in 1900. Also, along the back trail, a phantom horse rider is seen. The hiker will come up on the horse unexpectedly. A child has also been seen running through the swamp area, but disappears when followed.

This place has a connection to Central Falls. All but nine English were killed at the battlefield near Dexter's Ledge. The nine men were taken to the swamp in Cumberland and killed. The spot is called Nine Men's Misery and is marked today. The name tells of what happened and the ghosts of these men are said to still walk in the swamp.

EAST GREENWICH/EXETER/GREENE

In Greene, Arnold Spring Rock Shelter has shown archaeological evidence of use of the area for thousands of years. Many artifacts are found here. Exeter is the site of the oldest fort in the State. It was built by the Narragansett tribe during King Philip's War, called the Queen's Fort.

In East Greenwich, the eighth oldest town in Rhode Island, there is an area known as Dedford or Green Town. This town was settled by the Huguenots or French Protestants. The group started a silk production, but within five years, they left the area and no trace of that settlement remains today. The area is still called Frenchtown, and is a ghost town.

Main Street in town is part of the old Pequot Trail. The Narragansett Sachem, Pessacus, signed this land over to Charles II in 1644. That transaction did not seem to sit well with the Sachem in 1675. It was one of the first settlements destroyed by King Philip in King Philip's War.

JAMESTOWN

Conanicut Island, named for a Narragansett chief, is found at the mouth of Narragansett Bay, and has numerous lost treasures just waiting to be found. Not only did Kidd supposedly bury treasure here, but the pirate, Thomas Paine, is said to have buried loot on the island in Pirates Cove or Cave in the early 1700s. Paine was a known associate of Kidd's. It is said that he even visited Kidd here in 1699, right before Kidd was arrested. Paine told the authorities that Kidd asked him to hold his gold, but he refused. However, knowing what happened to Kidd, it is not really a surprise that Paine may have lied. Workers who were at Paine's home many years later found an ivory tusk and gold coins. Kidd's wife supposedly asked Paine for a large amount of gold after Kidd was hanged. What can be taken from these stories is that some pirate was on the island in the 1700s and that perhaps something was left near Pirates Cove or Cave. One thing to remember is that in that era, anytime a pirate was thought to be in the area, it was always said to be Kidd. If Kidd spent as much time burying treasure in all the areas that lay claim to him, he would not have had time to be a pirate. This island is also the site of an unfinished fort called Fort Dumpling. Military artifacts can be found here.

At the end of the island is the famous Beaver Tail Lighthouse. This was the fourth lighthouse built in the United States in 1749. The air-operated fog horn was literally powered

by a horse. This lighthouse was destroyed by the British in December 1775, but re-built. To stop the British, Beaver Head Fort was built by the residents in May 1776. However, it was occupied by the British in 1776, but American controlled the fort by 1778. During the occupation, Fort Getty was built, and parts of this fort still remain. The American Fort Wetherill was also constructed during the Revolutionary War era. The Lighthouse was ultimately destroyed in the 1938 Hurricane.

The Old Jamestown Bridge was built because of the above hurricane. The ferry, *Governor Carr*, which ran between Newport and Jamestown was driven ashore at Jamestown. This is why the old bridge was built. The ferry had been destroyed and deemed expensive to revive. The old ghost ferry site called South Ferry was located on South Ferry Road, about three miles south of the Jamestown Bridge. This bridge was known as the bridge to nowhere, the Jamestown Folly, and the Hail Mary Bridge. In the 1940s, the bridge would shake and rattle and lean southward. The bridge was not used by 1992, and on April 18, 2006, the bridge was destroyed.

The remainder of the old Jamestown Bridge, still sticking out of the Bay.

Someone did die while building the bridge, but was not buried under the bridge. However, sailors said that when they sailed under the bridge, they would get strange feelings and experience weird winds. People in vehicles crossing the bridge claimed to see apparitions and had premonitions

while driving on the bridge that saved their lives. This bridge was the longest bridge in New England until the Newport Bridge opened in 1969. That is now the longest suspension bridge in New England.

It is interesting to note here, that since this new bridge opened, there have been a lot of suicides. The area does have a strange feel to the air. I visited the bridge in 2009. I will admit that seeing the old bridge half sticking out of the water does make the visitor feel very strange indeed.

MIDDLETOWN/LINCOLN

In the town of Lincoln, the Conklin Limestone Quarry was established in 1640. It is the oldest and continually operated quarry in America.

This area was named Middletown because it is in the middle of the island. On December 7, 1776, eleven British ships landed and destroyed the town. Many people were able to leave before the attack, but when people leave quickly, sometimes artifacts are buried for safekeeping. When the person returns, the place where the item was buried may be forgotten, or sometimes the person does not return.

On Sachuset Beach near the Hanging Rocks, there is a legend that a treasure is buried. There is a 160-foot deep crack called Purgatory Chasm found outside town. This is a cave created by wave action where the sea rushes in and spurts out like a geyser in the cave opening. These types of caves are called "Spouting Caves" or a "Purgatory." A Purgatory is defined as an opening in the ground. According to lore, people would put food in these openings, so the people sent to purgatory could eat. This also was where the Devil went underground or the chasm was created when the devil chopped off the head of a Native American maiden. Since there are so many strange legends about this hole in the ground, what better place to hide something of value where no one would dare look for it.

NEWPORT

The first documented settlers in town were the Quakers in 1639. However, there is evidence of hunter-gatherer people living in this area between 10,000 and 12,000 years ago. Later, the Narragansett tribe, who were members of the Algonquian, and Wampanoag tribe lived here.

Pirates, smugglers, and wreckers also once thrived in this location. This was the place where molasses and New England Rum ran rampant. Both these products were considered the life blood of economy for Newport.

In writings from Cotton Mather, he states that "'The Devil's Seat'" is at the very edge of a precipice where, with his tail laid over his shoulder as a scepter, the devil would majestically direct the exercises." Apparently, this was where bad things happened.

It is thought that this may be the Viking site called Wampanoag. However, that is the name of the tribe who lived here, and not a Viking word. Still, this was one place where the Vikings supposedly landed.

The Bay when crossing into Newport, Rhode Island.

The Stone Tower in Touro Park is one of the most unique structures in North America. It was built as a windmill by none other than Benedict Arnold, himself. This is the same Arnold that became an American traitor later in life. It is known that he owned this property, but there is a question as to whether he actually built the windmill.

There is another version to the story. Perhaps the Norsemen built it between the twelfth or thirteenth

centuries and the tower is what is left of a medieval Catholic church. The structure itself is where the questions come from. The circular stone building is unusual for New England builders. Most of their structures are rectangular made with wood or brick. The building has eight columns and arches, which are very rare in New England construction. Whomever built the structure, it is believed that artifacts from that time still exist here. The town was also a safe haven for the accused witches from Salem, Massachusetts in 1692. It seems strange that certain places have more than one unusual circumstance happening there. There are reasons these are enchanted places.

Three miles from the State House is a battlefield that decided the fate of the Aquedneck tribe. Lots of arrowheads and hatchets have been found. This was a swamp before the Europeans came and the Narragansetts fought the Aquedneck, who became subjects of that nation. The seat of power was the Sachem, Miantunomu, who lived on Tomony Hill. Miantunomu's fate is gruesome. He was taken to Hartford, Connecticut, tried, and delivered to Uncas, Connecticut, for execution. He never made it back to Uncas. He was returning to Newport, and at the Sachem's Plain in East Norwich, Connecticut, in the field, he was tomahawked on the spot east of the road where many stones marked his grave for years.

By the 1690s, Newport was one of the principle ports in North America. The state's reputation as a haven for pirates earned the nickname "Rogues Island." Other nicknames for Newport are: City by the Sea, Sailing Capital of the World, Queen of the Summer Resorts, and America's Society Capital.

It was occupied by the British from 1776 through 1779. Before they fled, the citizens burned the city. This is the site of the only battle on Rhode Island soil between the American and British. In August 1778, General Sullivan withdrew his troops. He was pursued and the battle was fought at East Main Street and Butts Hill. Eventually, the Americans retreated to Tiverton, Massachusetts. In 1780, the French reclaimed Newport under Rochambeau, and for the rest of the war, Newport was the base of French troops. Also, many battles in French and Indian War fought here.

In 1949, a treasure chest was found at the base of Newport Cliffs, just south of city. It is thought to be buried by the pirate, Charles Harris, in 1723, however, the tide came back in and reburied the chest. That chest has never been recovered. Harris was a partner of Edward Low, so he did learn the piracy trade by a master. Harris did admit to burying a treasure here before he was hanged in Newport in July 1723. He was one of twenty-five pirates who were hanged on that summer day.

Pirates hanged here were tarred to slow the decay and left at Gravelley Point, overlooking the Bay. This was to warn people that Newport was no longer a safe haven for pirates. Later, they were brought to Goat Island and buried near Fort Anne; the ruins can still be seen at a mark half way between high and low tide, so the tide would forever flow over them, and they would never find rest. Perhaps that wish came true. It is said that the visitor can hear wailing and seeing glowing orbs here. This island was sold to Newport by Benedict Arnold for ten pounds. It is ironic that the fort here was built with the King's part of privateer (or pirate) money. A tenth of the privateers' stolen money was taken by the King of England.

Thomas Tew, the pirate also known as "the Rhode Island Pirate" is said to have buried $100,000 in Newport in the late 1600s. He claimed to have ancestors here since 1640, and considered Rhode Island his home. Tew was very popular here. There is a story that once when he came into port, the entire town went out and greeted him. So, how did Tew become a pirate or "go on account?" In 1692, he planned to sail his ship, *Amity*, to Africa to raid a French fort for the English as a privateer. However, the crew and Tew decided to search for treasure instead and became pirates. They went to the Red Sea, raided and captured the *Great Mogul*, a ship belonging to Aurangzeb, a wealthy leader in the area. There was over $100,000 worth of gold, silver, gems, pearls, ivory, and silk. He was mentioned by name in King William III 1695 Royal Warrant to Captain Kidd as a "wicked and ill-disposed person." Kidd was suppose to arrest Tew, but by this time, Tew was already dead.

In 1690, Tew became a leading figure in the illegal trade between Madagascar and Newport. The group was called the

Pirate Round. The Pirate Round was in force for about thirty years. By the end of the seventeenth century, the famous pirate takes of the Spanish Treasure Fleet had become scarce. The Fleet had become well armed and sailed at infrequent schedules. Also, the treasure taken by Spain out of South America was running low. Basically, it became hard to take the treasure. The pirates needed to look elsewhere, so they started to look to the Mogul and Arab treasure ships. These ships were even more wealthy than the Spanish ships of old.

The Round was a route that linked ports in the Caribbean and North American colonies, specifically, Rhode Island with Madagascar. That was where the treasures for the seventeenth century pirates would come from. Some famous pirates who were part of the Round were: Bart Roberts, Ben Avery, Thomas Tew, and Captain Kidd (though after Tew's time in the Round). The pirates were welcomed in the colonies because the British had enacted the Navigation Acts, which stated that only England could trade with the colonies. This created bad will in the colonies and the Roundsmen or Red Sea Men (the pirates of the Pirate Round) were embraced here. Rhode Island was the "clearing house" for the eastern treasure from the Round. The glory of the Round did not last long for Tew, however. In 1694, he was killed with a gun shot to his stomach when he attempted to board another Mogul ship. His sea chest, the only known sea chest of a pirate, can be seen in the Pirate Museum in the Florida Keys. The pirates Vane and Yeats also attacked ships off the Rhode Island coast in 1718 and are said to have buried treasure all along the shore. It is clear that pirate treasure did and does exist in Rhode Island.

There are four Lighthouses in the Newport area; Castle Hill, Lime Rock, Goat Island, and Rose Island. Rose Island, also known as Conskuet Island, has the ruins of a fort called Fort Hamilton, somewhere, but none of the remains are visible. It was used as a defense against the British in 1798 – 1800. It was considered cannon proof. It is called Rose Island because, at one time, wild roses grew all over. The lighthouse was built in 1870 and abandoned in 1971. It was re-lit in 1993. This island is owned by the Rose Island Lighthouse Foundation and is a bird sanctuary today. It has no water, phone, cable, or electricity.

The island is the site of mass graves and World War II ruins. It was used to store explosives during that era. There is no list of how many people are buried here, but Civil War era artifacts and skeletons were found in 1938. They were re-buried. In 1823, the cholera epidemic victims were buried here in a mass grave. Voices and footsteps are heard by numerous visitors. It is indeed a lonely place.

The *U-853* (a German submarine) was wrecked off the coast. The crew is still in the sub. This wreck is about eight miles off Sandy Point. Over $750,000 in jewels were taken from an American Express Office in Paris, France, in World War II that were on the sub, as well as about $1,000,000 worth of mercury. However, this is a military graveyard. There is no diving allowed on the site, however, there have been strange noises heard around the sub. It is considered a haunted place.

Fort Adams at Brenton's Point was destroyed in 1776 by the British, but then rebuilt by the British in 1793 and still stands in Newport today. Brenton's Point is also another place where the famous pirate Captain Kidd buried some treasure.

There have been numerous shipwrecks here. In 1912, the liner, *Commonwealth*, rammed the battleship, and the *USS New Hampshire* sank in the harbor in fog.

Not every story that has a ghost story actually is a haunted spot. Sometimes there are supposed hauntings because of the way a building was built. The story is told of an old house in Newport that was remodeled. An old saw was left on a wooden stud and when the wall was put up and a nail went through the board, just touching the saw blade, when the wind blew in a certain way, the wall would start to sing. Many families moved believing that the house was haunted. One owner lost his temper and blew a hole in the wall when he could not stop it from singing. He found the saw and realized what was happening. Nor do all vessels wrecked on Newport's shore have a reason. In 1750, at Easton's Beach, a vessel was discovered. No one was on board, and the ship was in good condition. It never hit anything but a dog and cat were found in the cabin. No one knows what happened.

There is however, a haunted tavern here called the White Horse. It is the oldest operating tavern in the United States. It was built in 1652 and became a tavern in 1673, owned by William Mayes, Sr. His son, William Mayes Jr., was a pirate. The infamous Captain Kidd was commissioned to hunt Mayes down and bring him in. Today, strange orbs and shadows are seen. Footsteps are heard, but no one is found in the room where the sounds occur. Many people have seen a figure standing at the windows of the tavern, when no one is there. Doors are locked and unlocked often. There is also a sense of a presence in the tavern. Exactly who is haunting this inn and why is unknown. As a pirate hang out, perhaps the ghost is guarding lost treasure.

NORTH KINGSTON OR KINGSTOWN/ SOUTH KINGSTON OR KINGSTOWN/KINGSTON

South Kingston is a Narragansett battle field. The tribe lost over 1,000 men during a King Philip's War battle in 1675. This area was called the "little rest" because the colonial troops rested here while on the way to the Great Swamp Battle during King Philip's War, where King Philip was killed.

South Kingston is called Quawawehunk, meaning "where the land shakes and trembles." The meaning could be for a couple of reasons. Many Native American names for swamps or bogs mean that the land shakes or trembles. What was meant was that when one walks on boggy ground, the ground bounces under foot. It could also be where minor earthquakes were felt, but because this was a swamp, the first meaning is probably the reason for the name.

There was a Narragansett fort somewhere in the area. This is the site of the Great Swamp Battlefield, found off State 138 and Route 2 East and part of the old Pequot Trail, where the last battle of King Philip's War occurred. On December 19, 1675, over 2,000 Native Americans and 80 settlers were shot or burned alive here. It is considered one of the most vicious battles ever fought on New England soil. There is no wonder that this is also a haunted place. It is now a battleground burial site (with a marker) where one can hear war cries,

gunshots, screams, and crying. There are even reports of seeing the Native Americans dressed in war regalia walking through the swamp.

It is said that the Native Americans were not prepared to fight the Europeans here. Was King Philip trying to lead his warriors to the Native American fort? It seems that the prediction of Panacos, a Native American Shawmon, came true. He said that King Philip would never fall to the white man. He died at the Mount Hope Fort, but it is said that he died in this battle. He was knifed by a Native American, who turned traitor. His severed head was sent to Plymouth, Massachusetts, where it was displayed for over twenty years. His body was quartered and hung on four different trees. The historic marker says, "Three quarters of a mile to the south on an island in the Great Swamp of the Narragansett, Indians were defeated by Massachusetts Bay, Connecticut, and Plymouth Colonies, Sunday, December 19, 1675."

Why was there so much conflict here? Perhaps the founder of Rhode Island said it best, "God Land will be as great a God with us English as God Gold was with the Spaniards." What

Swamps abound in the state of Rhode Island.

that meant was than owning land or gold at any cost was the true reason for English and Spanish exploration of the new world. That goal did destroy the way of life of the north and south Native Americans. Major conflict always occurs when the survival of people are at stake.

The North Kingston Lighthouse is located on Plum Beach, the west passage of Narragansett Bay. The Hurricane of 1938 was a fierce storm that destroyed many lighthouses in New England. The keeper and assistant here survived the gigantic waves of thirty feet or more by lashing themselves to the clock mechanisms in the fog bell room on the top. The lighthouse was completely restored in 1999.

This was where the discovery of an ancient Norse battle ax in 1889 lead this town to claim that the Norse landed here. It is part of the old Pequot Trail and the Post Road follows part of the path today.

The *Devil's Cloven Footprints* can be seen off this road since 1671. They can be seen off the Post Road, now Route 1, near the intersection of Devils Foot Road (Route 403), near Quonset Point. Go to the west side of Post Road, just south of the railroad bridge near the Point. There is parking available and the visitor can walk up the rock formation that overlooks the railroad tracks to see the footprints. The Native American legend states that a woman sold her soul to the Devil and brewed potions and spells here. When the Devil came to claim her soul, she ran off and the Devil left his footprints while he chased her. This area is also called the Devil's Foot Ledge, The Devil's Footprints, and Devil's Tracks. Only two footprints remain; the others have been destroyed over the years. The logical explanation is that they are dinosaur tracks. These fossils can be found all through southern New England.

PORTSMOUTH/PAWTUCKET

Pawtucket is a Native American name that means "place by the waterfall" or "falls of river." This is where the Blackstone River starts to descend. In 1650, iron ore was discovered. The first United States cotton thread was manufactured here at the Samuel Slater Mill using water power in 1793.

Portsmouth is the site of "Founders Brook" that was originally called Pocasset. There is a stone marker off Boyd's Lane to mark where the settlers first landed. The town was settled in 1638 and is the second oldest settlement in Rhode Island. It was settled by religious dissidents, who followed Anne Hutchinson and were expelled from Massachusetts. When the Europeans arrived, petroglyphs were discovered on the rocks in the area, but no one is sure what they meant or who carved them. Remember, the Native Americans really did not have writing.

The richest family, the Overings, in New England once lived near Union Street in Portsmouth. In 1710, the Overings' land was occupied by the British. Legend states that the British General Richard Prescott buried gold coins somewhere on the farm before he was captured by the Patriots. He is said never to have returned to retrieve his treasure. It is also said that General George Washington and Rochambeau marched through this area during the Revolutionary War. Anyplace armies camped would be a great place to find items that were left behind, either by accident or the item was just too heavy to carry anymore, and left.

In 1832, this town was rocked by the appearance of a werewolf. The story goes that a priest went insane and was murdered by the residents because he was a werewolf. The Portsmouth Poor Asylum closed in the 1920s and is now overgrown and in ruins. These types of stones tend to taint and stay with an area for a long time. Things seen and done can enchant a place.

So, do you think that sea serpents are only stories from a long ago era by people who were superstitious? Think again. On July 30, 2002, a sea creature was sighted on Teddy Beach in Island Park in Portsmouth. The creature was said to be fifteen feet long, green and black with a white belly and four-inch teeth. It was hissing, as it disappeared into the sea.

PROVIDENCE

This town is found in the north valley of the forty-six-mile-long Blackstone River. Water is critical to understanding the

history of any region in New England. It is the lifeblood of any early town. The Moshassuck and Woonsinatucket Rivers originally came together to form a great salt marsh, which was located northeast of the present site of Kennedy Plaza. Roger Williams was exiled from Massachusetts for religious reasons and settled here on the banks of the Seekonk River, near a fresh water spring in June 1636. He called the area "Providence Plantation" and purchased it from the Narragansett tribe. Williams also recorded the first documented earthquake in Rhode Island on June 1, 1638.

The Narragansett village here was called Chaubatick, which means, "at the forked river" or "the river which bounds." There was also another village near A'wumps Pond, now Wallum Lake. The Native American name is from the Pequot language, and was the name of the Quinebaog Chief who used to live here. The old Pequot Trail was once part of Weybosset Street. The name means, "narrows." It was the easiest place to cross the Providence River. From this point, the traveler would be able to continue into Massachusetts. The road is somewhat curved because it follows the old foot path. The Wampanoag Trail once passed near the Red Bridge, crossing near the Washington Bridge. It is here that ferries were first established. Ferries were necessary for the residents of this island community. In the vicinity of Stone Bridge, a ferry was established as early as 1640. In 1680, the narrowest place in the Warren River was near present-day Kelly's Bridge, so it is no wonder that a ferry was once established there.

Amethyst was found in Iron Hill Quarry, and Beryl was found in Johnston Quarry and in Spragueville area. There is also the Native American burial site near Narrow Lane. It is still a protected site for the Narragansetts and Niantics.

There is a legend about this town that starts in 1511. Petroglyphs found all through the state are said to be carved by the Portuguese explorer, Miguel Cortereal. The story is that Miguel was searching for his lost brother, who was shipwrecked in the North Atlantic. Miguel somehow sailed into Narragansett Bay, where he lived with the Native Americans and wrote on the rocks to tell others his story. It is said that he traveled throughout southern New England and carved messages into the stones. This even includes the

famous rock carvings in Dighton, Massachusetts. There is more about these carvings and area in the Massachusetts section of this book.

During King Philip's War, this town was destroyed and burned to the ground in March 1676. This town also fell to the British in late 1776, but there was a way to make some money during the occupation. Providence ships ran the New England-West Indies leg of the "triangle trade." Privateering or legalized piracy to seize foreign cargoes was another important income to the people who lived here.

Before the summer months in 1776, all gun powder in America was made in Groton and New London, Connecticut. It was decided to build a gun powder mill here in January 1777. To this day, the mill is still undiscovered. It was kept a military secret for a long while. It is known to have been located on Powder Mill Turnpike, which is Route 44 and the Putnam Pike, northwest from Providence.

There are no traces left of the nine forts that were built here during the Revolutionary War era. Fort Washington was built in 1775 and its location was known for a time, but recently the site was leveled when enlarging the port facilities. It is thought that more ruins can be found on Fox Hill between Field's and Sassafras Points. Fort Ninigret is found on Fort Neck Road and thought to be an earthwork fort built by the Native Americans. That is not true. This fort was built by Dutch traders early in the seventeenth century. It was used as a trading post with the Native Americans and the site of an early alliance between Captain John Mason and the Pequots and Niantics. The fort was dedicated in 1883 as a memorial to the Narragansetts and Niantic tribes and named for a great Niantic Sachem.

There is a legend of a old Huguenot settlement ghost town about fifteen miles south of the town. The first bridge was built here in 1710. In 1783, a peddler was walking the old road from Fall River to Providence and is said to have been carrying a very heavy load. He stopped at a house on the outskirts of town for the night. Months went by and the peddler was never seen again, though the family suddenly seemed to come into a lot of money. Years later, strange sounds were heard in the house, cries, groans, all coming

from the chimney. One day, the owner found a pair of pants there and in the pockets were wads of old Continental paper money. Apparently, the peddler had been found at last.

Gaspee Point is located seven miles below Providence. In 1772, the British Schooner, *Gaspee*, was wrecked here. The Patriots blew up the ship and debris was found all over the beach. This was one of the first overt acts of aggression of the Revolutionary War, and predates the Battle of Lexington and Concord. There were reports that at low tide, a hull of a wrecked ship could been seen off Indian Point.

Treasure Hunting Tip

Anytime reports by witnesses seeing wrecks off certain areas, may lead to treasure being washed up on nearby beaches

This was the town where the first American jewelry maker lived and worked. In 1796, Nehemiah Dodge was a silversmith who had a shop on the banks of the Moshassuck and Woonsinatucket Rivers.

The 1938 Hurricane came right over Rhode Island. Entire communities were literally washed away during that storm. All communications in the entire state were severed. A tidal wave hit this city reaching 13" and 8 ½" There was standing water in Market Square. Natural disasters also leave period artifacts in regions where they occur.

SCITUATE/POTTERVILLE

A Revolutionary War campsite is located in Potterville about one mile east on Town Farm Road. Wells and fireplaces can still be found here. The name of the town, Scituate, is a Native American word meaning, "cold running water." The Ganier Memorial Dam destroyed six villages that used to exist in the valley in 1915. Underwater or flooded towns, due

to the dam building, is a great source of artifacts of that era. One fun way for the treasure hunter to collect authentic relics is to look for it when the lakes that were created run low or when there is a storm and items wash on shore. Jerimoth Hill, located in town, is the highest point in Rhode Island. It is not really high, but 812 feet is a good hike. However, until recently it was off limits to hikers. The visitor needs to get permission to hike here.

There is a ghost town located near the Foster town line. An old dirt road lead to the colonial town in the 1700s, called Hopkinsville, or Cider Town, or Whip-O-Will Heights. There was a church, tavern and store at one time. There are many real physical dangers, including overgrown cellar holes, wild animals, old rusty machinery, and broken pieces of glass, and other ceramic items.

Treasure Hunting Tip

Always be careful when visiting any type of "ghost" place.

TIVERTON

Fort Barton, also known as Tiverton Heights Fort was located in Tiverton, and built in 1777. There is not much left of the earthen fort. It is considered a ghost fort today and in ruins.

This is also thought to be the site of another Norse landing and of the "speaking rocks" or "singing rocks." It was discovered in the mid-1700s. There are hieroglyphics carved into the boulders, but no one knows what they say or who carved them. Many theories have arisen as to the nature of the original six rocks found. It is said that the Norse, Native Americans, or early explorers must be responsible for the carvings. Only one rock remains today.

Sin and Flesh Brook in town is the site of a murder of a European settler by a Native American. Weetamoo Woods is named after a Pocasset Queen, which means, "sweetheart." There is the remains of a seventeenth century old mill and village on Eight Rod Way called Borden Mill. The cobbled road is lined with stone walls. This area was also known as Howland's Ferry for hundreds of years because a ferry once crossed at this point.

WAKEFIELD/SMITHFIELD

The green gem Bowenite was discovered in Smithfield. This gem is called Jade by early mineralogists, but it is really a form of Serpentine. Octahedrite has also been found in the lime rock in the area.

This is also the site of a ghost town called The Lost City or Island Woods. In 1836, the town was located in the north part of town. Relics abound here, but voices are also heard here when no one is around. It is believed that this was a Native American burial ground, so perhaps these are the voices of Native Americans.

There is a Narragansett legend about Sugarloaf Hill in Wakefield and a treasure buried that is guarded by snakes. As the seeker tries to take the treasure out of the ground, it just sinks deeper and the snakes seem to get more aggressive.

WARREN/WESTERLY

There was an old wreck reported on the beach at Misauamicut State Park located in Westerly. It was believed to be the American Merchantman ship, *Minerva*. There was no treasure on this ship, but plenty of era artifacts to be found.

This town is a mineralogist's dream. Granite and soapstone were quarried years ago. The quarries are closed, but the soapstone quarry was mined by the Native Americans before the settlers came, and re-discovered in 1878. There have been numerous artifacts found here. They include: copper, horns, stone, bone, brass and shells, arrowheads, knives, blades, spears, drill and ax heads, ceremonial stones, bowls,

pipes, and idols. A drill was a sharp stone with a knob to bore through skin and wood. In the Westerly granite quarry, the gem Beryl has been found.

Remember the eclipse of the moon in Mount Hope and the bad omen of the start of King Philip's War it is said to have herald? In Warren, another omen was seen and reported. On June 30, 1675, English troops saw a scalp that appeared on the face of the moon. This was seen before King Philip's War actually started, but the men had seen a horrible battle field. Poles were found which hung the eight severed heads and hands of Englishmen. The men were killed by King Philip at Mattapoissett, near the Kickamuit River, on June 24. It has been reported that these men do not rest, and will often appear where their heads were left, as if searching for their lost heads.

This town is located on the deep Warren River channel. It was considered a strategic position for the Native Americans against the Europeans during King Philip's War. It was also considered an important position for the Marquis de Lafayette in 1778 during the Revolutionary War. He and his army camped here near Windmill Hill.

Native American artifacts abound. This was the location of the Wampanoag village of Sowams. Oyster and clam shells have been found in abundance. Massasoit Spring is where the Massasoit tribe and Sachem camped. A tablet marks this historical place.

WICKFORD/WARWICK

Warwick was a Narragansett village from the Paleo-American era. The village was known as Apponaug, and located in West Warwick. It was the hub of the economic and political life of the area. Native American artifacts have been found near Pear Point, including, stone axes, mortars, pestles, platter, dishes, pipes, and stone bowls that are over 10,000 years old. There have also been railroad era relics found. Copper religious medals from the 1830s, iron spoons, and copper wires have been discovered in the Sweet Meadow Brook area. Native American relics have been found along Buckeye Brook and an ancient fish weir or water trap has been discovered along the Pawtucxet River.

In 1977, on the Forge Road near Greenwich Cove, there was a very rare Native American discovery made – projectile points from the late Archaic occupation (1600-500 BC) and post holes from a primitive shelter.

King Philip attacked the deserted town of Warwick in March 1676. The people fled to Newport after being warned of the attack. All the homes were destroyed. Though the town was re-populated, anytime a place is destroyed by nature or man or is deserted quickly, artifacts may remain from the era.

Strange unknown petroglyphs were found here on Mark Rock. Known as Cocumscussoc, which is Narragansett and means, "place of the marked rock," it is called "Devil's Foot Rock" and is located about a mile north of town. There are two legends telling why it was named. The first legend say that the devil left his print while chasing a Native American girl in the granite ledge. The Native Americans also had legends of strange stone markings that were left by demons or giants and the Europeans said that the devil left them. The second legend is that a Native American girl killed a settler, and as she fled the area and came to the rock, she met a nicely dressed settler who suggested she follow him to safety. She refused and called about her deity, Hobomoko, to help her. Hobomoko stamped his foot here before taking her to a place called Purgatory Chasm and flung her into the sea.

In March 1766, privateering became legal in Rhode Island. In other words, piracy was now legal here by an act of the Continental Congress. John Brown was a famous privateer from Warwick. It is said that in 1759, one-fifth of the male population in Rhode Island was made up of privateers.

In 1839, Geologist Charles T. Jackson found a boulder called "Drum Rock" south of the village site of Apponaug, now located behind the Cowesett Hills Apartment Complex. He said, "There is a curious mass of rock delicately balanced upon two points, so as to be moved with great ease by the hand, and it is said it's even rocked by the wind. As it rocks, a sound is produced audible at a great distance, perhaps six to eight miles. The conclusion is that this rock may have been used by the Indians to warn each other in times of great danger or to call people together."

Belleville is a ghost town found about eleven miles south of Warwick and one mile southwest of Wickford.

Roger Williams was canoeing to the original trading post in Wickford when his canoe overturned and he lost all his goods near the old Post Road about two and a half miles north of the town. There is also an area where stagecoach robberies took place called Robber's Corner on Highway 2, near Wickford Junction. It may be that some of the robbers left some loot behind.

Smith's Haunted Castle is a site of a mass grave of at least forty English soldiers, who died during King Philip's War in the last battle called the Great Swamp Fight. This is also the battle where King Philip died and perhaps as many as 500 to 1,000 Native Americans as well. It is a stone structure built in 1637. After the War, this trading post was used as a Native American slave selling place.

Though this is the smallest New England state, it is full of haunted treasure stories. This was a very important state from the beginning to modern times. The stories and history are truly amazing and this region will always be considered a magical and enchanted state.

Now, on to Massachusetts, the first state that was settled by the Pilgrims.

Leaving Rhode Island and its abundance of history and lost loot.

Chapter Three

Massachusetts

GENERAL

The Massachusetts nicknames are: Bay State, Old Colony, Puritan State, Baked Bean State, and Old Bay State. The town of Webster has the distinction of having the longest geographic name in the United States. Lake Webster's actual name is: Lake Chargoggagoggmanchauggagoggchaubunagungamaugg. This Native American word, means "you fish on your side of the lake, I fish on my side, no body fishes in the middle." Arrowheads have been found in the area, so perhaps it was the site of a Native American battlefield.

The Vikings are said to have landed in many places along this coast. It almost seems to be that the Norsemen landed all over New England. The places that claim to be landing sites are told throughout the book, but to name just a few: Andover, West Andover, Mendon, Webster, and Shutesbury, Massachusetts, all have claims to be a site of the Norsemen landing.

Treasure Hunting Tip

What is known is that the Vikings did come to this land. Their Sagas clearly document that they were here in the year 1000. Relics from that era may be hard to find after so much time has passed, but it is not unrealistic to think that something may be found in those places that have Viking legends about the area.

In bogs and swamps all through southern Massachusetts, clay Native American peace pipes have been found since King Philip's War in the 1600s. Perhaps they were left as the tribes fled the area, or maybe they were left during battles that occurred during that time in many places throughout Massachusetts and Connecticut. It could be that they were left when it was realized that peace was not going to be an option at that time. There were basically six Algonkian Massachusetts Native American nations, with numerous sub-tribes, when the Pilgrims first arrived. They were:

> The **Pennacook**, who were living in northern areas of the state. After King Philip's War, they went to Canada.

> The **Nipmuck**, who were found in the western part of Massachusetts. The town of Worchester was the site of their main village. This tribe sided against the colonists in King Philip's War and were almost completely destroyed by the end of 1676.

> The **Massachusett** were living in the Boston area. They were destroyed by a plague after the Europeans arrived. Only 500 were left and they became known as the "Praying Indians." The Native American name means "at or about the great hill," and this tribe who the state is named from.

> The **Pokanoket**, which included the Wampanoag and Mashpee, were living on Cape Cod, Nantucket Island, and Martha"s Vineyard. The Pilgrims first encountered this tribe when they landed in Plymouth.

The **Nauset** also lived on Cape Cod and the islands. They were a very friendly people to the colonists and assisted the colonists during King Philip's War.

There were many sub-divisions of the seven main tribes. Throughout the book, the sub-division name of the tribe is given at times, so it may become confusing. The list below is a partial list of the sub-divisions of the various nations:

Hoosac, Pocumtuck, Squakheag, Nonatuc, Waranock, Agawam (who had villages in Wareham, Plymouth and Ipswich), Nashua, Ninigret, Mashpee, Wamesit, Nashoba, Wachusett, Quabaug, Mystic, Naumkeag (from the Salem area), Neponset, Monomoyett, Nantucket, Pocasset, Nemasket, Mushawn, Pamet, Patuxet (this tribe was exterminated before the Europeans came in the Plymouth area), Ponoakanet, Namaskaket, Nobsusset, Pochet, Tonset, Nonomoyk, Pocumtuck, and Ponkapoag.

Treasure Hunting Tip

Always find out as much as possible about an area before starting to hunt. For Native American artifacts, you will need permission to be at the area, of course, but also it helps reduce confusion, if one knows that one group is a sub-tribe of another group, and why names may be different in various documentation.

There were Native American villages found throughout the area, though sometimes the actual site is imprecise. There was a Massachusett village called Woruntuck and another called Totapoag, meaning "twisted pond," but the exact locations are vague. The names refer to a location where the tribe used to dwell. At some point, Totapoag, the pond must have looked twisted when observed from a certain angle.

The treasure seeker should always pay attention to Native American words and places that mean shining or shiny. That may mean a place where some sort of gem-type stone is located. Somewhere in Franklin County on the Connecticut River, there was a village in 1663 called Wissatinnewag, meaning "shining hill" or "slippery hill." There also seems to be some sort of shiny stone or something that shined in Barnstable County. Near Wequaquet Lake there was a Wampanoag village, meaning "the shining place" or "torchlight place" or maybe "swampy place." The Weesquobs River in Barnstable County means "shining rocks." In Dukes County, there is a cliff called Wacobske, meaning "a shining rock."

Other interesting Native American places to search for artifacts may be as follows. In Bristol County at Weetamoe's Crossing is where one of the only Pocasset female chief or Suncksqua, called Weetamoe drowned. It was extremely uncommon to have a female Sachem in the New World. The word Weetamoe means "the lodge keeper." Also in Bristol County, Sassamon's Cove may yield some sort of treasure. This is a Wampanoag name for John Sassamon, who was Metacom's or King Philip's secretary. He was murdered in this place by the English, which is yet another reason for the start of King Philip's War in 1675. The name may mean, "cranberries." There is a legend about how cranberries came to Massachusetts. In the Mashpee area, which was inhabited by the Wampanoag tribe, missionary Reverend Richard Bourne converted many Native Americans to Christianity in 1660. (That was another major issue with King Philip. He did not like the Europeans changing the way of life of the Native Americans.) Anyway, in this story, during an argument with the Reverend, the medicine man lost his temper and chanted a bog rhyme, miring the Reverend in quicksand. They agreed to a test of wills which lasted fifteen days. The Reverend was not thirsty or hungry because it is said that a white dove placed a succulent cherry in his mouth each day. The medicine man could not cast a spell on the dove. He was exhausted and had not been able to eat or drink, so he fell to the ground and Bourne was free. Meanwhile, one cherry had fallen into the bog, grown, and multiplied. Hence, the cranberry came to Cape Cod.

Pokanoket, a Wampanoag word meaning "fort" or "refuge" was a favorite village or fort of King Philip found in Bristol County. Annawon's Rock in the same County is named in honor of the Wampanoag warrior and one of King Philip's most trusted Lieutenants, Annawon. He was captured near this rock in 1675 in the Squannahonk Swamp and killed.

Osceola Mountain and Island derives its name from Asiyaholo, meaning "black drink." It was a ceremonial potion and the place where this drink was obtained. One has to wonder what happened in the place in Middlesex County called Mashepagonoke Pond. It is a Natick word, meaning "at the place of the wicked destroyer" or "place of bad pestilence." A plague of some sort, perhaps? Is this where an entire village died or disappeared? The reason for the name is unknown. However, the village in the same area called Magaenak is Natick meaning, "where the Mohawks come" or "wolf place." The pond may be a battleground between the Naticks and the Mohawks.

Wahconah Falls and Park in Berkshire County, means "the old fort." In Barnstable County at Quanset Cove and Pond may be an abbreviation of Aqounset, meaning "boundary place" or "at the fort." Quaboag Pond and River in Worcester County is perhaps an abbreviation of a Nipmuck word, Msquboag, meaning "bloody pond" or "red pond." This may not be a battle site, in spite of the name. In Worcester County is a place called Agutteback Pond. This was originally called Qucuckpaug or Ohkeckpeg Pond. It is near a soapstone (steatite) deposit (quarry) where the Native Americans made kettles, dishes, and utensils. Perhaps Msquboag may be a place where the red material used in painting and such material was found. Either way, Native American relics can be found here.

Hoosicwhisic Pond in Norfolk County is a Natick word meaning "at the place of the small kettle" or kettle runs almost dry" or "place of the writings." What writings are being talked about is the question that comes to mind. Along old Native American trails there are two areas where strange markings or rock carvings have been discovered: Three Dagger Rock in Amesbury, Massachusetts, and Sword Rock in Westford on the Mohawk Trail. Who carved them and what they mean is still not clear, but the various theories will be discussed further in the book.

There are a few places in Massachusetts that may have made the Native Americans nervous to visit. Cheppipogut in Bristol County is a Wampanoag word meaning "spirits-place pond." Chaboken Pond in Worchester County is a Nipmuck word that means "hell pond" or "places of separated spirits." The town of Essex was named Chebacco by the Native American which meant "place of spirits." What happened in these places is not clear, but obviously something unnatural occurred creating the names for these places.

The Old Connecticut Path was a Native American trail through the state. This trail started in Cochituate, ran through the east part of Framingham, Hopkinton, and Grafton, to Woodstock, Connecticut. The trail came through the Bay (Boston), Watertown, Wayland, and Sudbury (Rice Hill is on path). Following the footsteps of Native Americans may yield items from their era.

A gem found all through Massachusetts is Beryl. It has been found on Pearl Hill in Fitchburg and a blue type called goshenite, and a rose type of beryl and Smoky Quartz have been found in Goshen. Another gemstone found all along the coast of Massachusetts is Porphyry. This word comes from the Greek, porphurious, meaning "purple or dark red." It is an ornamental stone that comes in the colors of black, red, fine green, and a rich chocolate. A rare earth element, Epidote, has been discovered in Woburn. There are two supposedly documented meteorite landings in Massachusetts, one in Lowell in 1846 and the other in Northampton in 1963. Various unusual minerals and gems can always be found at meteorite landing sites. It is great to find something that is literally out of this world.

Great ships were built on the shores of this state. Cleopatra's Barge, a pleasure craft, was built in Newburyport in 1816. It became the craft of King Kamehameha of Hawaii, the last Monarch of that state. There have been many, many shipwrecks on the Massachusetts coast and islands. Many will be named in the town that they were last known to be near. To start this long list, the schooner, *H.C. Higginson*, was wrecked near Nantasket Beach in a gale in 1888. During the 1938

Rivers were the best, fastest, and easiest way to
travel through New England.

Hurricane, the tanker, *Phoenix*, was dragged with anchors
attached, five miles up the Taunton River to Somerset.

There are many islands that dot the Massachusetts
coastline. This will not come as a huge surprise, but many
islands have tales about where pirate treasure may have been
buried. These islands will be covered in this chapter, but to
name a few: Grape Island, Hog Island, Swans Island, and
on Gallops Island, the story is that the pirate Avery is said
to have buried a chest of diamonds and gold coins. There
is also said to be a pirate treasure buried in Oyster Harbor
in Barnstable County, but the details are vague. The pirate,
John Breed's treasure is said to be buried on Swans Island.
Walker's pirate treasure is said to be buried near the East Chop
Light, and the female pirate, Mary Main's cache is claimed
to be on Plum Island.

A pirate's life was not easy, nor was his death. In 1684,
Massachusetts enacted a severe law against piracy. However,
it is only fair to mention here that the pirates were invited to
come here in the 1600s by Sir William Phipps, Governor of

Massachusetts at that time. In 1704, Captain John Quelch and six of his men were hanged in Boston. Quelch just came into Boston Harbor, walking through town, not really believing that he would ever be challenged. He was wrong. In 1724, Captain Archer White was hanged as a pirate in Boston. His body was put in chains and left on Bird Island as a warning to other pirates not to come there. In 1726, William Fly and two men were hanged and his body was bound in chains on an island called Nix's Mate. It is said that he even reproached the hangman for doing a poor job. He is said to have put the noose around his own neck.

Even the mountains have buried treasure. There are many abandoned farms and villages in these mountains, as well as Native American battlefields. The area called Red Rock may be the site of a Native American massacre, as well as an abandoned farm. Shelburne was named after the English Lord who sided with the Americans during the Revolutionary War. He sent this town a church bell as a gift, but it was intercepted, probably by the British. Whatever happened, it never arrived, nor has it ever been found to this day. It is thought that perhaps it was buried in the area. The town of Shelburne Falls is famous for the glacial potholes found in the river. There is a marble quarry found near Ashley Falls. The Boston Customs House and the Court House in New York City were built with marble from this town. The marble dust from here was once used as fertilizer for the potato fields in Aroostook County, Maine.

In 1901, the Alpha Mine in Hinsdale was said to yield small amounts of gold. However, this claim was said to be "planted gold." There is also the tale of Chief John Konkapot of the Machian or Stockbridge tribe. Somewhere in the Berkshire Hills is his lost gold mine.

On the slopes of Monument Mountain, in Risingdale, Smoky Quartz has been found. Jasper located in the Deerfield River in Conway. Six miles south of Forge Hill in Cummington near the Berkshire Trail Highway, the gem Garnet has been discovered. In Goshen, in the Barrus Mine, green Beryl and Tourmaline still exist. In Pelham and Westhampton in various township ponds, Pearls have been found, as well as on the Sudbury River in Concord. Three miles west of Marlin

Pond in North Reading, even more pearls have been found as well as on the Connecticut River in Franklin County. In the Rollstone Hills of Fitchburg, golden Beryl has been mined.

Mount Greylock, also known as the "specter" or "spector," and the highest spot in Massachusetts is located on the famous Mohawk Trail. This was a pre-historic trail used from the post glacial era to the modern era that travels through the Appalachian Mountains as a gateway to the west. This was a natural route from the Hudson Valley to the east over the Hoosac Mountains. In the earliest years, the Mohawk Trail was no wider that eighteen inches in spots – just enough room for one person to walk through or a group of people to walk in a single file. When it opened to cars in 1914, it was widened and covered with gravel and cold oil. This was one of the most heavily traveled trails in New England. King Philip is said to have traveled this path in 1676, while he was trying to recruit the Mohawks to help him win the war with the Europeans. His pleas did not work. The Mohawks did not help him and one wonders what may have been if the Mohawks had been willing to be part of the war effort.

Benedict Arnold traveled the Trail to Fort Ticonderoga, New York. He captured the cannon and brought it back to Boston via this path. There were also many stagecoach robberies here. Did the robbers bury the treasure along the route for safekeeping and the ability to make a quick escape? In 1914, the road was designated a scenic route.

There are a few towns, mentioned throughout the book in this state, where skirmishes from Shays' Rebellion occurred. The Rebellion took place between 1786-87. This episode was considered a major incident of the post-Revolutionary War era. The story starts in the time when there were serious economic issues after the war. The farming community was hit the hardest of all. There was no paper money, credit was hard to get, and foreclosure for debt was a common occurrence. Many towns were damaged or destroyed during the war, and places were abandoned for awhile. That will take a toll on any area. In Massachusetts, the farmers appealed to the Legislation for relief, but their request was not even considered. This rebuff created the result that the farmers armed and started to cause trouble in various communities.

They did not like to be ignored by the people they had put into office. Daniel Shays, a former Captain in the Continental Army, arose as a leader of the 1,200 farmers. He led an unsuccessful assault on Springfield and the Massachusetts army pursued him, caught him, thus successfully ending the Rebellion. The next Legislative session pardoned all the rebels, and responded to their request for help.

ADAMS/NORTH ADAMS

These towns are found on the Mohawk Trail, or Route 2, and were settled in the early 1700s. The haunted five mile $15 million Hoosac Railroad Tunnel was built in the nineteenth century had a station here. Hoosac is a Native American word, meaning "a stony place." The nickname of this tunnel is "Bloody Pit," for the over 200 people who died while building. The men had to tunnel through five miles of solid rock and it was the first time the new explosive nitroglycerin was used.

North Adams is the site of the only natural, water-eroded marble bridge and cave in North American created about 550 million years ago through erosion. This marble gorge is 475 feet long and 60 feet deep. The visitor may have to wade through Hudson Brook to get to the cave. The marble found here was a coarse grain marble. The quarry at Hudson's Cave or Falls operated from 1810-1917. There is also an abandoned and very hard to find lime quarry located on the outskirts of town.

In the notch of Greylock Mountain is the lost Notch Mine. In the 1880s, this mine is said to yield iridium. It was worked until 1902 and even small amounts of gold were found. In 1825, in a spring near the town there were diamonds discovered. They sold for $500, but no other diamonds were ever located. The diamond is not a common gem found here, but perhaps they were lost by someone or traveled down the river from another source.

In the early 1900s, a man was taking a piano down the mountain. Suddenly, he saw the reflection of himself in the clouds. This terrified him and he raced down the mountain,

leaving the piano where it was. The phenomena of "seeing a shadow of an object reflected in a cloud" is called Brockengespenst, meaning "specter of the Brocken." Brocken is the highest peak of the Hartz Mountains. This phenomena often occurs on Greylock Mountain and seemed to spook the Native Americans, as well as the first settlers.

There is a legend that there is a hermit treasure located on Greylock Mountain, the highest mountain in the state reaching the height of 3,491 feet. In the 1700s, a hermit lived here and used to pay for purchases with nuggets and gold dust. He never told anyone where he got the gold, and it is thought that he buried it all around his property. It is said that perhaps he even mined the gold from Greylock. He was found frozen in his hut. Experts say that there is a vein of gold extending north through New England and south into Georgia. The Berkshire area lies directly in that line, so perhaps there is more to this story then just a legend.

Greylock Mountain area was a Quaker settlement in the 1780s. In 1901, it was believed that the gold that is thought to exist was finally found, but it was iron pyrite, only "fools gold." There was also a Quaker copper mine here. The Quakers started to look for gold, then silver, and finally found copper and brass.

There are numerous "treasures to be found" type names in this area. Between 1765 – 1783, there is a story that counterfeiters built a cabin on the north fork of Money Brook. They were making fake Spanish dollars and Pine Tree shillings. They left rather quickly, right before they were caught, and it is possible that many relics of the era were left. Landslides, floods, and frost heaves all have helped to hide what may have remained. There is a collapsed cave near Money Brook Falls, where the Spanish created their fake money. The falls are 100 feet high, so perhaps a cave did once exist, and has since been buried, covering all the era artifacts.

Fort Massachusetts guarded the Hoosac River during the French and Indian War in 1745. It was located at the town line with Williamtown and over 1,000 Native Americans burned the post in 1746. The fort was ultimately abandoned in 1760, after being burned and re-built. There was a warm, soft water spring found in Williamtown. This water was found near the old Native American north trail and comes through deep volcanic deposits, sand, and gravel. The Native Americans believed the water had curative powers. This was a sacred place. Often when places were used for magic, it seems that they hold a supernatural feeling. Perhaps that feeling was always there, and that is why magic occurred.

This town also boasts of the Red Bat Cave, named for the black, red-headed bats that once lived in the 100-foot-long and 150-foot-deep cave. This cave may have been used during the Revolution by the Tories as a hiding place.

ASUCHNET/BEDFORD/BERNARDSTON/ BRIDGEWATER/ARLINGTON

Arlington may be one place where the lost village of Menotomy can be found. Here is the story. There is a statue of Menotomy, a Native American, at the Town Hall in Arlington. In April 1775, this place was called Menotomy. It was on the route to and from Concord. A very bloody battle took place here with many British and Patriots deaths. Paul Revere also rode though Menotomy on his historic ride. So, perhaps just the name of the town changed. However, it is also claimed that the lost village is actually hidden underground in Menotomy Park between Boston and Lexington. Why the settlement disappeared without a trace remains a mystery. All that is known is that numerous battles occurred in a place called Menotomy during the Revolutionary War.

Bridgewater was attacked by Tispaquin, also known as the Black Sachem, during King Philip's War in 1676. Tispaquin was Philip's best commander. Also, a paymaster was killed here in 1920. It is thought that his payload may have been buried in the area by the killers, so they could make a quick escape.

Bernardston is known as Falls Fight Township. There were four forts here in 1736. The settlers were in a continual fight with the Native Americans. Fall sites were the fishing lifeblood of the Native American tribes living in the area. When the Europeans dammed the rivers, the waterfalls disappeared, and so did the abundant fishing grounds. The Native Americans lost a vital food source and were fighting for their very existence.

These fights were all over New England. In the book, *Maine's Waterfalls, A Comprehensive Guide*, by Patricia Hughes, this is discussed as the main reason for many waterfall sites in Maine, also being major battle sites between the settlers and tribes in that state.

Bedford was a Native American trading post in 1637, and Asuchnet was a town destroyed during King Philip's War. After being re-settled, it then became a Revolutionary War battle site. Artifacts from both eras can be found in the area.

BEVERLY

This town was called "the Bass River side of Salem." Bean pots were made at the grist mill on the Bass River in 1647. Beverly is really called Bean Town, the real place of origin for Baked Beans, not Boston. The first Man-O'-War vessel, commissioned by George Washington during the Revolutionary War, was called *Hannah*, and built in the harbor here.

Not everything strange that happened here occurred in a previous era. On January 24, 1977, white smoke was spotted on Mingo Beach. The object that was found causing the smoke was taken to the lab for analysis. The results were that it was a "highly volatile material, produced smoke when it contacted water, looked like ice, but wasn't, it was not any kind of ammunition, and it was not radioactive." The U.S. Army landing vessel, *Page*, reported to the Coast Guard that there was a "flaming red object floating in the ocean" before the Mingo Beach material was discovered. No one knows exactly what this material is or was and why it was located on the Beach to this day, or at least no public report was ever given.

On January 27, 1984, witnesses saw something fall near Route 128. It was a green and white light that flew over the trees and crashed. Nothing was ever found. However, it was a clear evening with reports of meteor showers all over the East Coast, so perhaps unique minerals can still be found there.

BLUE HILLS/BERKLEY/CAMBRIDGE

The actual shoreline of Cambridge has changed due to the changing course of the river. The first name of the town was New Towne and changed to Cambridge in 1638. Fort Washington Park was an original earthen fort in 1775. The remains can still be found. It was a three- gun battery built directly on the riverbank, but the river changed course, and now the fort is hidden several hundred yards behind the M.I.T. campus.

The town was also an ancient burying site of the pre-Algonkian Indians. These people were known throughout New England as the Red Paint People. There is a place called Wallamanumpscook in Worcester County, which is a Nipmuck word meaning "at the rock standing in the red paint place." Is this another ancient village of these people or a place where the Nipmucks would gather red clay to use as paint? The answer to that question is unknown.

Grassy Island on the Taunton River in Berkley was another ancient village of the pre-Algonkian Indians well over 1,000 years ago. Blue Hills could also perhaps be the site of the ancient Native American village called Massachuset, though the exact location is unknown.

BOSTON

The Charles River was the canoe route and main means of travel for the Native Americans living here. The easiest path to Dedham to Riverside to Boston was along the river, the 85-mile canoe route from one part of the state to another.

Though it is said that Governor Winthrop actually tried to settle in Charlestown in 1630, he moved to Boston due to the lack of drinking water where he first landed. There was a Native American fort in Charlestown built by the Ninigret tribe. There was also an ancient Native American village here called Mishawum, meaning, "great landing place."

In 1634, Boston was described in a book, *New England Prospect*, by William Wood, published in London as "not having the usual three annoyances found in the area; wolves, rattlesnakes, and mosquitoes." There was once a high mountain, directly behind the state house, that was leveled in 1810. This was probably the mountain that the state was named for, not the Berkshires mountains to the west. The name, Boston, originally came from England from the old seaport. There was a song about a monastery, called St. Botolph's in the fields. Botolph was the patron saint of Mariners. In Saxon, the name means, "to help the boat." This whole area became a shelter to weary travelers. The long title of the song, "Botolph's fields," became "Boston."

Along the Charles River, between Newton and Brookline, the Norumbega Tower stands. Tradition states that this is where Thornwald, son of Erik the Red, a Norseman, walked on the river path to this site, and where he built a fort. There is said to be the ruins of a fort here, complete with a moat. Why is it thought the Vikings built this tower? The foundations were built with double-stone walls, which are only found that way in Iceland.

The ancient Native American village that was once here was called Totant. Beaver skins were used as currency, however, things changed in 1652, when the first United States mint was established. Instead of skins, the coins minted were called "New England" and the denominations were a shilling, sixpence, and threepence. These were flat silver pieces, stamped N.E. and the Roman numerals X11 (for 12 pence = 1 shilling).

Counterfeiting was easy and because of a shortage of coins, a process called "sweating gold" was started. This process was to put gold or silver coins in a box and shaking it violently to obtain the fine gold and silver powder deposit. Also, the clipping and/or shaving the edges of coins became widespread. Some coins were intentionally broken into small pieces, known as bits, to make "change" for lesser transactions. Copper was used for coins called the Fugio Cent. Fugio mean "time flies," also known as the Franklin Cent, said to be designed by Benjamin Franklin, himself. John Oldham reported to the Pilgrims that he had heard that at about 160 miles from the Bay, the Native Americans were mining black lead, probably somewhere in the Watertown, Connecticut area. Oldham was said to be murdered by the Pequot tribe in Maine. He was found floating in a boat with his hands and feet cut off.

Boston Harbor was a very important harbor to protect from attack. For that reason, there were many forts built here. If the remains of these forts would be found (the whereabouts are not known), it would be a major find for the era in the relics that may still be there. Fort Rukman was once a Boston Harbor defense fort. The Dorchester Heights Natural Historical Site is the location where, in 1776, the Americans built a fort in one night, March 4.

Fort Warren, also called the northern Bastille, is haunted by the Lady in Black. She haunts Georges Island in Boston Harbor, where the fort was built. Her name was Meline Lemere or Lanier and her story starts in the Civil War. Her Confederate soldier husband was a prisoner here. Meline got to see him and arranged an escape, but was discovered. During the ruckus, Meline accidently shot her husband. She was captured and hanged for treason and murder. It is said that she was buried in black and has been spotted hundreds of times in the dungeon of the fort. A woman's slipper footprints have been seen in the snow. Voices are heard saying, "Don't come in here," and the Lady in Black is seen dancing, or will roll stones in the room where the men are playing poker. Why does she remain? Perhaps it is the guilt in killing her husband, when she was trying to save him. During the construction of the fort, workmen found an undisclosed amount of silver coins in ceramic jars. Also, lead shot and cannon balls were found dating from the Revolutionary War period.

Fort Independence on Castle Island was built in 1634 by Governor Thomas Dudley, and now is in ruins. The fort was located on the tip of South Boston in Boston Harbor on the island. Much of this fort fell from Cushing Hill into the sea, though parts of it could still be seen in 1835. It was once linked to the mainland by a drawbridge in 1891. It is a place where many died and for very strange reasons. Is it cursed? The facts follow: In 1637, a gunner stationed at the fort sent a warning shot across the bow of a ship that was passing

close. The shot accidently killed a passenger, who was in the rigging of the ship. The fort was abandoned in 1642, then re-fortified in 1645. In 1655, Captain Davenport was killed at there while he was sleeping next to a powder magazine. A thunderstorm came up and lightning struck the room instantly killing Davenport. In 1665, the next commander, Roger Clap raised his fourteen children in this fort. One son, named Supply, died by an accidental cannon explosion on the island and is buried here.

As an interesting side note, Clap had some interesting names for his children. They include: Experience, Wait, Hopestill, Waitstill, Thanks, Desire, Unite, and Supply.

By 1716, this was considered the most important fort in British North America. However, it was never really used during the Revolutionary War, though occupied by the British during this time. It was used to fire on Boston at times. The British destroyed the fort in 1776, as they left the area. John Hancock took control of Castle Island in 1779, and used the guns to destroy the British ship, *Somerset*. In the 1780s, the fort was used as a prison. It became Fort Independence in 1799.

If the island itself is not cursed, there is a legend that all who dare to visit this island become cursed. Before the Revolutionary War, an English man lived with his daughter. She was in love with an American, but her father opposed the union. He wanted her to marry a British officer. The two suitors dueled and the American lost. The girl committed suicide and the British officer plunged into the water, uttering a curse to anyone who ever came to the island. This was the site of a real duel in 1817. Please note that the legend talked about earlier took place before the Revolutionary War. However, Lieutenant Robert F. Massie from Virginia was killed here in a sword duel. He was accused of cheating at cards, challenged to a duel, and died. In 1905, a skeleton was found in the dudgeon of the fort. Supposedly, it was Massie's opponent who was imprisoned alive in the fort. Sailors believe that the numerous shipwrecks here are due to the curse. There have been suicides, too. In 1903, a man jumped into the ocean. Another time, a man was found here with a bullet in his head.

There is also said to be a Spanish pirate treasure buried on this island in the early seventeenth century. In 1911, a clairvoyant dreamed of this island. She saw some people burying gold. Here is what the story may be. In March 1841, it is said that pirates destroyed the ship called *The President*. This ship left New York, headed toward Boston, but disappeared. Supposedly, a piece of the ship came to shore here. It was part of a wooden plank marked "PRESIDEN." In a West Pittsfield barn, a ship document appeared and was written by an unknown person. The document said that the ship was attacked by a pirate ship called, *Dragon's Tail*. The pirates took all the gold and silver before sinking the ship – though it is thought that not all could be taken by the pirates. Perhaps there is some to be found, if *The President* could be located where it sank off Castle Island.

In 1852, the *Star*, *Philadelphia*, and *Lizzie Williams* wrecked here. In 1896, on Farragut Day, during the celebration, there were children on the *Ella* heading toward the island. The children rushed to get off and the float turned over. Four boys downed and two of the girls were trampled.

In 1898, during the Spanish-American War, the United States took the fort from the city and made the island a mine and torpedo station. Four men were killed when one of the mines rolled against a seawall.

A cargo plane crashed on the island docks on March 10, 1965. The plane undershot the runway at Logan International Airport in Boston. All on board were killed.

A sea serpent swam right past this island in 1818. One hundred and fifty years earlier, a man was drowned here while fishing. It was reported that he had been caught in the mouth of "a whale."

As an interesting side note, the island's shape is the head of a monster, with the neck being the causeway.

There is also said to be pirate treasure buried on the South Shore of Boston Harbor on Nantucket Beach.

There are two other islands that used to exist here that have pirate connections. In 1634, men were found frozen on Bird Island. It is thought that they probably were from a shipwreck. Nix's Mate is found on maps dated 1636. The name of the island comes from a legend. Nix was a Captain,

whose shipmate was accused of murdering Nix. He was taken here to be hanged. Please remember that no executions actually occurred here. Anyway, the story goes that he stated that he would be proven innocent by this island disappearing into the ocean. That part of the story at least seems to be coming true. The island is slowly disappearing into the sea. What is interesting here is that even in 1636, there are records that document the island was slowly being washed away. In 1699, fishermen who were fishing off this island, drowned when a storm came up and ended up washed ashore on the islands.

Bird Island and Nix's Mate Island are actually burial sites of at least fifteen pirates. The pirates were brought already dead – again, there were no executions here. Bird Island Light in Marion, built in 1818, is located at the south entrance to Buzzard's Bay. The first keeper of Bird Island Lighthouse was said to be William Moore, a banished pirate put here as a punishment for his crimes. He is supposedly buried on the island, but no grave was ever found. The problem with this legend is that most pirates were hanged, not imprisoned for being a pirate. He is also accused for his wife's death on the island, and her ghost was seen on there as recently as 1982, though the lighthouse was turned off in 1933. The hurricane of 1938 destroyed most of the buildings on the island, except the tower structure of the lighthouse. The 130-mile-per-hour wind hurricane even blew off most of the topsoil that still existed. Bird Island is now part of Logan Airport, and only a small part of Nix's Mate still exists.

On Deer Island on Money Bluff, it is said that hoards of treasure have been buried. Coins from the nineteenth century are often discovered here. There is a legend that a headless ghost guards this enchanted treasure site. Others have stated that they have heard screams on the beach with no one on the island. At Deer Island, near Winthrop, 1,200 Mexican eight-reals were found in 1906. The beaches at Ipswich and Salisbury have frequently yielded Mexican silver coins dated 1715. Nahant and Revere are also said to also have pirate silver and gold treasures buried in these towns. On Apple Island the William Marsh treasure is buried. During King Philip's War, many of the "Praying Indians" were relocated here.

Wreckers once worked their crime on Nantasket Beach. They would show a light on Strawberry Hill and the ships would be drawn to the rocks off Point Allerton. Point Allerton is another place where it is claimed that the Norsemen landed. There are other areas nearby that also have that claim. They include, Winthrop, Great Head, Scituate Cliffs, Gurnet in Plymouth, Manoment (Cleft Rock), and White Horse Rock.

The first European UFO sighting happened in Boston in 1639 and witnessed by three men. The great light appeared over the sky near Muddy River and "it flamed up, and contracted into the figure of a swine." In 1909, a mysterious airship with bright lights was seen by thousands and remained over the city for ten nights.

The flying black giant was only seen in the Boston area twice during its long history. What it actually was is still not known and it is best explained by the witnesses. The first time this "giant" was seen was on August 14, 1765, documented in the *Boston Gazette* and *Country Journal*. Below is that article.

> Dry weather – a black cloud-like object approximating the shape of a human body hovered over Boston and remained until Sunset, and thousands saw it. At 7 p.m., the cloud landed, but quickly rose again and moved South only about 20 feet off the ground – down the main street, blowing a little vapor smoke intermixed with a few rapid sparks of electric fire, till it came before the Province House. Here, it flopped a few minutes, swelled, looked excessively black and fierce and suddenly discharged itself of three tremendous peals of thunder, which shook the lofty fabric and all the little houses, and hollow hearts did hear it. It shook and tore away a newly erected building said to be for a Stamp Office... It continued to behave in this ferocious manner until about 11 p.m., when it suddenly vanished and all was quiet once more.

A storm that lasted hours? Perhaps, but there was not even a thunderstorm in the area. A cloud that vented sparks and smoke and fire? Perhaps it was a freak tornado? It is really hard to know what that could have been. The only

other sighting was on April 11, 1778, and this "giant" cloud traveled from New Hampshire to the Boston area. According to the witnesses, this cloud "strode so fast as a good horse might gallop, and two or three feet above the ground, and what more than all we admired, it went through walls and fences as one goes through water, yet were they not broken or overthrown. It was black, as it might be dressed in cloth indeed, yet were we so terrified that none observed what manner if at all it was habited. It made continually a terrifying scream 'hoo hoo' so that some women fainted."

On November 12-13, 1833, "pieces of sky hitting the ground and dissolving" were reported. This meteor shower or storm seemed to be concentrated only over Boston.

There is still more Boston Harbor lore to be explored. Ships were continually wrecked at the entrance to the harbor at the reefs called Hardings Ledge, Graves Ledge, Shag Rock and Devils Back. A lighthouse had to be built. The first light-house was at Little Brewster Island, also known as Beacon Island or Boston Light. Little Brewsters Island, Grape Island, Hog Island. Swans Island, and Great Brewsters Island are all thought to be a burying site of a pirate treasure.

Boston Light is also thought to be cursed. The keeper and most of his family were drowned just off the light in 1718. The next keeper became a rum smuggler. Other keepers were tormented by ice, fire, and plague throughout the years. The British burned the lighthouse in 1775. Though it was rebuilt, the British blew up the lighthouse in 1776. Lovells Island reef called Ram's Head Flats, now called Man-O'-War Bar, was where a French vessel called *Magnifique*, carrying gold and silver coins was wrecked. This ship was covered with sand over the years, building a new reef and bar, thus a new shipping hazard was created. In 1786, a passenger ship wrecked and all died of exposure on the vacant wreck-built island. The boulder that the passengers were found huddled dead near is called "Lover's Rock" where two were found embracing.

The new reef may hold golden secrets. In 1902, the keeper here found over $7,000 in coins. People were still digging for the gold and silver coins in 1998. This lighthouse has been struck by lightning numerous times. It appears that lightning does strike twice. Keepers and the coast guard have reported that the radio will keep switching channels and there is a figure of a man seen sitting in the lantern room.

Still believe that Boston Light is not cursed? The story of the *Maritana* may convince you otherwise. In 1861, the worst shipwreck in Boston Harbor history occurred. The *Maritana* smashed into Shag Rocks in a horrible storm. The entire ship was utterly destroyed, wreckage and bodies kept washing ashore for months after the event. The bodies were buried on the island and twenty years later, the story continued. The keeper at the time, Joshua Bates, rented out a room to a middle-age couple, named Chardon. The woman had lost her memory, but was attracted to Boston Light and her husband felt that staying there would be good therapy. An English visitor to the lighthouse, Edward Moraine, was one of the twelve survivors of the *Maritana*. He had returned to the area to meditate and reflect on what happened there so many years earlier. One night, the woman suddenly screamed at the new visitor. She shouted that she remembered who he was. He was her husband and her name had been Alice. Edward nodded and reached for her. Alice was crying uncontrollably and ran into the dark. She must have tripped, though both her husbands believed she committed suicide. Her body was found on Shag Rocks where it was thought she died on the *Maritana*, twenty-two years earlier. If you think that is strange, there is actually more to the story.

The figurehead of the *Maritana* is a woman carved in wood. It is said that it resembles Alice Moraine Chardon. It was originally attached to the French warship, *Berceau*, which was captured by American privateers in 1812. It was a figurehead to the schooner, *Caroline*, which was wrecked at Boon Island, Maine in 1846. It then became the figurehead of the *Maritana*. Though the ship was completely destroyed, the figurehead was found floating without a scratch after the wreck in Boston Harbor. It was placed on display for all the see at Boston's Lincoln Wharf, but though a fire destroyed the wharf, again, the figurehead was spared. It was placed in the Old State House, and once again, a fire occurred, but the lady still survived. The figurehead remains in the Old State House in downtown Boston.

It is no wonder that this area is thought to be cursed. The *Rose* was wrecked here in 1713. The Great Storm of 1723, perhaps the most severe ever recorded in the eighteenth century caused the tide to raise to 16 feet. There were three recorded hurricanes in 1839. These hurricanes caused many wrecks, including the *Charlotte* and *Lloyd*. The keepers wrote in their logs of the large amount of bodies that kept washing up on shore from the wrecks. In 1860, the *Ewan Crerar* wrecked and in 1882, the *Fanny Pike* wrecked. In 1909, the *Davis Palmer* sank, the *USS Alacrity* was wrecked in 1918, and in 1919, the *A. Heaton* followed suit.

In the 1800s, a fisherman found a large chest of gold coins on Peddock's Island. Many coins have also been found scattered on the rocks here.

On Egg Rock in Boston Bay, about two miles south of Phillips Point, a young lover sailed to this place in 1815 to pick "forget-me-nots" because he was leaving his lover for awhile. A storm arose and he drowned. His girl died soon after seemingly from a broken heart.

Here is a great fish story. In May 1837, a large cod was caught by Ebenezer Philips here. It was purchased on shore and when cut open, a large eighteen-carat gold ring was found with the initials H. L. on it. Perhaps the fish ate the ring as it lay on the ocean floor from a shipwreck.

The sea serpent was also said to roam these waters in the nineteenth century. Today, seagulls live here.

There are some old taverns sites in town that may hold colonial artifacts. In 1634, the Coles Inn was located in what is now Merchants Row, across from Governor Winthrop's home. The Bunch of Grapes Tavern was found in what is now the New England Bank in 1640. It was on the corner of Kilby and King Streets. King Street is now State Street. The King's Arm was located on Dock Square in 1642, which is now the head of the dock. Castle Tavern was found on what is now the upper corner of Elm Street and Dock Square in 1656. The Royal Exchange was located on what is Merchant's Bank on State Street in 1747. The massacre of March 5, 1770, happened in front of the Tavern between the Tory Party and British Officers. The Blue Anchor or Blew Anchor, now the

Globe Newspaper building, was there in 1646. The Red Lion has been on North Street since 1654. It is the oldest tavern in the north end of town. The street used to be called Old Red Lion Lane, but is now Richmond Street. The Ship Tavern was found at the head of Clark's Wharf or on the southwest corner of North and Clark Street in 1650.

In the eighteenth century, Boston was the place where the best silversmiths in the country worked their magic. Railroad personnel have been known to find diamonds in town while working underground. It seems fitting to end this chapter on this strange note because no one knows where these gems originated from.

BROCKTON/BOLTON/CHESTER/ CHESTERFIELD/FITCHBURG/DOVER

The Dover Demon has been a legend only since 1977. It is said to roam the woods in Dover, near the Charles River. It is apparently 3 feet tall, with tan skin, and a large bulbous head with orange eyes. It seems that several teenagers in three separate incidents, saw this creature, though it is suspected that one of the witnesses may have been under the influence at the time of the sighting. These creatures are dwarf-like, which does bring to mind the Native American stories of the dwarf people in the woods that are usually a good omen, but could give the witness the evil eye if crossed. The Native American legend people talk about are called Mannegishi or Maymaygwayshi or Manitou. These stories were numerous, especially in northern New England. (I talk of these legends in *Lost Loot: Ghostly New England Treasure Tales*.)

In Fitchburg, green or milky-white Beryl crystals have been found. Chester, in Hampden County, is where Jasper has been located. In Chesterfield, on the Westfield River, deposits of Beryl, aquamarine, and dark green crystals were discovered. Bolton soil has yielded pink, lavender, and purple scapolite.

In 1932, a wealthy Brockton shoe manufacturer buried several caches of gold coins around his mansion, which was located on the east side of Stonehill College in Norfolk County.

BYFIELD

There is buried treasure to be found in this town. The oral legend begins in December 1799, with Captain Roger Hayman, who was a pirate in the Haiti area, before being mortally wounded. Before he died, he supposedly, in secret, sent two trunks to Massachusetts. The two men who were transporting the chests to Boston, felt they were being watched, so they buried the loot, $175,000 or $200,000 British gold sovereigns, in a pit four-feet deep, under a large rock that they marked with an "A" along the banks of the Parker Tidal River, west of the Blue Star Memorial Highway in Essex County. The trap granite boulder is covered with water during high tide. The "A" is thought to be at least six inches in height. The strange rock that the money was buried under is said to be a balancing rock, because it tips when you touch it.

Today, it is part of a Wildlife Management Area. Some coins may have already been found by workers who were digging a well here. It is also thought that perhaps one of the chests has been found. This exact same treasure is said to be perhaps buried on Kents Island. Where the seeker would dig, I suppose would depend on the story believed.

CAPE COD

This is the most southern area that the glaciers, specifically the Wisconsin Ice Sheet, came in New England. These great ice sheets helped to create the Cape 10,000 years ago. This entire place was created completely by sand formed in a body of standing water. Cape Cod did not exist before this ice age. The ocean dropped about 300-500 feet during this time. All the lakes on the Cape are ice-blocked lakes known as kettles. Since its creation, almost two miles may have been lost to the ocean. In the future, the Cape may actually be split in two, though it may also grow longer as more sand is deposited.

The Native Americans lived here 5,000 years ago and it was inhabited only 400 years ago by the Europeans. The

Wampanoag tribe was the group who lived here when the Puritans arrived. The tribes here called the Atlantic Ocean the "sea of darkness." What laid beyond this sea seemed to scare them. There were many prophecies about the coming of the Europeans in Native American legends. (There will be more specific information later in the book and more lore about the European arrival in *Lost Loot: New England Treasure Tales*.) Today, Route 6A is part of the Old King's Highway, one of the earliest foot paths of the Native Americans.

One group seems to be missing from the above paragraph and it is a controversial idea. It is also claimed that the Norse discovered and settled on Cape Cod, over 1,000 years ago. According to the Norse Sagas, Cape Cod was discovered by Bjarni Herjulfsson in 989 AD. In 1000 AD, Leif Erikson became interested in Herjulfsson's explorations, and supposedly arrived at Cape Cod in September. The story tells that he landed at Great Point off Nantucket Island. The Vikings sailed into a river that flows down from a lake. This is thought to be perhaps the Bass River. It is said that he landed at Follins Pond, which separates Dennis and Yarmouth today.

Anyway, one year later, Leif's brother, Thornwald came to this area or to the Boston area. (See the Boston section of this book for more details.) The story is that he sailed around Monomoy Island to Provincetown, where the shoals caused damage to the ship. He called this area Keelness or Kialarnes, meaning "Keel Cape." They repaired the ship and sailed into Bass Hole. Here they killed the Native Americans they found, and then were attacked by a larger group that the Vikings called, Skraellings at Nahant. Thornwald was killed during this attack and buried on the beach called "Crossness," loosely translated as Cape of Crosses. This place is thought to be in Hull or Gurnet Point.

In 1077 AD, Thorfinn Karlsefni, decided to settle in the New World with his wife. Later that year, a son was born, named Snorri, and he could be considered the first European child to be born in the New World. Thorfinn is said to have called this area, Furdurstandir, meaning "wonderstrands." Perhaps because of the mirage effect that often occurs here. The effect makes the land seem to tip up in front of the

person walking, making all the land (level or downhill) look like it is rising (or going uphill). It is said that the Native Americans and Vikings started to have issues and attacks became an everyday concern. These Vikings finally left in 1011 AD, but soon afterward, a new group came to the new land to settle. This group was split into two groups, who did not trust each other and tension grew between the groups. One of the groups killed all the men and women of the other group. The next year, that group left, and after that, no other Viking came to the New World.

Did the Vikings come here? That is what is so controversial. Viking relics have been discovered on the Cape. Rune stones were found in Bourne in 1658. The Aptucxet Runestone was used as a doorstop to a Christian Indian Meetinghouse. The Native Americans of the area said that it had been a sacred relic for many generations. An interesting side note is that the bogs and swamplands in Bourne yield a lot of iron ore. During the nineteenth century, this area produced many kettles, plates, and nails. The Pilgrims first trading post was called Aptucxet, now known as Bourne. This was the first trading post in North America. In 1627, it was built by the Puritans to trade with the Dutch. The site was also a Native American burial ground, used until 1810. Anyway, to get back to the Vikings, in the mid-1800s, an old Viking foundation was supposedly unearthed in Provincetown. A Viking shoring was said to be found in 1952 on the edges of Follins Pond and Viking mooring holes discovered in boulders on the banks of the Bass River. The question asked in the first sentence of this paragraph is still being asked today and perhaps there are Viking treasures just waiting to be unearthed. What is interesting to note is that there is a grapevine that is found in Buzzard's Bay area that is not native to the region. It is native to the Norse homelands. Perhaps the Vikings were here.

When Samuel de Champlain sailed around the Cape, he called it Cap Blac or Cape White. Tucker's Terror is a set of breakers on the Cape, named because a man called Tucker was frightened by them in 1602. It is said that Bartholomew Gosnold, Captain of the *Concord*, is the first Englishman to set foot in Cape Cod. He landed here in 1602 and found lots of cod, hence the name Cape Cod. He also found peas, strawberries, and hurtleberries.

The Native Americans here wore copper ornaments and had copper pipes. When the Puritans landed here in 1620, they reported a Native American burial ground north of Great Pond. No one is exactly sure where that site is today. Another Native American burial site is located in Yarmouthport near Long Pond. The area is marked with a boulder. The Pilgrims plundered some Native American graves in Truro. Why? It is said that the Native Americans wore copper as decorations, and that these objects were buried with the dead. The tribes living on the Cape were the Cammaquids, Nausets, and Pamets or Payomets or Pawmets. Aspinet was the Sachem of the Nauset tribe here in 1621.

Provincetown is also known as Helltown. The Native American name, Poquannoc, means "cleared land." There are even stories that the witch wind blew through Providence as it came toward Salem before the witchcraft trials. Wrecking was a recognized means of a livelihood in this town. Rum running and smuggling was also considered a good way to make a living.

This town is really a huge sand pile that was created about 30,000 years ago. There is no bedrock to be found under the entire area.

This town was abandoned during the French and Indian War, and there is said to be a pirate treasure buried on Money Hill. The details are somewhat vague. At Long Point Light, a submarine, S-4 wrecked here. At the northwestern tip of the Cape at Race Point, a large amount of British gold and silver was discovered in 1973. Thousands of coins have been found here dating from the late eighteenth century.

The Cape has seen many shipwrecks and horrible storms. There are numerous places named Devil here, most notably "Devil's Pillow" and the "Devil's Leap." The first documented shipwreck on the Cape was the *Sparrowhawk* in December 1626, near Nauset in a storm called a Northeaster. The crew were saved, and the wreck burned to the waterline. The remains of the ship appeared in the latter part of the eighteenth century in the part of the beach called Old Ship Beach. In 1863, the ship appeared again, and actually emerged

in good shape for being centuries old and underwater most of the time. The ship was exhumed and taken to Plymouth in 1899 where it remains today. On Orleans Beach, British brass coins were found. It is speculated that perhaps the coins came from the *Sparrowhawk*.

There are a huge number of ships wrecked here. In 1820, the *Rolla*, wrecked on Nauset Beach. The Bark, *Kate Harding*, wrecked near Truro in a gale in 1892. In 1893, the English ship, *Jason*, sank on Pamet Bar in Truro. In 1778, *Dead Mans Hollow* was attacked and destroyed by a British Man-O'-War, near Truro. The Schooner, *Job H. Jackson, Jr.* was wrecked off Peaked Hills Bar during a gale in 1895. In 1911, the barge, *Pine Forest*, also had bad luck in a storm on Peaked Hills Bar. In Chatham, there have been many ships lost over the years. This was also a wrecker's location. In 1870, the surf destroyed the Lighthouse here and unknown men were washed up on the beach and buried near the light. The *Katie J. Barnett* was wrecked in 1890. The *Jason* was wrecked in 1893, the *Cottage City* in 1890 off Morris Island, and the *Horatio Hall* in 1909 at Pollock Rip Slue.

The steamer, *Portland* disappeared here in November 1898, during the Great Portland Gale. This massive storm was really two storms that merged into one over southern New England. Wreckage from this ship and the other over 200 ships that were lost during this storm washed up on beaches from Provincetown to Chatham. The *Portland* was found north of Race Point in 350 feet of water. Divers have claimed to have seen a wreck in 144 feet of water about seven miles off Truro, but it is perhaps one of the other ships that sank that night. Some of the other ships lost that night were: *Lester A. Lewis*, *King Philip*, *F. A. Walker*, *Albert A. Butler*, *Addie E. Snow*, *Jordan L. Mott*, *Mertis H. Perry*, and the *James B. Pace*. Ship wreck items can be found on any beach in the area, especially after a storm. In 1901, the only two six-masted schooners in the world collided five miles off the Cape in fog. Off Provincetown in 1910, the schooner, *Estelle S. Nunan*, exploded. After unloading a cargo of gas, the crew lit a cabin light and the left-over gas ignited.

In 1778, Captain Ourry, of the British 64-gun war ship, was caught in the triangle of the Highlands, Chatham and

Pollock Rip Shoals. His ship headed straight for Peaked Hill Bar and many men were lost when the ship wrecked there. The Captain ordered everything to be thrown overboard. This tragedy was very profitable to the residents of the Cape. It is actually considered the most profitable wreck in the Cape's history. The exact location of the ship remains unknown.

Wellfleet has a pirate and ghost legend. It is a well-known fact that Samuel Bellamy's wrecked pirate ship, *Whidah*, was found in 1984 by Barry Clifford off Wellfleet. The ship struck a sand bar off South Wellfleet and sank during a storm in 1717, killing all the crew, including the Captain. This was the first documented wreck on a barrier island or sand bar in a storm in this area. What may not be known is that there is a story about the woman that Bellamy supposedly left behind years before, who is said to have cried out with joy as she watched the wreck that dark night. Maria Hallett, was also known as Goody Hallett to the residents in Wellfleet is the left woman. The story is that she had an affair with the famous pirate, and had a child, who died at birth. Bellamy never returned for Maria, but she lived in a shack on the beach awaiting his return for years. As the time passed, the rumors of her being a witch and consorting with the Devil were rampant. The townspeople said they saw her in the dunes cursing into a storm on the head of Bellamy. It was said that she screamed she would give her soul to the Devil, if she knew for a fact that Bellamy was dead. People along the beach on the night that the ship sank saw Goody Hallett standing on the bluffs screaming her thanks to the Devil for her vengeance against the pirate.

The legend is that she somehow found a chest of the *Whidah's* gold and buried it, but the curse backfired and she forgot where she buried it in Wellfleet. The chest of gold is still there waiting to be found. It is said that Bellamy's dead crew littered the beach for many weeks after the wreck. For years, local residents found gold coins on the beach thought to be from this pirate ship, especially after a storm. It is also thought that the ghosts of the pirate ship do not want anyone to find their sunken treasure and protected the loot, but in 1984, the treasure was found.

This is a Mashpee legend. On Screechams Island, also known as Grand Island, just off Cape Cod, two sisters, Hannah and Sarah, dealt with many pirates over the years that they lived there. Captain Kidd is said to have visited this island and dropped off some treasure chests for the sisters to protect. The legend says that Hannah kissed Kidd as he left the island, and directed the left-behind crew to put the chests in the hole that they had just dug. She pushed the crew into the hole, killing them, so they would guard the loot forever. It is then said that she screeched so loud that Kidd heard her on his ship and he knew that his treasure was safe. The hut where the sisters lived is on the left island in Witches Pond. That screech is heard today, so the story goes, when treasure seekers are searching for the chests. That sound brings out the ghostly pirate guards to deal with the treasure hunter.

There were other pirates who are said to have left treasure here as well. Samuel Bellamy, Paul Williams and a pirate named Baxter all are said to have visited this island at one time or another. Pieces of Eight have been found on the beaches, but whether they come from shipwrecks or buried treasure, it is unclear. The legend tells of another reason for the sister's terrifying scream. Though Hannah helped the pirates bury the gold, she could not touch it. It is said that if she tried to get the gold, the pirates she murdered would attack her. The screams, then, are said to be her frustration at not being able to get the treasure.

At Witches Pond, Sarah, the other sister and supposed witch, had her own issues. It is said that there was never a moon over this pond. Sarah cursed any hunter that came to her forest. Nothing could ever be killed by a hunter in her woods. The story is that she fell in love with a man, but he was terrified of her. To try to trick her, he invited her to his house, to perhaps kill her, or at least to get rid of her forever. However, she came as a horse and allowed him to shoe her. He used a silver shoe and tied her to a tree outside his yard, just leaving her there. The next day, the horse was gone, but Sarah had a silver horseshoe nailed to her left palm. It is said that the Mashpee Tribe of the region grew tired of Sarah and her evil ways. One member created a silver bullet and went to Sarah's woods. He shot the bullet through a deer and the next day, Sarah was found dead with a silver bullet through the heart.

The pirate, Captain Turner, is said to have buried two boxes of treasure on Strong Island. According to author Edward Rowe Stowe, he found a box with gold and silver coins exactly where Turner's treasure was said to be. He found about 316 coins, worth about $1800.

The bark, *Mayberry*, reported that on October 19, 1890, that a large meteor passed close to the stern of the ship off the Cape and plowed into the water. The crew called it a "sphere of fire" and that "a strong smell of sulphur filled the atmosphere as it disappeared into the sea." In June 1882, a meteorite was known to have fallen in Arkham, Massachusetts, on Nahum Gardiner's farm.

Native American petroglyphs have been found all through the area. What do they look like? Interestingly, they seem to look like an underwater sea serpent. Throughout history, there are many stories of sightings of a sea serpent off the New England coast. It is a fact that even today we have not searched most of Earth's ocean environment. We just are not sure what does or can exist there. Is it possible that some unknown large animal has lived and thrived for generations in the waters off the shore? Absolutely! It seemed to terrify our ancestors, as it does when modern people glimpse our ocean's best kept secrets.

Hyannis is an abbreviation of the Wampanoag word "Anayanough". The word means "he who wages war" and is in honor of a Chief who lived here in the early 1600s. He was the Sachem of the Cammaquid tribe and this was his seat of power. Squopenik was a favorite spot of the Native Americans. Numerous arrowheads have been found here. Tradition states that the hurricane of 1635 destroyed much of the area. The name comes from folk lore. It is said that a *squaw-broke-her-neck* here. It is obviously a play on words.

The Orleans Town Landing in Barnstable County is the site of the Battle of Orleans, where in December 1814, the militia repulsed a British landing party. In Sandwich, along the beach to Plymouth County, the mineral Jasper has been found.

CHELSEA/CARLISLE

In Chelsea, the old Wheat Tavern, found on Westford Street or Mass 225, was originally a stagecoach station on the Boston and Vermont Post Road. The treasure seeker should also try to visit sites that were once visited by people just passing through. It was in Carlisle that during the British siege of Boston, General George Washington's men camped. In 1908, a fire destroyed most of the city. Many valuables were lost. In 1921, workmen found about $50,000 in gold coins and silverware in a field in town.

CHESHIRE/DALTON

In Cheshire in Berkshire County on County 8, there is a legend of an unidentified pirate treasure buried on the banks of the Hoosic River. Supposedly, the pirate was hanged in 1717 but records are strangely mute about the details. A farmer did find two kettles full of gold coins at Sand Mill Hill in 1718. The kettles were found in a hollow in the heart of the mountain on a back road from Dalton to Cheshire. The farmer, Mesick, discovered a coffin-shaped rock in the hole, which sounded hollow when he hit it. There was said to be more treasure, but due to superstition and fear, he never returned. No one has ever been able to find it since.

That, however, may not be the true story. Dalton is another town located in Berkshire County on County 9. British soldiers, after being defeated at Sarasota in 1777, spent months plundering the settlements in northwestern Massachusetts. It is said that they buried three wagon loads of plunder somewhere near Sand Mill.

The Falls of Wahconah Brook has a Native American legend. A maiden is said to have finally won her brave after going through many trials in which an evil spirit was creating havoc. They were finally united here.

In Wizards Glen, which are giant rocks that look like a giant wall, there is also a Native American legend. There is a stone called the Devil's Altar Stone where the medicine men and tribal wizards were said to offer human sacrifice to the evil spirit, Ho-bo-mo-ko. Though this was the name of the Native American's evil spirit, in no other region was human sacrifice ever mentioned. However, the South American tribes did practice this ceremony. So perhaps fear caused this story to spread here.

Another story is that a hunter took refuge here during a horrible storm. Under the lightning, he saw the vision of Satan and his court. He started to recite a Bible verse in terror. A large crash of thunder occurred, and the entire scene vanished.

COHASSET

Minot's Ledge is located eighteen miles off Boston, and part of Cohasset Rocks. The Quonahassitis tribe believed that this area was inhabited by a demon-like spirit. These submerged rocks have terrified sailors for years and may have caused more shipwrecks than any other reef on the Atlantic Coast. The only time these ledges are dry is at low tide, and only for three hours per day. The world's highest waves have been recorded here, topping 170 feet. In just ten years, 1831-1841, over 42 ships were wrecked on these ledges. The first light-house was built in 1849, but was completely destroyed two years later, killing two of the keepers. That 1851 storm is still called the Minot's Light Storm.

Apparently, the reef wanted to continue to lure vessels to the area with no protection. These reefs have been known to create 100-foot breakers during a fierce gale. The entire island will tremble and rock, and the tower would sway two feet during a violent storm. To name just a few shipwrecks here: In 1693, A Sloop owned by a Boston merchant named Anthony Collamore wrecked. In 1754, a Dorchester merchant, George Minot lost a vessel with expensive cargo and all was lost. This is who the ledge was named after. The Danish ship, *Gertrude-Maria* hit the reef in 1793. The bark, *Sarah & Susan* was wrecked here in 1818. In 1847, the *Alabama* struck the reef. The *Jenny Lind* was destroyed by the ledge in 1848, and the brig *Saint John* sank in 1849 on Grampus Rocks with many lives lost. This ship carried Irish immigrants and was called one of the

coffin-ships. These ships were not considered sea worthy, but were packed with passengers to come to the United States. In 1898, during the Portland Gale, the schooner, *Juanita*, wrecked here. In 1916, in North Scituate, two barges, *Kohinoor* and *The Ashland* collided near Minot's Ledge. The Brig, *Marriel*, was completely destroyed on East Hogshead Ledge in 1852. There were no survivors. In 1853, the ship, *Maryland*, was wrecked on Gull Ledge. There are many artifacts to be found washed up on the reef, if one dares to venture close.

There was a strange beach boulder found here, perhaps washed up from another part of the shore or ocean. It was filled with white crystals of feldspar and tea-green porphyry stone. This is not the type of rock that would naturally be found in this region.

It is no wonder that this now-vacant area is thought cursed and haunted. Fishermen claim to see strange lights at night, as well as hear cries, moans, and pleas for help. The Portuguese crews stay away from this area believing that the spirit of their countryman, Joe Antoine, who died in 1851 when the lighthouse collapsed, warns them away. The fate of these keepers was found in a bottle by a Gloucester fisherman. The note in the bottle said:

Wednesday night, April 16 – The lighthouse won't stand over tonight. She shakes two feet each way now.
– J.W. and J.A.

The note and bottle now belong to the Hingham Historical Society. Shadow figures are seen in the new lighthouse; whispering voices and tapping signals are heard. After the Civil War, the keeper noticed that the lens had been cleaned, but no one living had cleaned it. This happened a lot. It was assumed that the two keepers who lost their lives were continuing to do their job. Passing ships still tell of strange noises, and report seeing ghost figures clinging to the lower section of a ladder to this day.

DEERFIELD/SOUTH DEERFIELD/DARTMOUTH

Dartmouth was another town destroyed during King Philip's War. In South Deerfield, the Mohawk tribe destroyed the Pocumtuck Fort at Fort Hill in 1666. The Pocumtuck tribe wanted protection from the Mohawk tribe, so that is one reason that they joined King Philip's War hoping King Philip would help them against the Mohawks. The tribe did not realize that the Mohawks had already refused to help King Philip or that he had sought an alliance with them when they joined his war effort. The area at that time was occupied by the Pocumtucks, meaning "swift river."

South Deerfield was first settled in 1669, and located in Franklin County on County 5. This town was literally on the frontier and a target for numerous attacks. Bloody Brook is the scene of a mass grave and battle site. The Native Americans killed eighty-five men who were taking grain to market. During King Philip's War, the "Bloody Brook Massacre" in 1675 caused the residents of the town to be evacuated and the town remained uninhabited for seven years. As mentioned earlier, any time an area is left quickly, even if it is re-populated later, many items of valuable may have been buried and forgotten for safekeeping.

Another battle called the "Great Deerfield Massacre" occurred in Deerfield in 1704 during the French and Indian War. Most of the residents were killed. The battle was between the French, commanded by Captain Thomas Lathrop, and the Pocumtuck tribe. There have been artifacts found from that era.

As an interesting side note, some residents of Suffield, Connecticut were captured during this raid and never seen again. They were either killed and no one was left to claim their bodies or they became part of the tribe as slaves.

DIGHTON

There was a tree here called the Council Oak. Tradition states that Metacom, or King Philip, and his council met under this large oak tree while discussing war efforts.

The Dighton Writing Rock was first documented by the Europeans in 1680. However, the Native Americans called this rock, Assonet, which is a Narragansett word, meaning "at the rock." The Taunton River rock inscriptions have been fading with constant water wear since 1903. The bedrock here is greywacke rock. The tide does leave the inscriptions exposed for a small amount of time. It is possible that these are Native American petroglyphs, perhaps recounting a battle? It is thought that there may have been a battle here sometime after King Philip's War, around 1680. Still, the question remains, who carved on this rock? There have been many theories, including that the Devil, Native Americans, Phoenicians, Libyans, Hebrews, Chinese, Norsemen, or Portuguese all may be responsible. It is said that a farmer dreamed for three nights about the chest of gold buried near the base of the rock. He decided to dig and found a chest. He saw the tide was coming in, so he ran to safety. The mist rolled in and he saw the Devil coming toward him, managed to escape with his life, but minus the gold. Most historians believe that the pictures are Norse in origin. The date said to be etched on the rock, however, is 1511.

To add more mystery to this rock, the Pokanokets tribe in southern Massachusetts have an ancient legend about a great white Chief who once ruled. The tribe was happy and prosperous then. They believed he was a God, who came from the east in a winged vessel. Before he died, he foretold that someday other white men would come. He told his people to treat the newcomers with respect and reverence. Was this a Viking who was left or stayed behind?

FALL RIVER/DRACUT/EASTON/FREETOWN/ GRAFTON/GRANVILLE

Grafton was called Hassanisco, meaning "place of falling stones." This was a praying-Indian town. There is an old Massasoit trail in Granville by the Little River Gorge. Freetown is found between Fall River and New Bedford. The east part of town was called "ye freemans land on Taunton River." King Philip is said to have spent his last night alive here in the "Rocky Woods."

In Easton on Rankin Farm, rocks can be found with hoof prints embedded in them. It is thought that the Native Americans somehow made these impressions. Native American relics have been found near Mulberry Brook. Dracut was once the capital of the Pawtucket tribe. The town was attacked during King Philip's War.

Fall River was first called Pocasset, then Troy, then Fall River from the Narragansett word, Quequechen, meaning "falling" or "swift river." In Sand Bank, a skeleton in full armor was discovered in 1831 on Fifth and Hartwell Streets. Longfellow wrote his poem, "The Skeleton in Armor" about this event. It was thought that perhaps it was a Norseman, but it really was a Native American decorated in armor. The skeleton can be found in the Peabody Museum at Harvard.

This town was once used by the Tories, who during the Revolutionary War, would aid the British by signaling to Taunton with flags and lights. A meteorite fell here on August 29, 1913.

Rolling Rock is found balanced on a ledge facing Layfayette Park on Eastern Avenue. The Native Americans discovered that they could roll this rock around and it would not lose its balance or fall off the ledge. Legends say that they used this as an unique torture technique by placing captives under a raised portion and rolling it on them crushing the flesh and bone.

FLORIDA

A beautiful twin cascade waterfall, 40 feet wide and 90 feet high, is found here. This town is also known as Hoosic Village and is the southern and highest part of the Hoosac Tunnel and Wilmington Railroad. The railroad was called the "Hoot, Toot, and Whistle." The Tunnel is 25,000 feet long and was completed in 1875. Almost 200 people died while building this tunnel. The area is considered haunted because of these traumatic deaths. Marble has been found near the Noxon farm site, also known as Idlewild, another place where a traumatic event occurred, yet treasure lies beneath the soil.

GLOUCESTER/CAPE ANN/ROCKPORT/GOSNOLD

This area was first named Le Beau Port by Champlain in 1606, while he was exploring the port. According to Charles M. Skinner, *Myths & Legends of our own land*, (1896), "Strange things had been reported in Gloucester. On the eve of King Philip's War, the march of men was heard in its streets and an Indian bow and scalp were seen on the faces of the moon, while the boom of cannon and roll of drums were heard at Malden and the windows of Plymouth rattled to the passage of unseen horsemen." The sounds and feelings of a bloody battle is said to have been known before the first attack of King Philip's men. This may be the beginning of what is known as "the spectre leaguers." It is said that a troop of French and Indian war group roamed the area who could never be caught, killed, or crippled, though many American troops tried. In 1692, it is said that this area must have been cursed to fight this troop of not flesh and blood due to the moral perversion of the colony. Who these American troops fought is still not known.

Rafe's Chasm, a narrow cut in the granite coast and when the sea is at high tide, it creates a booming sound, and Norman's Woe (not a public area), also known as Eastern Point Lighthouse was a site for smugglers and wreckers. Wreckers were the people who lured ships onto the rocks by false lights displayed from shore. The wrecking of ships was often a community affair. This was in the culture of "finders keepers, losers weepers."

As an interesting side note, the term wrecker was used in bygone eras, and originally it is a person searching for items on the beach from wrecked ships. The term ended up meaning a person who also may be the cause of the wreck and killing any survivors. Today, the term for searching for items from wrecks on the beach is beachcomber. Anyway, there was a great resistance to the building of lighthouses, this would cut down on the wrecking economic boom that many coastal communities had started.

The fishermen from Gloucester worked in the world's most dangerous waters, the fog-shrouded, berg-laden North Atlantic Grand Banks. Over 10,000 men who have been lost at sea were from here. Is it no wonder many tales of haunting and lost treasure occurs at these lonely, yet vital shores? In 1899, three schooners were wrecked on Norman's Woe, the *Hesperus,* the *Ellen M. Gleason,* and the *Elsie M. Smith.*

In 1692, while most New Englanders worried about witches, a UFO or aliens or perhaps even time travelers were spotted here. The story is that in the summer, a farmer saw two strangely dressed men run from his front yard into the cornfield. No one else in the family saw the men. The farmer quickly moved his family to the safety of the Cape Ann fort. He thought perhaps that the Native Americans were getting ready to attack. However, the farmer saw the same two men on a hill from the fort. Apparently, these men were following the farmer. The next evening, the same two were seen walking near the fort, one carrying a strange silver gun strapped to his side. Terrible loud sounds were heard outside the fort that night, and now it was believed that the Devil himself was involved. About 5 days later, these same two men walked toward the gates of the fort. The garrison shot at the men, and they ran away, but it is said that not a musket ball hit them. The men fired back at the settlers, and the "ball" that was dug out of a tree was a thinly pointed bullet, not the ball shape that was used as ammunition at that time. The men said that the language they heard they could not understand. These strangers started to stand their ground when confronted by the settlers, and never once, even when shot at numerous times, did either of them fall. After two weeks, the strangers disappeared, never to appear again.

Still think that perhaps the Puritans living here in 1692 were just edgy and exaggerated natural events? On November 26, 1984, the Coast Guard reported that residents saw a bright light over the ocean. The object was hovering over the water and shining a bright yellow spotlight into the ocean. It was a triangular craft that flew right over the heads of the witnesses only 100 feet above them. The sound was a muffled, yet constant humming, like a distant freight train. The craft was seen over Beverly and Amesbury, New Hampshire later that same evening. What was seen was never explained.

Sea Serpent lore abounds in this area. Columbus and his crew are said to have seen a sea serpent in the Sargasso Sea, as he sailed to America. It was reported by John Josselyn, the

English naturalist who described New England to Europe, that in 1638, an English boat reported seeing a strange coiled creature on a rock on the northeast shoreline of Gloucester. The English wanted to shoot the creature, but the Native Americans on board asked them not to; they would be in danger if it was wounded.

Ten Pound Island was purchased by Gloucester settlers from the Native American for ten pounds, and is the site of a documented sea serpent sighting. This serpent was seen by over 500 residents in August 1817 through 1886, some even stated that they saw it sunning on the island rocks. All ten people who saw this serpent in 1817 gave identical descriptions of the creature. The description was that it looked like a thick rope coiled on the rocks. It appeared to be around 100 feet long and the size of a barrel. The color was dark brown and it had two giant greenish-red eyes that protruded from its massive head. It seemed irritated by the people and slithered back into the sea. It was spotted again by the crew of the bark, *Pauline*. The crew of the American schooner, *Science*, in 1819, spotted the sea serpent where Eastern Point Light, constructed in 1821, now stands. An added description of white seen at the throat of the creature came from this sighting. They also reported a number of birds that followed the creature, perhaps eating the discarded fish killed by the serpent. In 1888, Granville Putnam author of, *The History of Rockport, MA* (Rockport is a town next to Gloucester), reported seeing the creature.

In the 1800s, the Linnean Society of New England did investigate this phenomena, hoping to prove the existence of a new species, called scoliophis atlanticus, or the Atlantic humped snake. A baby serpent was supposedly found by a group of boys, but it was found to be a black snake with tumors. In 1957, off Cape Cod, another monster was sighted. Six men from the scalloper, *Noreen,* saw a creature with a large body and a small alligator-like head. In August 1962, a sighting of this monster was supposedly reported off the coast of Marshfield by fishermen. In May, 1964, fishermen reported a sixty-foot sea snake off Nantucket Island. It was described as having a large head shaped like an alligator, tail of a lobster, and a spout like a whale. In 1970, it was reported that a sea serpent was found dead on Mann Hill Beach. In May 1975, the monster was seen by the crew from the *Debbie Rose*, about fifteen miles off the coast of Gloucester. In 1978, a crew on a fishing vessel reported that they saw a large head ringed with white swimming near them. No one knew what the creature was. They had never seen anything like it in all the years they had fished the area. In 1980, a 450-pound creature washed onto the shore of Plum Island, an extension of Newburyport. The Smithsonian Institution concluded that the monster was a large squid.

As an interesting side note, it is reported that giant squid breed north of the New England waters, off Nova Scotia, perhaps even off the coast of Maine. As recently as 1997, a serpent creature was described being seen in Fortune Bay, Newfoundland.

There have been numerous shipwrecks here. Some of the coins found here date from the mid-1600s. In 1704, pirate John Quelch is said to have buried a large amount of gold on Snake Island off Cape Ann. Treasure hunters have found a small amount of coins, but none dating from the 1704 era. The haunted cursed ship, the *Charles Haskell*, was wrecked here. This ship has the same lore as the *Flying Dutchmon* ship or *The Dash* ship of the Maine coast. The doomed ship is to forever sail the waters warning modern sailors of impending crisis and destructive storms that are approaching.

Off Point Allerton, the three-master vessel, *Howard*, was wrecked at Grape Vine Cove at the turn of the nineteenth century. It is said that crowds gathered there to see what the sea was giving them. The Brig, *Persia*, sank in 1829. All hands were lost just a short distance from the Cape Ann Lighthouse. Perhaps it was not only storms that caused ships to wreck here. The coast of this area has felt the rumbles of earthquakes. In 1755, Cape Ann shook with a minor quake.

Dog Town has been a ghost town since 1830 and can be found between Gloucester and Rockport on Cape Ann. There are ruins still to be seen in the deep woods. It was reported as being "a blasted Heath," which is a rolling moor strewn with glacial boulders. There are about forty cellar holes all through the area. Fishermen and families lived

here in 1650. The widows and children were protected by vicious watch dogs (hence the name of the town).

Witches were also said to live in Dog Town. One of the witches was very annoying. It is said that one particular witch could bewitch an oxen team to stop at her house with grain. Old Peg Wesson would disguise herself as a black crow and follow soldiers, annoying them so much that the crow was finally shot with a silver bullet. A that very moment, Old Peg fell in Gloucester and broke her leg. She died soon after, and some say with a silver bullet in her heart.

This site is said to have been cursed and some people who go there have never returned. There are reports of murders that have taken place here and strange voices have been heard over the years.

Rockport is the site of an old fort that was built during the War of 1812 and was attacked by the British. There are granite quarries throughout the area. Though these are coastal towns, minerals have been discovered. The Pomeroy Quarry in Gloucester has yielded smoky Quartz. The Babson Farm Quarry in Rockport has yielded citrine Quartz.

Gosnold on Penikese Island was once a leper colony. The state purchased this place in 1907 to be used specifically for this purpose. It was later abandoned.

There is a pirate legend about Tarpaulin Cove on the east shore of Naushon Island, that Kidd stopped there on his last voyage and buried treasure. Naushon Island is now privately owned.

The French Watering Place, which is found southeast of the Cove is named for the French privateers who were based here.

GREAT BARRINGTON

The Great Road or Mohawk Trail traveled through this town. It was the route of the French and Indian War expeditions. Near the Housatonic River (Bridge Street) was the site of an old Native American fort in 1676, called the Great Wigwam. This was the place of the main Machian Council Fire. The village name was Mahaiwe, a corruption of the word

Neh-hai-we, meaning "place down stream." The Housatonic River is a Native American word meaning "the river beyond the mountain." The Narragansetts were over taken by Major Talcott here in 1676 and this town was the site of a skirmish of Shays' Rebellion.

There is also a Native American legend. A girl hurled herself off the cliff on Monument Mountain, when her love for a person was not returned. This place is found in the north part of town, and is really a rock cairn. It is on an old Native American foot path. There is, however, a darker version of the story. It is said that the Native American girl fell in love with her cousin. For that transgression, death was the penalty. She was pushed over the cliff or she jumped because she had to. Either way, it must not have been a pleasant event.

There are other names for this area, Ice Gulch or Purgatory. It is freezing cold here all year long. The gulf was created by an earthquake. Another part of the tale is that it is that the Native American girl tried to save herself by holding onto a branch as she fell, but when she finally could not hold on anymore and let go, her screams were heard throughout the mountain valley.

Still another version of the legend tells us that Kankapot, Chief of the Machians, declared this spot as a boundary of land between his tribe and the Mohawks. This rock memorial or pyramid, six feet to eight feet in diameter, was said to be here before the settlers arrived. Those rocks marked the boundary.

Whatever happened here, this is a place the Native Americans deemed very important – and something absolutely happened here.

This is another town where a robber supposedly inhabited a cave. It was also called an ice cave because there was ice here in the summer (Ice Gulch?), but this particular cave does not seem to be here anymore. No one knows exactly where it was located. The cave is called Robbers Roost, though perhaps it is the same as the cave above. On May 27, 1875, bank robbers of the "Red" Leary gang, attempted to rob the National Mahaiwe Bank and hid here. (See more of this story in the Stockbridge part of this book.)

HADLEY/SOUTH HADLEY

Hadley, in Hampshire County is the place where in 1683 Mary Webster was accused of bewitching and murdering Deacon Philip Smith and hanged, then buried in snow. She actually survived and died several years later of natural causes.

A battle in King Philip's War was fought here and the town people actually won, repelling the Native Americans. This was the site of a Native American fort. Skeletons have been found on the bluff overlooking the Connecticut River. It is thought they are from the battle.

Dinosaur tracks were dug up by farmer brothers, Harlan and Carlton Nash in 1802. One of the tracks found in 1941 measured twenty-three feet long. They are over 200 million years old. This is where the Nash Quarry was created in 1955. Many dinosaur tracks have been found since that time. Today, those tracks reside in museums throughout western New England.

There is a story of gold bullion being buried in a cave in South Hadley on State 5. South Hadley was settled in 1659. The Pass of Thermopylae is a colonial-made narrow rock passage through the foot of the 995-foot Mount Holyoke near the Connecticut River. The passage was created by pouring water on the rock in the winter and taking away the granite when it split. Now, the settlers would not have to climb over Mount Holyoke.

Titans Piazza is a volcanic bluff that is found here. It is classified as a world's major natural phenomena. Fossil footprints have been found here. The Devil's Football is a 300-ton magnetic boulder. Geologists say that it was carried here by glaciers from Deerfield or Sunderland. The legend is that the Devil kicked the boulder here from the Devil's Garden at Amherst Notch. This town was abandoned during King Philip's War and was known as Swampfield at that time.

HATFIELD/GROTON

In March 1676, a band of Nipmucks attacked and destroyed Groton during King Philip's War. It is said that

many men, women, and children were killed here. The ghostly screams of those killed can still be heard if one listens closely. There is a Native American legend in Hatfield. In 1675, over 800 Native Americans were slaughtered here. The woman who supposedly betrayed them was thrown to dogs who tore her apart. Native American attacks caused the town to be abandoned in the 1670s, but it was re-populated.

HOLYOKE/HINGHAM/HOLLISTON

There are remains of a settler fort in Hingham. The details of exactly where this fort is are very vague. In Holliston, a strange unknown plague struck only this town from 1752-1754, killing one eighth of the population. It never spread beyond this town and it is still not known today what it was. It was a logging town on the Connecticut River. There has been a dam here for many years; in 1848, it was made of wood and in 1900, it was rebuilt in stone.

Native American arrowheads have been discovered in Holyoke. In 1869, while building factories, a Native American burial site was found. All the Native Americans were buried in a sitting position, with all their belongings surrounding them. They were buried near the falls, but there was no known village here. Since that time, those who crossed the Williamansett Bridge report seeing ghosts of Native Americans, pioneers, river men, and loggers who died while doing their job. It is said that the ground will shake here for no reason, though the railroad has long since gone. Dinosaur tracks have been found on the West Bank of the Connecticut River. These tracks are over 150,000,000 years old.

HUBBARDSTON/LAKEVILLE/
LANCASTER/HUNTINGTON

Lakeville is the site of a Native American village and burial ground. Lancaster was attacked during King Philip's War. Hubbardston is the place where Nonesuch apples were discovered in 1790. This is a special variety of apple found

only here. The town of Huntington was a skirmish site in Shays' Rebellion.

IPSWICH/SALISBURY/NAHANT

The town of Nahant was settled in 1630 and is part of Essex County in the eastern part of the state. This is a high rocky island that is now connected to the mainland. When first settled, the island was covered with trees.

A cave exists here that has been haunted since King Philip's War. A fissure in the rocks is called Swallow's Cave. This is now private property found on Swallows Cave Road. It is a natural recess in the rocky shore. It is said that the witches who were hunted in 1692 hid here. The ghost of the witch that haunts this cave, however, has nothing to do with the witch trials of the region. It was here that forty Narragansett tribe members hid in 1675, after crossing the Bay to raid the settlement at Lynn during King Philip's War. The story goes that they hid for two weeks and were never discovered by the British. The Captain of the British troops consulted the Nahant witch called Wonderful to find the fugitives. She told him where to find them, but she warned them not to kill them. They would surrender, which turned out to be true. She died and was buried overlooking the cave. It is said that her ghost still haunts here.

The Schooner, *Jennie M. Carter*, wrecked off Salisbury Beach in 1894. Graves Ledge is also known as Salisbury Pinnacle. There is a legend about $175,000 that was buried in Salisbury. The details of what happened in Salisbury are vague, or who burned it.

Ipswich was the scene of a strange historic event. In the early 1700s or 1635, the dates differ, Reverend George Whitefield from the First Parish Church, which became the Congregational Church, was preaching about fire and brimstone in church. He was giving such a powerful speech that it is said to have drove the Devil out of the Church. The story goes that the Devil leaped out of the church and left his cloven footprint in the solid granite rock below. The Church was destroyed by lightning in 1965. As mentioned earlier, most of the "Devil" type footprints were, and are, dinosaur fossils or footprints. They are remarkable discoveries and are noted because if one footprint was found, it is possible that more still exist awaiting discovery of the patient treasure hunter.

The Schooner, *Mexican*, wrecked at Ipswich Bay in 1890. Coins have washed ashore.

LANESBOROUGH/PITTSFIELD/ WEST LANESBOROUGH

Baker's Quarry Cave is a 140-foot marble cave found in West Lanesborough. This solid white marble cave is considered one of the most beautiful caves in New England. Along the Massachusetts and New York border, there are three caves in the Taconic Range that were used by counterfeiters near Lanesborough. On the western shoulder of Constitution Hill, the caves are named: Crevice Cave, Counterfeiters Cave, and Belcher's Cave. The road that leads to these caves is called Silver Street, because of the "fake" silver coins that were made here. In Counterfeiters Cave, there was a seventy-five-foot waterfall that seemed to guard the entrance to the cave. The cave is now crumbled and inaccessible. This is the lost cave located in Pittsfield State Forest. In the 1890s, counterfeiters used melted silver to make fake coins. During a flood, a slab of rock fell over the entrance of the cave. It is possible that there may still be fake silver coins left in the cave. Crevice Cave is one large room opening above a brook. Constitution Hill got its name from the historical speech given by Jonathan Smith, which is said to turned the tide of Massachusetts adopting a national convention. Belcher's Cave is thirty feet long located on Bung Hill. This was the cave where the largest and most brazen counterfeiters in New England history set up shop. It is where the money was made and named for the leader of the group, Gill or Gil Belcher. Fake coins dated 1834 were found in a sack by boys exploring the area on the rattlesnake-infested mountain.

In the north section of Lanesborough, there was an old house called the Bradley House. This was a British headquarters

in 1777. When Burgoynes' soldiers passed through after the defeat at Saratoga stopped here, it is said that the quartermaster hid a bag of gold. When they returned, the bag vanished and no gold was ever found. Did they forget where they hid it or was it found?

In 1900, the Hamilton Mine in South Mountain claimed to take out gold worth $10 per ton. The extraction cost was $3 per ton, so it was considered a profitable mine. However, one must be careful when gold is declared to be discovered. In Hinsdale, in the 1900s, a gold vein found in the nearby hills created the Hinsdale Mining Company. The ore was said to be assayed at $35 per pound. Unfortunately, it was all a ruse.

Another balance rock can be found here. This 350-ton boulder stands on a small pedestal. The Native American legend said that this rock was a plaything of an Iroquois champion, who tossed it there to show the Mahican youth how to play quoits. It is now in a park owned by the City of Pittsfield. There seems to be many balancing-type rocks in Massachusetts. It proves the amazing power of glaciers and how that ice shield literally moved mountains and drop them anywhere.

A Tory is reported to have hidden in Diamond Cave. He later changed his mind, emerged from the cave and fought for the colonies during the Revolutionary War. Why would this cave be called diamond? There is no family by that name here, but the cave is diamond-shaped. It was carved by water running through it. The walls sparkle and glitter (just like diamonds) when the light hits them just right. Perhaps that is the reason it was part of an abandoned colonial road from Pittsfield to Bennington, Vermont. It is now a hiking trail.

Silk was manufactured in town on the Housantonic River. The original name for Pittsfield was Pontoosuck Plantation. There was a lot of attacks from Native Americans in this area. Ghostly voices are heard around Pontoosuck Lake. It is said the voices speak in the language of the Native American and are thought to be the lovers, Moon-keek and Shoon-keek. A jealous intruder killed them here.

This is also the town where the visitor can view the marble that still exists underground. Leopard Rock is found in one of the chambers of the Great Radium Spring Marble Cave. The water has washed over the hard white marble and yellow limestone creating a white leopard with yellow spots. The marble quarry in Pittsfield is really a marble labyrinth. White marble is found at the mouth of the cave. It is also known as Coon Hollow Cave and found behind Laurel Hill. All the old farm houses have disappeared, but the visitor can find relics of a bygone era throughout the area. The marble mined here was used in making the Capitol in Washington D.C., the Berkshire County Courthouse and the Berkshire Anthenum in Pittsfield. Laurel Hill was where the Native Americans held their grand council meetings.

In the northwest of town, there is a Native American tradition around Lake Onota or Lake of the White Deer involving a pure white doe that no hunter would shoot at. It was an omen of good fortune. The Machian legend stated that as long as the snow-white doe came to drink at the lake, no famine would blight the harvest nor would pestilence come to the lodge nor foe would lay waste to the country. During the French & Indian War, Montalbert, a French Officer, wanted to bring the snow white pelt back to Canada. The doe was killed while drinking at the lake. As he started to take his prize back to Canada, an angry red moon rose over the lake. It is said that he met his death somewhere along the Long Trail to Canada, and the prophesy came true as the tribe members diminished, and prosperity vanished.

LEE

"Peter's Cave" on Orchard Street was the hiding place of Peter Wilcox, Jr., who was condemned to die for his participation in Shays' Rebellion. He was caught here, but eventually pardoned.

There are numerous lime and marble quarries found in Lee, also known as "Marbletown." The marble was a grey-veined type and unusually hard. It is the hardest marble found in the country. This marble was used for headstones at Arlington National Cemetery, Grants Tomb, and Saint Patrick's Cathedral in New York. The pits today are deep and filled with water. One pit, called the Philadelphia Hole, yielded two million cubic feet of marble. It is used as a swimming hole today.

During the Civil War era, the Lee Paper Mill discovered that the paper they were printing was marked with a "C.S.A." Mr. Linn, who created the bank-note paper, was summoned before the District Court in Boston to explain. At that time, the initials meant Confederate States of America. According to the story, he was carrying out a plan given to him by Union sympathizers, who planned to flood the south with quantities of counterfeit bills. The value of the southern currency would be destroyed and the war would be over. The case was postponed and never tried. Mr. Linn disappeared and the truth is still a mystery.

LEYDEN/BECKET/HARVARD/ LITTLETON/LEOMINSTER

A silver mine was found in Harvard in 1783. In Leyden, copper was mined on the Green River. In Becket, copper has also been discovered. Yokum Pond is named for the Native American Chief who is said to have drowned himself in this water. A mound on the shore is said to be his grave. The Porter Road Bridge in Littleton marks the site of an old mill and a crossing of the Acton-Groton stagecoach.

There is also a legend that this is an ancient, extinct waterfall site. The Tophet Swamp and Chasm (found at the lower end of Oak Hill) was created by a glacial lake or it may have been created before the ice age.

Native American relics have been found in Leominster. There is also a claim that this town is a Viking landing site.

LYNN

This town was settled in 1629 and named from ancient Briton, meaning "place of the spreading waters." Lynn Beach was where the Native American gathered to prove skill and strength. It is also the site of many shipwrecks – the Bark, *Vernon*, in 1859. Also, the English Merchantman, *Pembroke* was lost here in 1766. That ship carried $200,000 sterling in silver coins. Coins can sometimes be found on the beach after high tide or a large ocean storm.

Dungeon Rock is where pirates are said to have buried many treasures. It is a park today and searching or digging for this treasure is highly discouraged.

The legend is that a huge cave existed at the mouth of the Saugus River and was destroyed forever by an earthquake in 1658. It is said that pirates hung light signals from Lantern Rock for small boats to come to secretly hide their loot. The pirate, Thomas Veale or Veal, was said to have been buried alive or crushed by the enormous rock that tipped over the entrance of the cave during the earthquake. His ghost is said to now guard the treasure to be sure that no one leaves the cave alive with the loot.

Before 1658, Veal set himself up a cobbler (or shoemaker) as a cover. Veal was one of four pirates said to be trying to escape from British forces, and three were captured and hanged, but not Veal. It is said that his cobbler shop could still be seen as late as 1844. There were also stories of outlaws who would hang out in the area. It is said that they captured an English Princess and murdered her here.

As an interesting side note, there are claims that the earthquake of 1658 occurred in the middle of a hurricane. Whatever the truth may be, something catastrophic happened in this spot. In the 1830s, two attempts were made to blow up the rock covering the entrance. All that happened was that the entrance was totally destroyed.

In 1852, Hiram Marble, a member of the Spiritualist Church and the new owner of the property, said that Veal's ghost told him where to find the loot, but he never did. He built many structures all around the area, some can still be found today. It is said that a tool shed was built near the tunnel entrance, but no one knows where it actually is. Hiram's son, Edwin asked to be buried here and it said that a stone marks his grave. Many years later, four men are said to have sailed the Saugus River and stopped at the Saugus Iron Works to buy digging tools. They asked that the tools be delivered to a place called Pirates Glen and that payment in silver bars would be waiting. The tools were delivered, but no one was around. The money was there, so the tools were left, and no one ever saw the men again.

On the Circle Trail, there are unusual minerals and glacial deposits that are only found in the Lynn Woods. The exact location of a factory called Lynn Ironworks is unknown, but did exist in the woods. Strange sounds are heard here. It is said that it sounds like someone is walking beside you when walking through these woods.

MARBLEHEAD

A legend in Marblehead states that "our ancestors came here not for religion. Their main end was to catch fish." This old fishing port is full of strange tales. Ghosts, hobgoblins, will-o'-the-wisp, apparitions, and premonitions were most common existing here according to the United States Supreme Court Judge, Joseph Story, a native of Marblehead in the 1800s. Early residents claim to meet the Devil riding in a coach and some were chased through streets by a corpse in a coffin. Old "Mammy Red" from here was hanged as a witch in Salem in 1692. It was said that she knew how to turn enemies' butter into blue wool.

There is a military ghost that haunts the Old Burying Hill Ground, where over 600 Revolutionary War soldiers lay.

The Great Neck, also known as "the churn" or the "spouting horn," is the site of Marblehead Lighthouse, about four miles south of Salem. This port was considered "a good harbor for boats and safe riding for ships," according to the *New England Prospect* in 1633.

Halfway Rock is where it is custom for the fishermen to toss pennies to buy good luck and a safe return. Many privateers and mooncussers or wreckers made their living in the Barnegat District, and many pirates and smugglers were welcomed and stayed in hiding at the Fountain Inn. In July 1722, pirate Edward Low plundered thirteen vessels near Marblehead. John Quelch is also supposed to have buried treasure here as well as on Snake Island, nearby.

There is an offshore island called, Satan Rock, a place where ships wrecked numerous times. Treasure hunters have found large amounts of late eighteenth century English and Spanish coins in the area. The Steamer, *Norseman*, wrecked off Tom Moore Rock in 1899.

The story of the screeching woman started on Oakum Beach in October 1680. A strange Spanish ship loaded with treasure is said to have come into harbor when the men were fishing on the Grand Banks. The ship had been attacked by pirates and all crew and passengers were killed, except one. The pirate crew, for reasons not really known, rowed her to the beach, cut off her ring finger, perhaps because she would not give them her ring, and murdered her on the beach. The woman screamed on the beach for help, but the residents left in town could do nothing. They would only be murdered by the pirates if they went to give aid. The next day, the residents found the body and buried the woman on the beach. To this day, people have reported hearing cries for help on this beach in October.

There is also a legend that an ancient burial ground for the pre-Algonkians exists in town. Perhaps the tribe was related to the Newfoundland Beothunk Indians. This tribe was also known as the Ulno, Skraelling (remember that is what the Vikings called the Native Americans they supposedly met on Cape Cod), and Red Indians.

MARLBOROUGH/LUDLOW

During King Philip's War in Ludlow, a band of warriors, led by Roaring Thunder, leaped over the cliff, now called Indian Leap, into the Chicopee River to escape those in pursuit. The Native American Plantation was called Okammakamefit in Marlborough. The English called the town Whipsufferage. It was one of John Eliot's praying Indian towns and destroyed during King Philip's War.

MARSHFIELD

In 1789, Stuart Alton went into the banking business, married, and had three children. In 1807, he learned the harpsichord, and purchased an organ built by George Astor, brother of John Jacob Astor. He played the organ each night. In the War of 1812, Stuart's wife was lost on the frigate,

Constitution. Stuart was devastated and vowed never to play the organ again.

Time passed and he eventually moved to another place in town. He put the organ near the fireplace and started to play again. He again played for years, and one day while his entire family was there, he died in the middle of playing a piece. Nothing was ever found of his vast fortune that was said to be in the form of $10- and $20-gold pieces. His granddaughter, Lucy, moved into the home. She also learned to play the organ. She said that she had a dream about her grandfather. He was seated at the organ, playing an original piece. He then walked over to the fireplace and tapped the left side with a poker. As she awoke, she heard the organ playing, but by the time she got to the top of the stairs, the playing had stopped. Lucy found $37,600 worth of $10- and $20-gold coins exactly where her grandfather told her they were.

MARTHA'S VINEYARD

This triangle-shaped island was first discovered by English explorers, John Breneton and Bartholomew Gosnold in 1602. Why the name Martha? No one is really sure. It may have actually been called Martin's Vineyard? Why is it called Vineyard? That is an easier question to answer. The discoverers found huge amounts of vines here.

This is indeed a magical place. At the east end of the island, the tides actually flow east to west. The area was first settled by Thomas Mayhew in 1642. There is a well-known Native American route or path here called "The Savage Path." It is three feet wide and deeply worn from centuries of use. The ancient name was Nope, an abbreviation from the Wampanoag word, p'nopsquessaugamaug, meaning "menhaden fishing place." Another ancient name was capawack, which means, "enclosed harbor" or "place of refuge." There was a Native American village south of the landing place, about a half mile past what is now the Courthouse.

The Viking, Leif Erikson, wrote in his Saga of a long westerly passage and the keel-shaped Cape, which is thought to be Cape Cod. He also mentions the Straumey or Island of

Streams, thought to be Martha's Vineyard. It is said that he camped for the winter here and an attack on his two camps is thought to have taken place at Menemsha Pond, which does open out into the sea. A dolmen, or cromleach, or table stone, also known as stone monument, stands here supposedly erected over the burial places of those Vikings 1,000 years ago. It could be a Norse marker, or a Native American marker, but the first settlers found it already here. In the peat bog just out of town, human remains have been found. Though no one is sure where they came from or who they were, it is known that they met a violent death.

It is believed that the tribe of the island was a branch of the Wampanoags. However, the first tribe members who came here are said to have come from the north floating on an iceberg. The dialect spoken here was that of the Algonquins of Maine, they worshiped a white rabbit, which was unknown here, and they really did not want anything to do with the mainland tribes.

The western tip of the island, called Gay's Head, is where yellow amber has been discovered. There are also traces of volcanic formation found.

Black Brook is known for the strange sounds that occur. Twigs snap as though someone is walking over them after dark. Lights are seen where no lights exist. There were burial stones found near Miltark Rock. There is a presence that is always felt. It is said that a headless man stands north by the Brook and there is also a horse ghost seen here.

The last witch to die at Gay's Head was a Native American named Patience Gashum. She was a Wampanoag herbalist. It was believed at the time that you could kill a witch with a silver bullet, and that is how she died. If one can avoid the spirits here, there is a treasure to be found. Ikis Hill dreamed that she saw pirates bury a treasure near the cliffs. The site was marked with sticks. This description is rather vague and hard to follow.

Prehistoric whale, shark, and shellfish were found near the Gay's Head cliffs. It was believed to be the monster Moshup who lived here. The settlers called the area Devil's Den. Teeth are still found in the ravine to this day. What is interesting is that a lizard of some sort is often seen off

these cliffs. It is described as being sixty feet in length with a cow or horse head, with paddle legs and a long slender tail. The first documented sighting of this creature was by a British Man-O'-War in 1700. The last known sighting was in 1930 by fishermen.

There is a geologic beauty to the cliffs. The colors are amazing: Red, white, yellow, blue, indigo, and black cover over 6,000 feet of area. The Native Americans used the clay to make pottery, and would use the wood from shipwrecks to have warm fires when winter came to the island. This practice became the reason for a murder. In February 1823, the brig, *Pilgrim*, was wrecked at Devil's Bridge, a sunken shoal, near Gay's Head Light. The wood was taken by members of the tribe, and one woman, Mary Cuff, was found with her head caved in on the shore. The man accused of her murder was found innocent, but five years later was hanged for murdering another woman in New York City.

The Elizabeth Islands lie just south of the Vineyard. The Native American name for the collection of islands was Nashanaw, meaning "our father's islands." The islands were named by Gosnold for his Queen. Gosnold is said to have set up a settlement on Cuttyhunk, also known as No-man's Island. He landed or really wrecked here on May 21, 1602. He built a home, but was attacked by the Native Americans, so he abruptly left the area, taking nothing with him. The islands are named west to east as follows: Cuttyhunk, the last of the island chain, which is also known as Elizabeth Isle and may have a fort or home on it built by Gosnold; Penikese; Nashawena; Pasque; Naushon; the largest of the chain, Weepeket; Uncatena; and Nonamesset. Gosnold reported that he found orange bark fruit trees on Cuttyhunk Island that felt smooth to the touch. No one is sure what those trees were. The Native American name for this island was poocutohhunkounoh or "place of departure." His ship, *The Concord*, was wrecked here and the hulk could be seen as late as the 1900s.

In the blizzard of 1866, the schooner, *Christina,* was wrecked off Cuttyhunk, also known as No-mans-land or Norman's Land. It was here that an inscription in rock was found in 1929. It is said that the translation stated, "Leif

Erikson's island thirty men." Was this a hoax? Or did the Norse land here many years ago? Since the 1938 Hurricane, the boulder with the inscription has fallen face down underwater. This however is not the only Norse writing found here. A member of the clergy in the late nineteenth century found a runic inscription at Oaks Bluff. The boulder was originally high on the bluffs, facing the ships sailing west into Nantucket Sound. The boulder had toppled and landed on a beach. The rock soon was named Lover's Rock, because couples carved their initials into it. It is now entirely underwater.

No-mans-land is also said to be the site of a buried treasure. A seance told a couple where the treasure was. They found a rock with inscription on it and behind that they were to find a treasure at the center of a deep, muddy pond. (There are rocks that do have marks on them; see paragraph above.) They tried, but though they could not raise the treasure. There are those who insist that a treasure still exists there.

The Elizabeth Islands have a legend surrounding them. It is said that a father owned all the islands of Cape Cod, and his legacy to his three daughters were the islands. The eldest called all the islands after herself, Elizabeth. The middle daughter took the largest island, and named it after herself, Martha's Vineyard. The youngest, Nancy, had to take Nantucket, in other words, "Nan took it."

In 1689, Thomas Pond was captured in Vineyard Sound after a sea battle with the British around Tarpaulin Cove. He was one of the few pirates who was acquitted, and later became a commander of a King's naval ship.

The 270-foot *City of Columbus* wrecked on the west tip of Martha's Vineyard in January 1884 at Devil's Bridge, with 103 crew and passengers lost. Many ships met their demise at Devil's Bridge. This one in particular is considered one of the worst marine disasters of that era. *Gate City*, the sister ship of *City of Columbus* wrecked off Naushon Island in a dense fog in 1886. In 1924, the schooner, *Ruth E. Merrill*, grounded on L'Hommedieu Shoal. This ship was one of the largest schooners in the world at that time. The *Emma* wrecked here in 1899. In 1856, the brick house was always damp and was torn down. It was thought that this was the reason for the often fatal unknown diseases and mysterious

illness that occurred here. Perhaps mold was a reason or perhaps it was something else.

Edgartown was first called Nunnepog, meaning "fresh pond." It was named for Edgar, the son of King James II of England. A large number of silver English coins were found near Great Pond dating from the late 1700s. The *Mertie B. Crowley* was wrecked in 1910 on the Wasque Shoals. This was the largest and longest schooner ever built in Rockland, Maine. She had wrecked two times before this, but always managed to be repaired. This is also the site of a Native American burial ground. Human bones have been found. What is strange about this site is that sometimes giant bones have been found, much larger than present-day man.

Native American lore had a sea serpent on this island. The tale was of the sea woman named Squant, with hair of seaweed and a body of a seal and eyes shaped like squares. She lived in an underwater cave off Aquinnah (Gay's Head) where the spirit of Maushop lay asleep, enchanted by the sea woman's song that led him from the dry land to her watery cave. Benjamin Franklin's uncle saw a serpent off the Cape in 1719. It had a head of a lion, large teeth, long beard, and floppy ears. In 1886, a sea serpent was seen off Provincetown. This creature was 300 feet long, and 12 feet wide. A sulfuric odor was said to come from the beast. It also came ashore and had a 20-foot tail. An article at the time made an interesting comment: Perhaps the sea serpent was awakened by recent earthquakes felt in the area. Also, a water spout was seen here in 1896. Maybe that stirred up something from the deep.

During the Revolutionary War era, a French Galleon was wrecked on the south side of the island. It carried a large amount of money, part of the payroll for the French troops. The money was salvaged by the officers, and said to be buried for safekeeping. The story is that they never returned for the money. There was an undisclosed amount of money found here many years ago. A horse broke through to a treasure cave or pit and the federal government took most of the loot, but the rider did get some substantial reward.

There were no banks on the island for many years. The settlers, when they had money, would have to find other places to conceal their wealth. After all, pirates, smugglers, and wreckers were common here. Hidden places often included cellar walls, false doorways, or just a hole in a back yard. Knowing and researching where people once lived on the island and receiving permission to dig on private property may yield amazing results. Many residents quickly hid precious items when strangers were seen coming to the island. Coins have been found in tree hollows, people have thrown items into Beck's Pond, and it is said that a pirate once told of burying loot along the north shore of the island where two brooks emptied into the Sound.

The Blue Rock of Chappaquiddick is an enormous boulder located near the shore where the Cape Poge Light stands. A farmer stated that he saw pirates come ashore here and bury a chest under this rock. The leader of the group killed two men and threw their bodies into the pit with the treasure. The farmer quickly left, and came back the next day, but strangely could find no sign of the treasure pit or the murders.

MENDON/MEDFIELD/METHUEN

Mendon was also known as Quinshepauge and destroyed during one of the first battles of King Philip's War as was Medfield.

Methuen was named for Lord Paul Methuen, who was an English official in pre-Revolutionary War Days. This was also the birthplace of Major Robert Rogers, commander of the famed New Hampshire Rogers' Rangers, who destroyed the St. Francis Tribe in 1759. I discussed this lost treasure and his journey in my first book, *Lost Loot, Ghostly New England Treasure Tales*.

In the nineteenth century, Mark and Nathaniel Gorill buried a treasure around Tenney Castle. They courted the same woman and she rejected both of them. They became hermits, never speaking to each other again, but both lived on the Hill. After they died, a resident of the town dreamed of a treasure hidden in a wall in the castle. It was searched and $20,000 in bonds were found in the cellar in one of the towers. The ruins of this place can be found on Danny Fryes Hill in Essex County.

MIDDLEBOROUGH

Middleborough was settled by three shipwrecked French sailors. This town was destroyed during King Philip's War, and then rebuilt.

A rock in the area is called Hand Rock, where an impression of a hand can be found. It is the spot where people claim seeing a Native American waving at them at various times, but no one is really there.

The people of this town built a fort on the bank of the Nemasket River to protect them from Native American attacks. In 1675, during King Philip's War, a band of Native Americans were seen on the opposite bank, near Hand Rock. Over the next few days, one Native American kept coming there gesturing something, seeming to want to provoke an attack by the settlers. Something needed to be done, so the Captain of the fort shot the Native American, where he died at this spot. Is this the person that is seen at different times?

This is also the site of an ancient stone quarry. Rock Village in the area gets its name from a massive ledge. There are also caves, and one of the most haunted and famous is King Philip's Cave. This cave, during King Philip's War, was said to be large enough for King Philip and his horse to hide in. Much of the cave today is under Walnut Street and not readily accessible.

MILLS/MAYNARD/MONTAQUE

In Maynard, in 1720, Thomas Smith is said to have buried a cache of silver and gold coins in the woods north of his home on the Assabet River. Mills was settled in 1657 near the Charles River in Norfolk County. A legend exists about Union Street in town. The Dinglehole is a pit formerly filled with water where Puritans heard the ringing of the bell that was said to summons witches to their evil rites and they actually saw on moonlit nights a headless man keeping vigil.

Turners Falls is the main village in Montaque located on the Connecticut River. Elisha Mack built the first dam on the Connecticut River here. An ice jam in 1936 swept away three bridges, including the longest covered wooden bridge in the state belonging to the Boston and Maine Railroad. This is one of the few places where the northern tribes and southern tribes came together to fish, trade, worship, and socialize.

It is said that Kidd also buried a treasure here on Captain Kidd's Island just above French King Rock. This iron chest is full of gold and jewels. A dead pirate does guard this treasure and the story was told by the African cook of Kidd's ship. Why French King Rock? This was where King Philip would sun-bake shad (a type of fish) that were caught by the falls. Still, King Philip was not a French King, so perhaps this is not the real reason for the name.

MOUNT WASHINGTON

This town is the site of Bish-Bash Falls in Berkshire County. These are spectacular falls, settled by the Europeans in 1692. The falls are a 200-foot drop that overlooks Profile Rock on top of a perpendicular cliff. The pool below the falls has a Native American legend attached to it. It is said that the "spirit profile" of a Native American girl, White Swan, can be seen under the water in the pool. She was the daughter of a witch, who is said to have lived beneath the falls. The girl was married to a handsome young brave. Because she could not have children, her husband took another wife. White Swan pined for her husband, gazing into the pool for hours, and one day, she heard her mother calling her from beneath the water. She jumped in, and her former husband jumped in after her. They both died there, but she can still be seen.

This is the smallest town in the state. The southwestern part of town is called "Boston Corner." It was probably named because it was as far as you could get from Boston and still be in Massachusetts. The nickname was later changed to "a corner of hell" and in the nineteenth century, the name changed to "Hell's Acres." There is an old superstition here that the soil is underlaid with minerals and is always hot. "Hell's Acres" had a reference to the number of horse thieves and counterfeiters who used the area as a hide-out in pre-Revolutionary times.

The Mohegan tribe were known to have buried large amounts of treasure in the seventeenth century in the area. The treasure was obtained by the numerous raids on the English settlements in the area. Bish-Bash is a Mahican word, meaning, "she is shot." Basha or Mombasha, a Native American, was shot at these falls during the Esopus War. The Esopus Wars were two wars fought between the Dutch settlers and the Esopus tribe of Lenape Indians from New York during the seventeenth century. This place was a battle site for that war.

Alander is kind of a ghost town found here. In 1647, it was the central village area of Mount Washington. The road to this place passes through thick woods. It is also said that the Black Grocery Gang buried treasure in this vicinity.

NANTUCKET ISLAND

The Native American name of this island was Canopache, meaning "The place of peace" or "far away land at sea" and is located about thirty miles off the south shore of Cape Cod but only a six-mile canoe ride from Rhode Island. It is the most southern island of New England. This island was settled by Europeans fleeing religious persecution in June 1661. There is a Native American legend about this place. It seems to talk about a serpent, but here is the story. An evil ogre did not want the Native Americans to live on the island. The evil spirit had a serpent with legs and it was very large. He controlled snakes and when he was mad, he could cause earthquakes. He was called Pootar, meaning "whale" or "whale spouting." The name still exists on the island in Pootar Pond. The Native Americans did settle the island after they killed the evil monster. It is really a tale of good versus evil and good triumphs at the end.

There were various Native American villages located here, though the last wigwam disappeared in 1797. One village was called Occawa or Orcawa and was located near Siasconset. There was also a village at the northern part of Miacomet Pond and on the west side of Squam Pond called Ahapahant. South of Abrams Point near Sawkemo and north of Secacacha

Pond were also the sites of Native American villages. It is said that north of Shimmo is a Native American burial ground.

Whaling did play a huge part in the islands' economy. It could also be said that the whales here may have seemed more aggressive. In 1820, the whaling ship, *Essex*, was rammed by a whale. It is thought that perhaps a sound from within the ship caused the sperm whale to attack. The ship sank very quickly and only eight of the crew survived for three months in the open whaling boat. This story is also said to be the basis for *Moby Dick*, by Herman Melville. In 1846, a great fire ended the whaling industry here. It destroyed the entire town and the last whaling ship had left that year, never to return.

Gibbs Pond is the islands' haunted lake. It was named after the Nantucket tribe member John Gibbs. In 1665, John Gibb was a Harvard lawyer who spoke the name of the dead leader of the tribe, Massasat, a crime in Native American law. King Philip took offense at this slight and arrived at Nantucket Island at Low Beach at Tom Nevers Head, heading toward the largest Native American village called Oggawam by Gibbs Pond. The village was near the east end of Great Pond and Swamp called "sconset" or "siasconset." He was looking for John Gibbs. The tribe was hiding him, but managed to pay off King Philip with eleven pounds of silver and gold. He left along a stream called Philip's Run today. There were actual deadly battles about this issue, however. More to this story can be found in the East Hartford, Connecticut part of this book.

A French corsair landed here in 1695 and used the island as a base of operations. A corsair is a pirate ship sanctioned by the country to which it belongs. It is different from a privateer ship, which is a privately owned ship that is commissioned to seize, sink, or destroy enemy vessels. A corsair can seize, sink, or destroy any other vessel, whether at war or not. The French corsair is said to attack a house owned by the Bunker family. Tradition says that the family buried all their gold, but after the corsair left, the family was so shaken up that they could not remember where they buried it.

There have been numerous remains of ships found on the beaches near Long Pond, Siasconset, and Wauwinet. Siasconset is a Narragansett word, meaning, "at the place of bones," or "great bones place," or "Near the Great Bone."

It is thought that perhaps this was where massive amounts of whale bones were found. The bones are gone, but where they went is unknown.

There were over 269 shipwrecks in just the year 1910 alone. The value of the cargo that was lost just that one year is said to be $809,020. Some of the treasure was salvaged, but it is thought that $125,285 is still missing. That is just one year's worth of information. There are said to be over 500 wrecks by the year 1877. The following is just a small list of some of the shipwrecks that occurred here: The English ship, *Sir Sidney Smith* in 1812; the brig, *Poinsett* in September 1870; the British Barque, *Minmaneuth*, in 1873 on the south shore. The Steamer, *Republic* sank in 1909 with about $3,000,000 on board about twenty-seven miles southwest off the island. It collided with the Italian liner, *Florida*. This was the first time a wireless radio was used to radio for help. The signal for a distressed ship before that time was to fly the national flag upside down. In 1914, the schooner, *Alice M. Lawrence*, ran into Tuckernuck Shoal in a gale. In 1924, schooner, *Wyoming*, wrecked near the Pollock Rip Lighthouse during a blizzard. Also in 1924, another schooner, *Evelyn & Ralph* wrecked in fog. In 1936, two freighters, *Canadian Planter* and *City of Auckland* collided near Horseshoe Shoal in dense fog. In 1944, the American steamer, *Oregon*, sank by the Nantucket Shoals Light with over $8,000,000 on board. The Italian Steamer, the *Andrea Doria*, sank in a collision with a Swedish motorship, the *Stockholm* in July, 1956. She sank forty-five miles southeast of the island with diamonds and china still on board.

The vicious and violent pirate, Edward Low, plundered these waters. He really hated New Englanders and would do horrible things to passengers or crew who were from New England. It is said that he witnessed Captain Kidd's hanging in London in 1701. It had a huge impact on him. He vowed that he would never allow himself to be murdered that way. When did he become insane? It is said after the death of his young wife. Paul Williams is said to be the only pirate from Nantucket Island. He was a partner ship with Samuel Bellamy.

Garnet grains can be found on Sankaty Head. Shell fragments, some absolutely perfect specimens of Ostrea,

Petricola, Pholadiformis, Venus Merrenaria, Myaarenaria, Ilyanassa, Odostomia have been found here. There are also rare species of shells found called Chrysoldomus, Pilsby, and Stonei. There has been an extinct species discovered here called Miocene Pandora. Amber is one mineral that has been discovered.

NEW ASHFORD/NEW BEDFORD/ NEW MARLBOROUGH

New Ashford, in Berkshire County, is the site of a blue and white marble quarry discovered in 1822. The town was settled by Methodists from Rhode Island. They settled high in the mountain area because they believed that the valley mist caused a fever. They built a fort called Ash Fort, named after the town. The site is marked today and was built to protect the town from the Native Americans. The fort was found near the crossing of the old Stagecoach Road from New Ashford and the Rockwell Road to Greylock Mountain.

New Bedford is located on Apponagansett Bay and founded in 1760. There are ruins of colonial buildings still here. This was a rendezvous for American privateers during the Revolutionary War era. It was also an underground railroad station, which was a stop to smuggle southern slaves to Canada during the Civil War. Fort Rodman was built here after the Civil War. Numerous hulls from shipwrecks can still be seen in the muddy ocean bed all around this area. Artifacts from various eras have all been discovered in town.

New Marlborough was a station of the famed Red Bird Stagecoach line. This is also the site of the Cleveland Gold Mine in 1867. Copper and nickel were discovered around the southwest part of Harmon's Pond. It is currently a lost mine, since all the roads leading to the mine are covered, but there are old buildings all around the region. Be very careful when exploring old mine and building sites. They are very dangerous and can be deadly.

NEW SALEM/NATICK/NEWTON

Newtown, in Middlesex County, was settled in 1639. The Native American village called Nonantum was here. It was also the site of Echo Bridge, that went over the Charles River. In 1876, it was the largest triple-stone arch bridge in the world. Natick was a Praying Indian town and burial site. New Salem was a trading center for stagecoaches running between Brattleboro and Worcester. U.S. 202 and Mass 122 is an old stagecoach road.

NEWBURYPORT/NORTHFIELD/GREENFIELD

Newburyport was settled in 1635. Since colonial days, there was a silver plant and mill in Essex County. It is also the site of the treasure of Plum Island. This place has an unique connection to East Haddam/Moodus, Connecticut. It is here that it is believed that the earthquakes that are felt in East Haddam, causing at least some of the famous Moodus Sounds originate from here. Moodus Sounds are deep booming sounds coming from the mountains. This phenomena is recorded all over the world and thoroughly discussed in my first book.

Northfield and Greenfield can be found on the Mohawk Trail. Beer's Plain and Beer's Mountain were the sites of Native American battles during King Philip's War in 1675 with the settlers. There was also a Native American village and burial site.

Between Northfield and Greenfield, lies King Philip's Hill. It is thought that there was a fort where King Philip once lived. The remains of something could be seen here, but it is still unclear whether it was a Native American fort or something else. Native American relics have been found in the Greenfield area.

NORTHHAMPTON/EASTHAMPTON/NORTON/
PEABODY/PEMBROKE

Pascommuck Boulder is the site of a Native American massacre in 1704. There was a battle between the settlers and Native Americans in Easthampton. Northhampton is another site of a battle between the settlers and Native Americans. The town was abandoned in 1747 but was resettled.

Norton was settled in 1669. There were two witches who were said to live here, Dora Leonard and Naomi Bunt. It really is not too surprising that witches would be alleged to live here. A legend of the area is that Major George Leonard sold his soul to the Devil for gold. In 1716, the soul became due and the Devil carried his body off by jumping off the roof of his home. Devil's Footprints are found on a rock below the eaves where he landed.

In 1650, Pembroke settlers built a fort to ward off attacks from the Native Americans. In Peabody also known as Salem Farms, is where those who were accused of witchcraft in 1692 lived. There is still a pond called, "The Devil's Dishfull."

PLYMOUTH/QUINCY

Quincy was a non-stop party site known as Mapole Park in the 1620s. The residents drank beer and danced constantly. The other name for the area is Merry Mont, for obvious reasons. The Native American name for this area was squantum. There is also a legend that the Vikings landed here.

Martin Pring was the first one to visit Plymouth. He loaded his ship with sassafras to bring back to England. He told the English of immense forest fires he saw. No one is really sure what he actually saw. The Native American village of Pakanokick was here when the Pilgrims arrived. The ancient name for this area was Pathigget or Patuxet, meaning "falls at the mouth" or "falls in the brook." The only survivor of the village – a plague killed the rest of the tribe – Squanto, also known as Tisquantum, helped the Pilgrims survive that first winter in this new environment.

There may have been ancient rock writings found here, too. Humarock is a Wampanoag that means "shell place" or "rock carving." Cromesit Point in Plymouth County is a Wampanoag word, meaning "deserted fort." These are the reasons that the treasure hunter must learn ancient names for areas and regions. Names meaning "deserted fort" and "rock carvings" may lead to major discoveries.

Five miles north of Gurent Point in Green Harbor on Plymouth Bay, the British warship *H.M.S. Hazard* was totally destroyed during the hurricane of 1714. Over $100,000 of sterling gold coins were lost. There have been some coins found in the sand over the years. During the Revolutionary War era, the British Frigate, *Niger*, was wrecked here. In 1899, the schooners, *Massasoit* and *Golden Eagle* sank. There is also a story of a ghost ship that haunts the harbor. During the blizzard of 1778, the armed brigantine, *General Arnold*, tried to survive, but many of the crew were found dead on board after the storm. There was a mass grave dug for the crew, but people today claim to see the ship still sailing in the harbor. Usually seeing a ghost ship is a bad omen.

RAYNHAM/REHOBOTH/STOW/ SUNDERLAND/SWANSEA

Sunderland was abandoned during King Philip's War. Swansea was the first Massachusetts town attacked by King Philip in King Philip's War on June 24, 1675. Rehoboth is just one of the many King Philip War battle sites. This is also a haunted battle site. Ghost fires can be seen burning on the rocks and voices can be heard.

Raynham is located in Bristol County and settled in 1652. This town was left untouched during King Philip's War because the local forge repaired his weapons and the town supplied him with tools. This forge is said to be the first in America built in 1652 by the Leonard family. Earlier, before deciding to help King Philip, this town had many battles with the Native Americans. The victims are buried on Squawbetty, the west bank of the Taunton River. Though it seems that King Philip did not fight here while he was alive, his ghost may be here today. Perhaps this is where he feels safe.

King Philip is said to haunt here every three to five years. He is seen in the swamps and woods, apparently looking for his head. He was quartered when he was killed, and according to the Medicine Men of the tribes today, in order for him to move on, his body needs to be whole. His head was sent to Plymouth, where it was impaled as a warning to others. It is said that friends of Philip in Raynham took Philip's head and buried it in a cellar in this town in a jar.

As an interesting side note to this story, a head in a jar was found in a courthouse in Taunton and it was determined to be the head of a Native American. It is known that the swamp in the area near Fowling Pond was Philip's hunting area. Raynham was also part of Taunton at one time. According to Narragansett legend, it is said that every third generation Medicine Man will see Philip's ghost and he tries to reveal the location of his buried head somewhere between Taunton and Mount Hope. It is hoped that one day, he will be understood and he can be reunited with his head and finally rest.

REVERE/ROCKLAND

The corner of Revere Beach Parkway and Railroad Street is a battle site. The Battle of Chelsea Creek, now known as the Mystic River, was fought here in May 1775. The British needed food and tried to buy from the local farmers. The Patriots moved their livestock and food from Hog Island, and were going toward Noodle Island when the British schooner, *Diana*, opened fire. Israel Putnam and his men waded in the waist-deep water and returned the attack. The *Diana* was abandoned and then stripped and burned by the colonists.

Rockland, in Plymouth County, was settled in 1730. It was once a Native American encampment. There have been many Native American relics found here. The encampment site is now the Rockland Shopping Plaza.

Doane Falls on Lawrence Brook cuts through Granite Gorge. This is also the site of Forbes Falls, also known as

Royal Falls. Reynolds Mine in Royalston has yielded smoky Quartz and beryl. The aquamarine beryl is almost as blue as sapphire.

SALEM

One of the reasons that this town is well-known is for the witch hunts and trials of 1692. This event did darken the history of Salem and it is no wonder that hauntings and treasure stories abound here. This book will not go into that particular history; there is really no treasure to be found in those tales.

But there is one interesting side note to that time. In those days, it was believed that clever folk could outwit the Devil with a tough riddle and a quick answer. "Neck Riddles" gave the condemned person a chance to escape the gibbet. Today, we pay tribute to that time by using the line, "I could not think of the answer to save my life."

Salem was occupied by the tribe called Naumkeag. The village was called Nanepashemet, a Nipmuck word meaning "he who walks at night" or "the moon." Nanepashemet was the great moon chief of the Naumkeag tribe in 1616. The English name, Salem, ironically comes from the Hebrew, Sholom, meaning "peace." It is thought that the name is ironic because of the dark history that Salem has. Salem was heavily involved in privateering during the Revolutionary era.

Bakers Island Light is located about six miles in the harbor. Supernatural issues here began when a tree fell, killing a visitor to the island in the seventeenth century. There is said to be an evil force roaming the island called the Beast of Bakers Island. Details describing the creature are vague, but ominous. The fog bell warning alarm would turn on by itself. The foghorn would sound on crystal clear nights and it was hit by lightning in August 1877, causing it not to run right ever since. It was replaced, and was again hit by lightning in July 1879, and replaced again. Why this occurred, no one knows, but in 1898, one of the former keepers, named Walter Rogers, went to the island for a reunion of past keepers. As the keepers were getting ready to return to the mainland, the fog bell started. The men left as the bell kept ringing and were caught in an unexpected storm. The ship sank, all the former keepers, except Rogers, drowned. He always wondered if the bell went off to warn the keepers of the storm or to keep them on the island away from the storm.

One of the fifteen islands found in Salem Harbor is called "the Miseries" because of all the shipwrecks there. The Steamer, *Monohansett*, known as the fastest sidewheeler on the coast and used in the Civil War as a dispatch ship, wrecked in fog in 1904. The mineral corundum, also known as ruby and sapphire, have been found in the area.

SANDWICH/SCITUATE/SHIRLEY

Two granite lighters, the *Benjamin Franklin* and *Potomac*, were lost in a gale in 1909 off the Sandwich coast. They were carrying granite to build the Cape Cod Canal. In Scituate, the pilot boat, *Columbia* smashed through a house during the Portland Gale of 1898. A ghost ship is often seen offshore here.

There is an old fort treasure in Shirley worth over $400,000 in gold and silver coins. The fort was located on County 111 in Middlesex County. There is also a legend of a $100,000 hoard that was buried on the site of the Willard Tavern.

SOUTH EGREMONT/SOUTHFIELD

There is a place in Southfield in Berkshire County, called Rock Ledge, also known as Cook's Ledge, that boasts of yet another Tipping Rock. This is a forty-ton boulder so delicately balanced that the pressure of the hand will sway the stone, but not dislodge it.

In this Berkshire County region lies the location of the second largest cave in New England. Eldan's Cave or Eldon's French Cave was found by a boy exploring Tom Baldwin Mountain in South Egremont in 1875. This 450-foot cave under the mountain is a water-worn marble cave. The marble comes in five different colors with seven different hues.

There is white, purple, ochre, and red marble near the five waterfalls found under the earth. It is indeed an amazing natural treasure. No wonder the Native Americans had a village here in 1734.

SPRINGFIELD/RUTLAND/SHEFFIELD

A marble quarry is found in Sheffield. This was where the last battle of Shays' Rebellion occurred. In 1802, a shower of stones occurred here. Why it happened and where they came from is unknown? Unexplained mysteries are why these places are magical and enchanted. Many events seem to occur in these areas.

Rutland was the village where General John Burgoyne's troops camped after the defeat at Saratoga, New York. This was also the headquarters for Shays' Rebellion.

It has been said that donated and bequeathed church treasures stolen from the church in the area are buried in Springfield. There is said to be a crown of amethysts, worth over $5,000 buried somewhere in town. Even an entire railroad may lie under a cave-in here. Between 1864-1910, the magnetic iron ore mines here were used to make iron during the Civil War for the Union. These Emery mines helped win the war for the Union soldiers. There are stories that a railroad car was lost during a cave-in. Pearls have been found in the Connecticut River here. In January 1787, the first battle in Shays' Rebellion took place here at the arsenal.

This was the state with many tales of witchcraft. The main thing that terrified the Puritans was consorting with the Devil. This was a strange and scary place to the Pilgrims. Everything that was unusual was associated with the Devil and considered evil. There are legends that one way to prove witchcraft in some homes was to see if there were stairs, called witches stairs. These were narrow staircases used to facilitate the witches coming and going. These stairs went up the opposite side of the house, then the regular human staircase. If this type of staircase was found in your home, watch out!

Two witches were arrested in Springfield in 1651. In 1652, this town brought the first male witch, Hugh Parsons, to trial for witchcraft. He was found guilty, but the execution verdict was overthrown. The truth was that Parsons was well-liked by many of the woman in town and that made the men angry, so they called him a wizard, warlock, or male witch.

STOCKBRIDGE/WEST STOCKBRIDGE/ SOUTH MASHPEE/TAUNTON

On the West Stockbridge-Alford town line lies Tom Ball Mountain. This is the highest point in the area and on the western slope lies Devils Den. This is a cavern, but wide enough that a load of hay can be driven in. In the cave is a stone altar. It is fashioned out of strangely arranged boulders. The stone seems to be stained red. It is said the vision of Satan appears on the side of the altar. There is also the legend that the Native Americans sacrificed here. This is where the Devil's Den buried treasure is said to be found. The details are vague about what this treasure may be and also who actually buried it. This is another place said to be the site of human sacrifice, though not the usual practice of New England tribes. But they did fight amongst themselves and killed each other as prisoners of war. It is hard to tell what happened here, if anything.

There is also marble to be found. The marble from Alford built the State House in Boston and the Law Building in Albany, New York.

In Norfolk County on County 102, in Stockbridge is a Native American burial site in the southwestern part of town. It was founded in 1766 and attacked during the French and Indian War. It is said that the residents buried all their valuable belongings before the attack. Many of the residents were killed and are thought to have never recouped their treasure.

Stockbridge once boasted a marble quarry. The marble deposit was discovered in 1824 by a farmer who fell into an open vein. The marble was pure white with a dark blue tint resembling granite. It was also used in the State House in Boston and City Hall in New York.

Stockbridge was the site of a Machian Native American village called Qua-pau-kuk. This tribe was a branch of the

Algonquins. The name is a corruption of Mukhehaneew, meaning "the people of the over-flowing waters."

There is a legend that an unknown traveler or peddler came to the Stockbridge Tavern from New York in a raging storm. He paid his bill with a large amount of money and left. He was never seen again. His murdered body was found near the road after the snow melted. His ghost is said to roam there.

A cave purgatory between Lenox and Stockbridge between Bear and Little Mountain is a place called "ice glen." The crevices here keep winter snow and ice long into summer. It can be entered from the Laurel Hill end and exited half mile south. It is said that a robber hid his loot here, stolen from the Housatonic National Bank in Stockbridge. He was captured and it is said that others found his money, worth thousands of dollars, and vanished. (See Great Barrington for more information—different stories, but strangely seem connected.)

During the Revolutionary War, a Taunton wealthy merchant is said to have concealed a cache of gold coins and jewels near Watson Pond in Bristol County. He died before revealing the location. Taunton is called the "silver city" for the many Silversmiths who once had shops here.

There is gold to be found in South Mashpee, if one dares to retrieve it. The story is that a Frenchman made a deal with the devil for a kettle of gold. Though he sold his soul, he got scared and buried the treasure. However, the curse already occurred and the man died. The kettle remained filled with gold buried in the woods. Later, a Native American found the money, spent some it and died, though the remainder of the money was still buried. The cursed kettle of gold is said to still be buried in the area.

TURNER FALLS

This is the first dam found on the Connecticut River. It is also the site of a battle between the English and Native Americans in 1676. This was the territory of the Pocumtuck tribe who shared the fishing and hunting grounds with the

Mohawk tribe. Turner Falls was one of the disputed sites and often fought over. The Europeans also wanted this land, so a "peace" conference between the warring tribes and Europeans was arranged. A member of the high council of the Mohawk tribe was killed, by whom is not recorded, but the Mohawks blamed the Pocumtucks, came over the Mohawk Trail and annihilated the tribe settlements. The English were now able to expand up the Connecticut River Valley and the Dutch took the opportunity to move up the Hudson River Valley. The Trail was named after the victor of the war, the Mohawks. Part of this original trail can still be hiked today. This was one of the sites where all the northern and southern tribes would gather to fish, trade, worship, socialize, and share. Many Native Americans and settlers were also killed during King Philip's War here. This site is considered the greatest Native American battle site in the entire valley. Knowing the history, it is not a surprise that numerous arrowheads have been found.

TYNGSBOROUGH

This town is found in Middlesex County and settled in 1661. On Tyng's Island, also known as Wickasuck Island of Tyngsborough, located in the Merrimack River, was a Native American village. The island is about a half mile north of North Chelmsford. A 1936 flood uncovered a large amount of Native American artifacts. This sixty-five-acre island was formerly occupied by the Merrimack tribe. There is a legend that the Native Americans stole two little boys and brought them here to be raised as tribe members. This was a frontier town, and the garrison or fort was commanded by Jonathan Tyng, who faced whatever foe arrived in his home, which is also known as the haunted house.

He gave the island to the Pawtuckets, also known as the Praying Indians, after King Philip's War. The garrison stood on a little hill, close to the road, opposite the ferry landing about a mile upriver on Holden's Brook. This is the area where it is said that Joe English was shot to avoid being tortured by his Native American captors by taunting

them to kill him. He was the grandson of the Sachem of the Agawam tribe.

There is an even stranger legend here. It is said that the Native Americans held off an attack by the Knight's Templar before the Europeans arrived. Due to the many legends and tales that Native Americans did meet and interact with people from across the dark ocean years before the Europeans officially arrived, it is impossible not to reflect that perhaps there is more to the stories about ancient people sailing to these lands and having either good or bad relations with the people already living here. Perhaps the prophecies about the arrival of the Europeans were really memories of what happened long ago. Oral communication is not always the best way to hand down tradition. Think of the game called telephone. It does not take long for the meanings and even the words to change when handed down orally.

UPTON/UXBRIDGE

There are Devil's Footprints found on the southern slope of Pratt Hill in Upton, located in Worcester County and settled in 1728. The impressions are found in solid rock over two miles apart. Both prints are about five feet long and two feet wide and both are pointing south. This is also an alleged Viking landing site. The town of Uxbridge was a Nipmuck Praying Indian town, called Wacannuck by the Native Americans and settled in 1662.

WALES/WARE/WEST CHESTERFIELD

There are cellar holes all around Veineke Pond in Wales. These are from an old Hessian village named Veineke, who was one of the Hessian soldiers taken prisoner at the surrender of Burgoyne's army in 1777. This area is not accessible by car.

Ware is located on the Ware River and settled in 1717. Ware is a loose translation of a Native American word, Nenameseck, meaning "fishing weir." The term applies to areas where weirs once caught fish for the tribe.

The Quabbin Reservoir, meaning "many waters" is found on the west side of Ware. This is the largest man-made body of water in the world created exclusively for drinking water. There were parts of three towns flooded when this was created, Enfield, Greenwich, and Prescott. These are underwater/flooded ghost towns. Era artifacts are found on the shores of man-made lakes.

A slab stone marks Alden Culiver's grave in West Chesterfield, and he is buried above his chest of gold. He died in a battle with the Native Americans, but they buried him with his treasure. It is said that he even dug his own grave! There is actually more to this story. His daughter is also buried somewhere around this area and she has the key to the chest around her neck. Smoky Quartz and Tourmaline has been found in this town.

WEST TISBURY/WESTBOROUGH

West Tisbury can be found in Dukes County and was settled in 1669. Every wild flower known to exist in western Massachusetts has been found here. The Native American name for this place is Tackhum-min-Eyi or Takemmy, meaning "the place where one goes to grind corn." In 1659, this was a praying Indian town called an Algonkin word, Manitouwattootan, meaning "Christian-town."

Westborough was settled in 1675. Ruggles Street was a Native American path prior to 1630. Jack Straw once lived on Jack Straw Hill. He is believed to be the first Massachusetts Native American to be converted by the Europeans to Christianity. He was also one of the two Native Americans to be taken to London by Sir Walter Raleigh and presented to Queen Elizabeth.

Hoccomocco Pond was named by the Native Americans after an evil spirit. The name may not fit the area because is was also the place where Tom Cook, a highwayman in 1738, used to rob the rich and give to the poor. This rich would pay Cook large amounts annually for immunity from his robberies! Perhaps it was a proper name after all.

WESTFIELD/WESTWOOD/WILMINGTON/
WINTHROP/WORCESTER

The ruins of a Revolutionary War gun shop owned by Richard Falley in Westfield is located not far from the Belcher Cave in Pittsfield. He was the great-grandfather to President Grover Cleveland. The shop was called "secret armory." The grindstones used for musket-making are still seen in the area. In the Lane Traprock Quarries, amethyst has been found in the north part of the Armory. There is also a Native American cemetery near the Westfield water supply reservoir.

Westwood is located in Norfolk County and is known for the rock called Devil's Mouth. This is a large rock formation that was used as an arsenal and bake oven.

In Winthrop, a large amount of Spanish and British eighteenth century coins were found in the sand between Short Beach and Grover's Beach. This is also the site of the treasure of Shirley's Point, Willard's Taproom Treasure and the Captain's buried treasure.

Worcester is the location of Sutton Purgatory, now a state park, a solid gneiss cave about half mile long that was created by the Earth's movement that opened a hole in the ground. The legend is that Simon Such of Northbridge crawled deep into the cave known as Devil's Tomb and killed himself in November 1930. It is the only known cave suicide in New England. This is a battle site of Shays' Rebellion, and the site of a Nipmuc village.

There are so many enchanted, haunted places with lost treasure to be found in Massachusetts.

Treasure Hunting Tip

Remember that not all treasure is silver and gold. Lost towns, relics and artifacts from a historical era, can help the seeker on the journey to explaining an unknown mystery and unlocking the secrets from our past.

Chapter Four

Connecticut

GENERAL

The Connecticut River is where the story begins for this state. The Native Americans called this 410-mile-long river various names, but all meant "long river" or "long tidal river." Some of the names were Sokoquois, Connittecock; Quinnehtukgut; Quonehtacut. This river flows from Canada to Long Island Sound. Adrian Block, the first explorer of the River called it Versch, the Dutch word meaning, "fresh water river." He was also the one who drew the first definitive map of southern New England called the "figurative map." The term fresh was used to distinguish it from the brackish tidal rivers of New York. He sailed up the River on the ship, *Onrust*, meaning "restless" in Dutch. Block found a Native American fort half-way between Hartford and Windsor, called Nawaas. The French called this incredible river, Riviere des and it was called "South People's River" on Aubrey's map in 1715.

The mighty Connecticut River.

Native American legends states that the Connecticut River once ran through the entire Connecticut Valley and reached Long Island Sound at New Haven, instead of Old Saybrook. However, geologists state that perhaps it could be true, but it would have to flow through Hartford and New Haven, and that means it would have had to come through the Metacomet Ridge. That would be a very difficult journey and water always finds the easiest route to flow through. The Metacomet Ridge, by the way, was named for King Philip. Metacomet was his Native American name.

There is a red sand or soil found in this state, unlike any other soil in New England. It is an attractive Brownstone; geologists call it Arkose. It is a type of sedimentary rock that erodes very easily. Connecticut's Central Valley is known as the Copper Valley. As you will see as you read through the book, there are many copper mines worked here. The metal vein was found running through East Granby through Bristol to Cheshire. There is also a Marble Valley in the state. This vein of marble runs from Kent to Gaylordsville.

By 1830, there were over fifteen marble quarries. Twin Lakes, Wononskopomuch Lake, Robbin's Swamp, Lake Candlewood, Cornwall Bridge, Falls Village, New Milford, Danbury, and along the Housantonic River have all been places where marble was discovered. There are even marble caves found, one is the longest in New England called the Bashful Lady Cave in Salisbury. In New Milford, the Tory Cave is also a marble cave. Both caves are now closed to the public. There are also two magnificent Marble Valley waterfalls, Kent Falls and the Great Falls of the Housatonic. Connecticut gemstones are Garnet and almandine garnets; yellow and green Beryl; rose quartz; and Tourmaline.

Other minerals are also found in Connecticut. They are Limonite, Malachite, Pyrite, Gem Quartz, Topaz, Tourmaline, Garnet, Beryl, and Torbernite. Limonite is a brown hematite or bog ore and an important ore in iron. It can be found near Ore Hill, Lakeville, Salisbury, Mount Riga, Sharon, Cornwall, Lantern Hill, North Stonington, and Kent. Malachite is a green copper ore. It is found at Granby, Simsbury, Bristol, Cheshire, Mount Carmel, Canaan and Boardman's Bridge. Pyrite is "fool's gold." It can be found in Orange, Derby, Roxbury, Middletown, Haddam, Trumbull, Monroe, East Litchfield, and Danbury. Gem Quartz, including Rose, Chalcedony, and Smoky can be found at Southford, Monroe, Meriden, Farmington, Woodbury, Branchville, Portland, and Glastonbury. Topaz can be found in Trumbull, Middletown, and Willimantic. Tourmaline is a gem stone that comes in a variety of colors. Connecticut rivals Maine and California in the excellent gems that have been discovered. Gems can be found in Haddam Neck, Portland, Haddam, East Hampton, Brachville, Danbury, Trumbull, Middletown, Monroe, Newtown, Bethel, Waterbury, and East Litchfield. The gemstone Garnet is found in Norfolk, Portland, and Glastonbury. Beryl has been discovered in Trumbull, Woodbury, Ridgefield, Haddam, Haddam Neck, Middletown, New Milford, Monroe, Southford, Branchville, Willimantic, Glastonbury, Portland, and East Hampton. Tobernite is an ore of uranium and radium. It was mined in Portland, Glastonbury, Haddam Neck, Monroe, Southford, and Branchville. In Bethel, there was a tourmaline quarry, as well as rose quartz and beryl.

It is really no wonder that the Native Americans here called this valley "the smile of God." The Massachusetts tribes told the Pilgrims that their God, Kiehtan, gave them the Connecticut Valley to show his favor to them. The entire Algonquin population was about 90,000. Kiehtan was their God of Love, Hobbamock was their God of Fear, and Manitou was their God of Thought.

This can be considered a magical place. At three different times, three different sheets of lava flowed over the state. Those sheets are called traprock. The second lava flow is over 500 feet thick. The upward edge of the second sheet created some of the mountains around the state, including, Granby's Newgate Mountain, Avon's Talcott Mountain, Farmington Mountain, Meriden's Hanging Hills, Berlin's Lamentation Mountain, and North Guilford's Tokoet Mountain. Connecticut was created by the removal of a band of weak rocks by erosion, which elevated and tilted south. This event caused a peculiar mineral to have formed here – a very coarse grained granite called pegmatite that is radioactive.

Some of the major, though not all, Native American tribes in Connecticut were as follows: The Nipmuck, this tribe was found in the northeast corner of the state. The name means "away from the river." The trail called the Nipmuck Path, roughly went from East Hartford to Union. Today, this path is roughly represented by the Tolland Turnpike. The Sequin tribe was found in western Connecticut, and they were known as the River Indians. The Matabesec or Wappinger were found in the Wethersfield and Rocky Hill area. The Connecticut River was called Siccanum here. The meaning is not clear. It could mean, "pond," "beaver," or "hard fish" (perhaps meaning clams?). This tribe lost a lot of members during the Dutch War from 1640-45. They also manufactured wampum, which was the currency of the Native Americans.

The Pequot, meaning "The Grey Fox" tribe was located in southeastern Connecticut along the seventeen-mile long Thames River. This tribe originally came from New York, but eventually took over much of Connecticut. After being defeated in the Pequot War in the early 1600s, the settlers relocated to many of their abandoned village sites. This was considered the most formidable tribe in New England. The tribe's symbol is framed against the sky; the lone tree on a knoll represents Mashanucket, the "much wooded land" where the Pequots hunted. Displayed on the knoll is the sign of Robin Cassasinnamon, the Pequot's first leader following the 1637 massacre at Mystic Fort. The fox stands as a reminder that the Pequots are known as "the fox people."

The Mohegan tribe was located in southeastern Connecticut along the Thames River. However, before the Sachem Uncas, the Mohegans lived in the East Hartford and East Windsor area, along the Connecticut River. The Mohegan trail went from Norwich to New London. The Wappinger tribe lived in Central Connecticut and the Western Nehantic (Niantic), meaning "those who live at the point" and the Eastern Nehantic (Niantic) lived on the shore.

The Thames River in Connecticut.

As with the other states in the book, there were also sub-tribes for each nation. Some of the sub-tribes were: The Tunxis, a sub-division of the River Indians. They were also known as the Sepous on the Farmington River. Other tribes were Poquonnuc, Podunk, who were found in East Hartford and East Windsor, Wangunk or Wongunk, Machimoodus, Hammonasset, Quinnipiac, Pootatuck, Wepawaug, Unocwa, Siwanoy, Potatucks, who were located in Guilford, Milford, Madison, and New Haven area. Other sub-divisions were the Scatacook, Mattabesic, Naugatuck, Pangusset, Massacoe, Quinnebaug, Saukiog or Sicaog, Poquonock, Namercoke, Scanticook, Hockanum, and Wabaquasset.

The Mohegan and Pequot language consists of 446 words and it is an oral language only. Pequot is said to mean "the destroyers," but it means the grey fox people." The other name was probably given by to the Pequot by the Mohegans. Mohegan means "wolf people" or "at the great woods." Some words and meanings that may be helpful when searching places for Native American artifacts follows. Debe – jeebi means "evil spirit." Pagessin means "it falls" (usually meant lightning or a thunderbolt. Melted glass is often found at a lightning strike area. Petroglyphs or Pictographs are strongly associated with shamanic practices. It is a form of visual literacy. Most of the art is found on rocks jutting out into the water. When a carving is found, it usually meant something special happened – a battle, a boundary, or an unusual event.

Native American forts were a circular stockade of upright logs about ten feet to twelve feet high. Three feet of the logs were buried in the ground and Earth was thrown against the inner side of the logs for greater protection. Gaps were filled with small trees and branches, leaving only enough room for bows to shoot through. The entrances were limited to narrow openings at opposite sides of the fort. Bows were made with witch hazel trees and strung with animal gut. The eighteen-inch arrows were made with brass, stone, or eagle's claw.

The Abenaki words of Mteoulin, Madeluno, Madewahun, Manrigwa, Magermette, or Majalmit all mean "one who drums," "soothsayer," witch," or "sorcerer." These terms were used all through the New England tribes, but were suppressed or changed after 1630 by European religious authorities. Places that were named this are lost in time, but the areas that were named these words may have mystical amulets or other artifacts hidden beneath the earth.

Fort Shantok wildlife. This place is a Mohegan battle, fort, and burial site in Connecticut.

There are a few known Native American trails through Connecticut, the Pequot Path, which is now U.S. Route 1, that were also called the Boston Post Road, or the King's Highway. This old trail runs through Pontiac, Apponaug, East Greenwich, Tower Hill, Westerly, Stonington, and New London. Also it should be noted that nowhere in New England did the Native Americans use caves as hiding places and dungeons as much as the tribes in Connecticut. In 1638, there was an earthquake that rocked southern New England. On October 27, 1727, there was a great earthquake. These events could cause caves to be buried or landscapes to change, as seen in the other chapters.

Many ancient Native American trails led to great waterfalls where all could gather for incredible fishing. Many Main Streets today (or Center Streets or River Roads) can find their origin on a Native American path. It is always a good idea to search for relics along old trails or paths. Some of the old paths are

marked. In Preston on the Quinebaug River by Old Jewett City and Zion Roads, are the remains of old fishing weirs. In New Canaan, the Pomus Monument is an inscribed boulder on Ponus Ridge Road that marks a path taken by the tribes when going to New York. There is a Native American burial site across from this site.

Unidentified Flying Objects or UFO sightings have occurred in Connecticut as well as Massachusetts, even in the modern era. Over 2,000 people in southwestern Connecticut saw a "well-lighted hovering boomerang on the evening of June 11-12, 1984. No explanation for this sighting was ever given.

It is not possible for the esteemed and misunderstood pirate Captain Kidd to have buried as much treasure as he is credited with. However, he is the one pirate that everyone knows and when a pirate treasure legend begins, it usually ended with Kidd. Throughout the book, Kidd's treasure will be mentioned in the specific towns where he supposedly landed and left his ill-gotten goods.

The Trolley routes in Connecticut may be a line that one could find relics from that era. The trolleys were horse drawn in 1863. The first electric trolley in 1888 in Hartford was also known as The Hartford- Wethersfield Railroad. Only three miles of the original 200-mile-long track remain, and it is used by the Connecticut Trolley Museum in East Windsor. Some of the names of the towns where trolleys used to ride through are Thompsonville, Somers, Suffield, Warehouse Point, Windsor Locks, Stafford Springs, Windsor, near the Rainbow area, which is a park in Poquonock section, East Windsor Hill, Rockville, Bloomfield, East Hartford is still used today as railroad. In Manchester, South Manchester, Hartford, Glastonbury, Unionville, where a very serious crash occurred with car #1 on August 10, 1908, and Jackie Walsh the motorman was killed. In Bristol, near the Riverside Avenue car barn, Lake Compounce, New Britian, Berlin, Rocky Hill, Plainville, Southington, and Middletown are the areas where artifacts from that era can usually be found. Most relics are discovered near abandoned railroad, stagecoach, and trolley lines.

The Connecticut ghostly fox tale has been told since before the Europeans came. Whenever a hunter is in the

Connecticut woods, beware of the Black Fox of Salmon River. It is said that once seen, the hunter is lured deeper into the woods, with a desire to own the fur. The hunter always returns empty-handed, but also hunters have been found deep in the woods, dead from exposure.

Some of the state of Connecticut nicknames: Constitution State; Provision State – given because the people living here provided supplies during the Revolutionary War; Nutmeg State – because the colonist craved this as fruit, however it is a hallucinogen. Peddlers would often substitute wood chips for nutmeg to sell to the colonists living here; Land of Steady Habits; Blue Law State; Brownstone State, and Freestone State. Connecticut residents were called Connectiocotians by Cotton Mather in 1790. Other names for residents of the state are: Connecuicutesian, Connecticutter, Connecticutian, or Connecticutile.

The Blue laws were a supposed legal code of the short-lived New Haven colony. They, signifying gloom and forbidding feelings of the colonials, were written as though the law still prevailed in the extinct colony and were overly strict social laws. Where did the 45 laws come from? The answer is many sources: some private prejudices of extremists, some from common legislation of all civilized society, some from social censorship, and perhaps others invented by the author, Samuel Peters. Some of the most strange laws were:

17. "No one is to cross a river, but with an authorized ferryman."

18. "No one shall run on the Sabbath Day, or walk in his garden, or elsewhere, except reverently to and from meeting."

19. "No one shall travel, cook, make beds, sweep house, cut hair, or shave on the Sabbath Day."

20. "No woman shall kiss her child on the Sabbath or fasting day."

31. "Whomever wears clothes trimmed with gold, silver, or bone lace above two shillings by the yard, shall be presented by

the grand jurors, and the selectmen shall tax the offender at 300 pounds."

35. "No one shall read common prayer, keep Christmas or Saint's Days, make minced pies, dance, play cards, or play any instrument or music, except the drum, trumpet, and Jew's harp."

45. "Every male shall have his hair cut according to a cap."

If you think those laws were tough, in 1642, there were ten crimes one could commit to receive the death penalty in Connecticut. They were:

1. Worshiping another God than the Lord God.

2. Being a Witch.

3. Blaspheming.

4. Murder.

5. Slaying another by poison.

6. Kidnaping.

7. False Witness.

8. Conspiring/attempting an invasion or rebellion against the Commonwealth.

9. For a child above 16 years old to curse or smite his mother or father.

10. For a son above 16 years old, who will not obey his mother or father, after he has been chastened by them.

AVON

This town was named for the Avon River in England. Talcott Mountain, also known as Avon Mountain, is made of oxidized trap rock and is red in color, like most of Connecticut rock. Here lies the site of King Philip's Cave. It is said that it was in this cave where King Philip watched the sacking of the Farmington Valley by the Narragansett tribe during King Philip's War. The war is discussed in detail in the Rhode Island part of this book. The visitor can get to this spot, but it is very dangerous and not recommended. Rocks have been tumbling down from here since 1665 and the entire area is usually slippery with mud. All that is left is a narrow, level shelf at the back of the cave, where it is said that the King once sat in March 1676 and watched the destruction of the valley below.

On Route 185, on the crest of Talcott Mountain in Simsbury, there is a gorge called Hell Hole. This is where Captain Wadsworth is said to have hidden after hiding the Connecticut Charter in the Charter Oak. On Bald Mountain, elevation 1,200 feet, there grows a rare trailing evergreen known as Arctostaphylos uva-ursi, or bear-berry. It was used as an astringent by the Native Americans.

BEACON FALLS

The yellow reason the settlers first came to the New World, also known as gold, has been found in Beacon Hill Brook in New Haven County. Spruce Brook is one of the most beautiful ravines in the state. Under the cliff along the Paugusset Trail are the remains of a Native American chipping ground where they made arrowheads. A lot of arrowheads are found here. It is interesting that a chipping place for the Native Americans is where Thomas Sanford invented matches. The Diamond Match Company bought the invention for $10.

BERLIN

The town was named after Berlin, Prussia in 1785. Tin was first manufactured in America here in 1740. Remains of the tin factory can still be seen on Spruce Brook Road, north of the Meriden border. Yankee peddlers actually began their trade in this town in the mid-1700s.

The town was also known as the Great Swamp, Kensington, Worthington, and Farmington Village. There was a fort on Christian Lane in 1686-87. East Berlin is the geographic center of Connecticut. Amethyst has been found, but it is considered very rare. The discovery was about 5 ¼ miles southwest of West Peak, close to the New Haven County border. A silversmith shop was located across from the Academy in 1801.

Mount Lamentation rises about twelve miles from Wethersfield and is where Leonard Chester wandered looking for a place to build a mill. For two days, he wandered, lost, and a bit scared. On the second night, he said he saw a dragon, and followed it to the mountain. He climbed the ledges and suddenly heard his friends and family, from Wethersfield, calling him, so he climbed down and met up with them. The mountain gets its name from this event.

BOLTON AND BOX MOUNTAIN/ BRANFORD/NORTH BRANFORD

Black Sal's Cave on Box Mountain was the home of a family of Native Americans from the Mohegan nation. The cave is part of Bolton Notch. The highway and railroad blasted through a pre-glacial steam channel, but this area was an outlet for a glacial stream after the natural drainage area to the east was blocked with debris. The rock type here is known as Bolton Schist. This entire area has many Native American associations. In the state park, there is a Squaw Cave, where Wunneeneetmah's Dutch husband was killed. He was a deserter from one of the ships on the Hudson and shot by people looking for him. The old Spring that the tribe used is still there. A Native American workshop has been found on the east side of Middle Lake. East of Bolton Notch are some abandoned quarry sites, which were mined for flagstone.

An old iron furnace lies at the foot of Lake Saltonstall in Branford. This was used to make cast iron. The lake can be found under a ridge. Beware when exploring this area; both the lake and ridge harbor black snakes and they abound here. About a mile north of Stony Creek is the abandoned Norcross pink granite quarry, complete with a railway system.

The Thimble Islands are just offshore in Branford. There are over 100 small islands here, but most are just rocks protruding from the water, basically boating hazards, more than anything. The Native American name for these islands meant "beautiful sea rocks." However, there are some islands that are just large enough to have some lost loot buried on them.

One of those island is High Island. It is here that a Kidd treasure was buried in 1699. He is said to have hidden his ship near this island in the natural harbor and that he used it for his Connecticut headquarters. Another island that harbors Kidd's treasure is Money Island. Here, he buried treasure in an underwater cavern.

There are tales that an old fort was built here that was five miles long. Totoket Mountain is said to be named for Native American who is said to have "cut his foot" here. Obviously, it is more a play on words than an actual event. Indian Spring Trail can be hiked in the Great Meadow, and always led cold water. The Bluff Head Spring is a spring that is always warm water, so cold water was needed for the settlers and tribes living in the area. The warm spring is in the southwest part of town known as Jaffery's Point, which was also the site of a Native American village.

In Sackett's Cave in North Branford, valuable Native American artifacts were discovered. However, the use of dynamite, perhaps to open the cavern, has blocked part of the main entrance to the cave.

BRIDGEPORT

This town, also known as Newfield and Stratfield, is located in Fairfield County, and the Native American names, Pequonnock, Paquanocke, Pequannocke, meant "cleared field." A battle with the Pequots is said to have been fought near Porter's Rock. This was the site of a Native American village.

During the Revolutionary War and in the War of 1812, Grovers Hill Fort protected the harbor. Old ruins are found throughout the area. The American steamer, *Lexington*, was shipwrecked here. Bridgeport also claims to be the landing site for the Norsemen. They landed on the mouth of Pequonnock River.

Gold color has been found in the rock formations near the north end of Broad Street. A silversmith shop was located at 262 East Main Street around 1815.

The Old Remington Arms Factory has been abandoned for years and is off limits to visitors, though dark shadows are seen here and loud, strange noises are heard at night and no one knows why. However, due to fire, accidents, and explosions, many workers died on this site.

BRISTOL

This town was also known as New Cambridge. The Native American trail traveled through this area, running west up Chippans Hill. The town is best known for its brass works, because copper is the principle element needed to create brass. The Bristol copper mines found on the border of Bristol and Burlington were discovered in 1790 by Theophilus Botsford. He wondered why the vegetation along the stream died on his property and why were the stones green? He found the copper, but did not do anything about it.

It was later that Asa Hooker got the rights to the mine, and in 1800, the mining started. Many people were killed in the mine; some of the bodies were never recovered due to cave-ins. The ruins of the mine and dam can be found off Mines Road. There are deep levels of copper to be mined

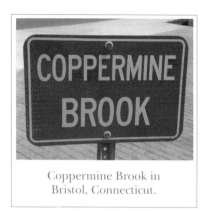

Coppermine Brook in
Bristol, Connecticut.

Sometimes it is easy to follow
the signs to a mine.

here, but none of the veins are continuous. This type of copper is called, "purple copper" because of the iridescent color it has.

However, the spring found in Bristol apparently has crystal clear water. It really does not make sense, and men did die from drinking the sparkling clear water. That fact clearly proves that clear water may still carry deadly chemicals. When knives were placed in Copper Mine Brook, a layer of copper would appear over the knife after time. Clear does not mean safe.

This mine had a strange history; investors committed suicide, the dam that held the Mine Pond burst in 1896 and destroyed all the bridges between the mine and Forestville. The flood washed out the embankment on the New England Railway causing a major train wreck.

The Bristol mines were said to be jinxed, but really the issues were that the mine had money mismanagement problems, there were heavy rains and floods, ice jams and when the dam was destroyed, the problems just escalated.

Now, the Mine Pond is part of the New Britain water system. One of the mines was called Penny Pat, named after one of the girlfriends of a miner. It is considered a rich site, but hard to get to. Two of the most distinguished mineralogists in American scientific history, Professor B. Stillman and Professor James Dana Whitney, both from Yale, examined the mine in 1855. They were amazed at the great quality of the copper.

Lead has also been found here. It is always exciting to find lead because gold and silver can sometimes be found with

Copper was discovered here in Bristol, Connecticut.

lead. Gold was discovered, about 23 feet underground in the adjoining meadow by Everett Horton in 1896 near his shop on Oak Street. In 1907, workmen excavating for the Wallace Barnes Plant found six gold nuggets. This was on West Oak Street, so perhaps the nuggets were washed down from South Mountain by Ivy Brook.

There was once a soapstone quarry here, according to Native American legend. On Goose Street, relics of unfinished soapstone pieces were found. Native American relics, basically arrowheads, were unearthed on Grove Street and on top of Kelley's Hill. These were thought to be the artifacts of the Tunxis tribe, a typically non-warlike tribe, but they used arrowheads as protection from the feared Mohawks of New York. South Mountain was called Morgan's Swamp, where a Native American named Morgan was killed and is said to be buried here. Between Bristol and Farmington, there is a place called, Scott's Swamp. This is where a settler named Scott was tortured and killed by the Native Americans.

This town was a known hiding place for British sympathizers during the Revolutionary War. Moses Dunbar was hanged here for recruiting British soldiers. The Tory Den cliff is part of the ledges where large bands of Patriots sought refuge as a hiding place, but no one has actually found the place where they hid. Many of these men died in the New England winter and campers have reported strange lights and a heavy breathing noise in the woods. Chippins Hill is a corruption of the Indian name, Cochipianes, the warrior who was a great hunter.

Witches Rock is an area where cellar holes have been found near Fall Mountain. The name comes from a Baptist Church that had a supernatural event occur. Early in history, witchcraft had supposedly taken place in town, people were being possessed by witches, and they even saw their oxen being torn apart in front of them. The event here in the 1800s was that Elijah Gaylord would drive his ox team past this rock and the cart tongue would drop to the ground. It was said that he had incurred the ill will of Granby Olcolt, a known witch, and she supposedly caused all his trouble. Also, there were reports of people being tormented by having pins and needles stuck in them by the witches here. As you can see by the dates, this was well after the witch trials and hysterics of the late 1600s. If the story seems familiar, like you have read it earlier, you would be correct. These types of stories occur all through southern New England; just the people's names and towns change.

In 1822, an assault, then a murder, took place near Peck Lane. The criminal was never found, and even today, at night, when a person goes up Peck Lane, a light would appear and travel with the person until they reached the dead woman's home site, then disappear. Eventually, people just stopped using this lane after dark.

When first seen by settlers, there was a beaver dam at the southern end of Cedar Swamp. The name comes from the fact that the entire swamp was covered with white cedar. When the man-made dam was first built, it flooded the entire area and the forest filled with water. It became a floating forest.

Burlington Brook has two fall sites that can be found west on Route 116. Some abandoned roads exist on Johnnycake

Mountain, where the forest is finally reclaiming the land. There is also a rock-lined gully called Devil's Kitchen, about one mile north of Whigville. The Whigville Copper Mine was the largest in Connecticut in 1847. It is known for finding excellent Chalcocite, and the specimens found are considered the finest in the world.

CANAAN/BROOKFIELD/BROOKLYN/CANTON

Canaan is the area to find ruins of the failed Farmington Canal. What happened is that the builders did not use mortar and the canal leaked. The ruins are near Main Street. Marble quarries were mined in town in 1915.

Limestone beds are found in Brookfield. There is also a lead mine, and the minerals galena and sphalerite were discovered in the mine. There is a Native American legend here that Waramaug, a Native American Sachem, dwelled in a palace here. Lillinoah was his daughter. She is said to be the reason for Lover's Leap in New Milford. That story is told later in the book.

A large pirate treasure is hidden in the town of Brooklyn in Windham County. Amethyst has been found in Canton. During the Revolutionary War, this town was called Unionville. The legend states that a French paymaster was carrying a bag of gold to pay the troops in New York. He stopped at the Canton Inn, but that was the last that was ever heard of him again. The Innkeeper said the paymaster left that morning, and he never heard or saw him again. Many years later, the inn burned down, and a skeleton was found. It was thought that this may be the paymaster, who was killed and his gold taken.

After that, many people met a lone headless horseman here at night. Even when automobiles came to the area, people claimed to see a headless figure in the headlights. Why is the ghost headless though? It was not said that the skeleton did not have a head. There is another historic figure that does not have a head that roams southern New England. That is King Philip. The story in Raynham, Massachusetts, explains the story for his ghost.

CHESHIRE

Copper was mined in this town. This is a barite copper vein, which is a white mineral that is used as paint. In 1670, the mine was opened in the southeast part of town, but the ore samples were somehow lost at sea. There is also a dark story about the mine. It is whispered that one of the mine officials was murdered and dropped down the shaft. In 1854, the old mine shaft was re-discovered with a beech tree, over two feet in diameter, growing over the shaft opening. There were relics found at the bottom, including an iron bucket, wooden dipper, handles, crowbar, picks, drills, and hammers. The copper was found on Milkingyard Hill that was owned by John Parker in 1711. The barytes found are perfect and found in museums all over the world.

The gem, Amethyst, have been found on Roaring Brook. Townline Road was originally a Native American path to Mount Sanford, crossing Roaring Brook.

CORNWALL BRIDGE
(Also Known as Dudleytown)

This spooky ghost town is found just south of the 1,500-foot Coltsfoot Mountain, northeast of Cornwall Bridge. The farming area is also known as Owlsbury. By 1899, no one dared to live in this cursed place. This town once sat on a hill above the Housantonic River in 1738. However, the place was a dark region, poorly lit due to the hills surrounding it. Though close to the river, there was a strange lack of water here and there was always a high wind blowing. The Dudleys arrived in 1747, and this is when the curse began.

It started with Edmund Dudley, who was be-headed when he plotted to overthrow King Henry VIII in England in 1510. This act created the curse of the whole family. Four Dudley brothers founded the town: Gideon, Barzilla, Abeil, and Abijah. First, an epidemic raged through the town in 1774. The town was struck by lightning in 1804. Mary Cheney was born in the town, and she committed suicide in 1872. Late in the 1800s, entire families died here of consumption.

Children have gone into the woods and never returned. Numerous homes have been burned with no explanation. In the 1920s, William Clark's wife went insane, while living here. She told everyone that something terrifying came out of the forest. It is said that the curse would cause a death at least every seven years.

There are remains of the town and it is illegal to enter the area. There is a heavy fine, if anyone is caught here for any reason. One modern reason for the supposed "curse" is that the rocks contain a large amount of lead. That lead may have leaked into the groundwater, and caused the inhabitants to go insane.

As an interesting side note, the Mohawks hunted here undisturbed for many years before the town ever existed. There are pleasant things to find in the area. There is a marble vein that was discovered. Ironically, there is a place near here called Cathedral Pines, a virgin stand of white pine, considered the "finest in the eastern states and not surpassed in the Lake region." Another place named Cornwall in Connecticut is known as Cornwall Hollow. Only by a canoe on the Housatonic River can one see this place.

CROMWELL/NORTH CROMWELL/COS COB

Many gems found in Cromwell are not found anywhere else in New England. The types of gems are various types of Garnet, Beryl, and Tourmaline. Many Native American relics have been found on the Connecticut River in North Cromwell. Cos Cob is located on the Mianus River. The name comes from the name of a friendly Native American Chief who is buried in the Old Indian Burial Grounds. Just north of this point, on Strickland Brook, there was a very bloody battle between the Dutch and tribe who inhabited the region in 1646

DANBURY

This town was also known as Pahquioque and Beantown. Why Beantown? It was due to excellent beans found. There is also a legend that states that the land here was bought from the Native Americans with one bag of beans. There are some interesting place names in the area that may be worth more research to find lost treasures: Pinchgut; Mashing Tub Swamp, Squabble Hill, Cat-tail Mountain, Monkeytown, and Dodgingtown.

In 1707, there was a fort built. This town was raided in April 1776 by the British, known as Tryon's Raid. The terrified townspeople hid in a surrounding swamp, perhaps taking valuable artifacts with them, or perhaps hid them before leaving. Danbury was actually the British headquarters for a time. The British finally retreated, but as the site of a military battle, unfortunately there were casualties. The Connecticut militia was led over Wooster Mountain in an attempt to cut off the retreat of General Tyron's forces after they attacked Danbury.

Between 1780-1782, George Washington came through this town while on the march from Yorktown. General Rochambeau's army camped here in Plum Meadow Grove. Today, it is a cemetery.

Treasure Hunting Tip

This trail may be worth exploring; often military troops leave artifacts behind. Either the items are too heavy to carry or they need to move faster, so they unload items that they no longer deem necessary.

Candlewood Lake was created when the Connecticut Electric Company dammed the Housatonic River. The entire Big Basin area was drowned in 1927 when the dam was built and the two villages of Jerusalem and Leach Hollow were flooded. Though the villages were burned, witnesses to the flooding of the valley stated that the water rose over the

left farm implements, bikes, old cars, and two cemeteries; though the bodies had been removed prior to the flood, a schoolhouse and the foundations of homes. Artifacts from those two towns are sometimes found on the shore of the Lake.

There are legends in the area. In the 1900s, apparently after 1927 when the dam was built, Perry Boney came to the Candlewood Lake area. It is said that he always seemed to be watching things that no one else could see. He owned and operated the smallest store in the world, on the hillside near the New Fairfield and Sherman line. He just disappeared one day, but some say that they can still hear his flute in the woods near Greenwood Mountain. There is marble found here. A silversmith shop was located south of Court Street in the 1800s. In 1793, another shop was found on Main Street, opposite where the Hotel Green is today.

The honey yellow Danburite was first discovered here in 1880. This gemstone is named for the town of Danbury, where it was first found.

DANIELSON/DARIEN/DERBY

Aspinock Quarry is found in Danielson. This quarry was used by Native Americans, as far west as Michigan, as a source for whetstones for shaping arrowheads.

At Rowayton, in Darien, there is a place on the Five Mile River called the Old Landing Place. This is where a ship would dock along a rock ledge during high tide.

On Contentment Island, west of the mouth of the river, is the site of a Native American village. Rocks can still be found that were used for grinding corn. Tories Hole is a cave that legend states once hid Tories during the Revolutionary

Treasure Hunting Tip

Anyplace an area was used to unload goods and items may be a great place to search for lost artifacts.

War era. It is located between Delafield Island and Tory Hill Roads. The entrance was blocked by blasting years ago.

The Native American name for Derby, was Paugasset or Paugasuck. There was a Native American fort here on the east bank of the Housatonic River. The fort was located about 500 feet from the southwest intersection of Seymour Avenue and Division Street. A new fort was built by the settlers on the east shore of the Housatonic River, about a quarter of a mile above the dam.

Eight miles from Derby, copper was discovered in Oxford at the Stevenson Mine on Bower's Hill. Today, the shaft is filled with ice cold water that is said to never freeze.

EAST HAMPTON/EAST HARTFORD/
EAST HAVEN/ENFIELD

East Hampton was also known as Chatham. The gem, Beryl has been found here, as well as rose Quartz, in the Slocum Quarry. Pyrite, Garnet, and perhaps some gold flakes have also been discovered in the area.

Comstock Covered Bridge crosses over the Salmon River. It is one of Connecticut's last remaining covered bridges and is limited to pedestrian traffic only. The bridge is now part of Salmon River State Forest. The hiking trail, called the Airline Trail, follows an old railroad bed. A solitary grave in the area belongs to a soldier. Though the stone is weathering, one can still see the name, date, cause of death, and age. The Salmon River Covered Bridge, built in 1873, originally was not used as a road, but just a foot bridge for someone to cross the river from Colchester to East Hampton. It was the only link between the two towns at that time. Before the bridge, the only way to get to one place or the other was to ford the river! Perhaps building a road later over the bridge was not such a great idea. During the Prohibition Era, a truck loaded with illegal whiskey struck the side of the bridge and all the liquid spilled into the water.

Pocotopaug Lake has a Native American legend about The Ledges in Markham's Bay. The Wangunk Native American word means "divided water." Many Native Americans have drowned in this lake before the settlers came to the area. It is the place where a Native American spirit lives. The Medicine Man said that the only way to stop the drownings was to sacrifice the Chief's daughter, Na-moe-Nee or Cochica. She died by jumping off the eastern bluffs. The sacrifice seemed to work for a while. There was never a report of a drowning in this lake until 1885, when someone fell through the ice. It is thought that there must be an ancient trail from Indian Hill to the lake, though the exact location is not known.

There is an old ironworks and cobalt mine road here. Part of Grover Lane, now Forest Street, is the road that led to the mine. Though this mine was not a success in 1743, the French and American armies used these roads during the Revolutionary War era.

Silver Lane is named for the silver coins that can be found in East Hartford. In 1781, General Rochambeau was marching through here to meet George Washington's army. The soldiers were followed by wagons carrying chests filled with silver. The center of his camp was on the present day Silver Lane. The troops were paid with silver coins. Even in recent years, silver coins have been discovered. This road was also a Native American path through the town. There are many artifacts that may still exist beneath the earth.

There was also a Native American battlefield near Fort Hill. In 1656, there was a battle between the Mohegans, with Uncas as the leader, and the Podunks, the leader was Weaseapano. A Podunk member killed the Middletown Sachem, Mattabaseck. Uncas wanted the murderer and when refused, he attacked the tribe. However, this matter was ultimately settled in Massachusetts on Nantucket Island. The rest of this story can be found in that chapter of this book. The story on Nantucket Island and King Philip may on the surface appear not to be related, but it was this murdered chief's name that was spoken.

The Native American name for this area is Podunk. In 1675, the village was found at the north end of the Meadow and the south end near Hockanum River. This was the site of the last Podunk tribe, which vanished from the records in 1760. It was from this village that one of the Sachem's visited

Plymouth in 1637 to request help from the Europeans with the Pequot Tribe. His name was Waginnacut, which meant "Brave man who likes big noise." They ended up joining King Philip during his war, and were killed or dispersed after losing.

Amethyst and Beryl have been found at the Burnside Crossroads in East Hartford. The quarry is about 1/4 of a mile southeast on SR-17 in Howe Quarry.

In East Haven, the British invaded the east side of the harbor in 1779. There is an ancient cemetery on the site of a Native American fort that was used by Quinnipiack tribe. The Totoket path is one of the earliest Native American paths found in the state. Totoket is probably a corruption of the word, Lonotonoket, meaning "tear of the Great Spirit."

Adriaen Block's exploration of the Connecticut River ended at Enfield Falls. These falls are actually 5 ¼ miles of rapids. A settler fort was built on the east side of Enfield Street, near Allen's Corner.

The Connecticut River.

ESSEX/HADLYME/NOTT ISLAND/SELDON ISLAND

The Native American tribes living in Essex were the Hammonasett and Nastic, before the Pequots and Mohegans arrived. Native American names for the town were, Pautapaug, Pettipaug, Poattapoge, Potabauge, and Potopaug. It was also known as North Cove on the Connecticut River. The village was located at the point that juts into the River north of Thatchbed Island.

Emeralds were supposedly found on the west bank of the Connecticut River opposite Gillette Castle in Hadlyme in 1919. Emeralds are not a native gem for Connecticut, so it has been suggested that perhaps smugglers buried items here. There is a legend that somewhere on the Gillette Castle grounds is a cache of buried emeralds.

In 1812, a British force landed at the exact spot where the Essex River Museum is today and destroyed twenty-two ships at the dock. The British quickly took over the town and many colonial and Victorian era artifacts are found here. This

This is the exact spot where the British landed
in Essex, Connecticut.

place was actually a dumping ground or garbage heap, and everything dumped was buried.

This is the site of the steamboat, *New England,* explosion in 1833. Fifteen of the passengers were killed in the explosion. There are pieces of pottery found from the steamboat period all around. Under Lion Rock in Roger Lake is said to be another Kidd treasure.

This is Nott Island.

On Nott Island, on the Connecticut River, right across from Essex, a cannon ball was discovered. It was probably from the War of 1812.

On Seldon Island or Neck, though there is no longer a neck to this island it has been washed away, Native American artifacts are found in the northern part. There is also an unsolved murder here and the ghost of the victim tries to tell the story, if anyone could understand.

FAIRFIELD

Just east of the present-day town, lies the site of the famous battle of 1637. The colonists defeated the Pequot and it was the final battle in the Pequot War. The Pequot War was an offensive war against the Pequot tribe ordered by the General Court in Hartford on May 1, 1637. The Pequots were originally from the Hudson Valley in New York. The Mohawks, also from New York and who were friendly with the Pequot in earlier times, sided with the colonists and killed Sassacus; the Sachem during this time, and over 600 members of the tribe were killed at their Mystic Fort. The remainder of the tribe from the fort fled, but were overtaken in this town by the English. This was a Native American village site called Uncoway. This fertile valley was settled by the Europeans, who returned after the area was discovered by the military, who went through here chasing the Pequots to Sasqua Swamp, which was the final battle of the Pequot War. This war ended in 1637. Though there is a marker explaining this event, the swamp is completely filled in today.

The Native American name of the swamp area was Totomak, a Mahican word that means "a meadow that trembles when walked on." Perhaps once a bog or underground water source? There is also a place here that the Indians called, Samp Mortar Reservoir. This Natick name meant "corn bruised in mortar and boiled." Samp was a favorite New England meal until at least 1945.

The town was attacked by the British in 1777, and the village burned during General Tyron's raid in 1778. As an interesting side note, the raid and burning all took place during a severe thunderstorm.

In 1888, George Hawley found five large caches of gold and silver coins all dating 1795 at the beach near Penfield Reef. This treasure is said to be from a pirate ship that landed or wrecked here in 1882. In 1931, documents were discovered that reported pirates did take crocks and bury them on a beach near Penfield Reef.

The Penfield Reef Lighthouse, constructed in 1874, is part of the National Register of Historic Places. This Reef is considered one of the most treacherous areas of western

Long Island Sound and numerous shipwrecks have occurred there. This place is also considered very haunted. In 1916, the keeper rowed to the mainland to join his family for Christmas. The sea was rough and his boat capsized. The keeper died, and it is said that he started haunting the place about two weeks after his death. It has been noted in various keeper's logs that his ghost floats down the tower stairs and the light acts "strangely" when he appears. In 1942, two boys were supposedly saved by this keeper after their boat capsized near the Lighthouse. After being rescued, they identified the person who saved them from a picture of the dead lighthouse keeper.

FARMINGTON/FRANKLIN

In 1658, the Stockbridge tribe attacked the Tunxis tribe's fort. In Farmington at Little Meadow on the east side on the Farmington River. Many Native American artifacts have been found here, which include arrowheads, war axes, wampum beads, and stone bowls. On the old Farmington to the Naugatuck River Native American trail, there is a cave in the east part of an area called Indian Heaven. It was used as a sleeping chamber, also known as Jack's Cave.

Bill Warren's glen or cave is located about two miles south of the town near the top of Rattlesnake Mountain. He was a bandit during the Revolutionary War era who used the cave to hide in. In the 1800s, a visitor to this cave found an old canteen, tin cup, and bayonet. The owner of the cave during the 1860s did not want people to explore the cave further, so he filled it in.

The Farmington Canal was the longest canal ever built in New England. It was completed in 1835, but it was a complete failure. Ruins of the canal can still be seen today all along its route. The entire canal ran from Greenfield, Massachusetts, to New Haven, Connecticut. The main reason that it was discontinued was due to the constant landslides that occurred, but also it was poorly built.

Silversmith shops were located at the head of Main Street about 150 feet west of the Elm Tree Inn, now 200 feet north of the Country Club.

Connecticut is well-known as the state where peddlers began. So naturally, there must be a peddler curse and treasure somewhere. That place is in Franklin. In November 1759, a peddler arrived in Nine-Miles-Square, which is Franklin today. He carried many valuable items, and a heavy silver-laden purse. He was lucky to find lodging at the Micah Road Farm, but the next day, he was never seen again. Winter, spring, and summer came and went, and the *what happened to the peddler mystery* remained. The next fall, the apple blossoms at the Micah Farm were streaked with red, not the usual pink or white. Then, the peddler's corpse was found under an apple tree. This proved to the residents that the peddler was trying to tell them something, but the crime and why these apples have a red streak in them to this day remains an unsolved mystery.

GLASTONBURY/SOUTH GLASTONBURY

The soil of Glastonbury is Triassic Age and trap rock from the lava that flowed. The town was a huge glacial lake during the last ice age. Minerals can still be found in the Husband Quarry about half mile before the Portland town line. It is really no wonder that the early settlers called this place Glassenbury, meaning "glistening town." The spelling Glastonbury comes from the town Glastonbury in England. That town was said to be the home of the first Christian Church in England.

There are many Native American names for places here. Hoccanum means, "fishing place;" Naubuc means "plains on the east side;" Nipsic means "place of water." This area was once a lake, but it was drained. Minnechaug, means "berry place;" Wassuc means "place of paint or between brooks;" and Kongscut or Honksit means "goose place." There were also lots of rattlesnakes found here. Mesomersic Mountain is a Native American term meaning "great rattlesnake" or "abundance of rattlesnakes." Whenever a person is searching for artifacts, knowing what a place was once called with help in the search and in what dangers may still lurk.

Main Street was once the Native American trail called "Long Path" or "Country Road." The path was part of the trail from Hartford to Norwich. The other roads in town that were once part of the trail are: Hopewell, Griswold, Niepsic, Chestnut Hill, and New London Turnpike. Along the New London Turnpike, 3,500-year-old clay pots were found, while laying sewers in 1975. The workers also found spear points, hand axes, arrowheads, and charred bones. Why charred bones? This was also where a Native American burial ground was discovered but why were the bones burned? No one knows. The road was the trolley line route and the site of a bad trolley accident in the fall 1915. It was a head-on collision when a passenger car forgot to wait at Hales Siding. The passenger car motorman was instantly killed.

In 1971, along the old coal dock in the Meadow Hill area, another Native American burial site was discovered. This site was used from 500 B.C. to 500 A.D. Many copper implements were found, including: knives, pottery, and pendants for the neck and ear. Red Ochre was also found in the graves. Perhaps the tribe was part of, or had ties to, the mysterious Red Paint People of Maine. (This group was examined in detail in book one: *Lost Loot, Ghostly New England Treasure Tales*.) In 1938, over 500 Native American artifacts were found at Ferry Lane, many fashioned with copper. It is believed that some artifacts in this area could be over 10,000 years old.

There was a Wongunk fort located at Red Hill on the river bank on present day Stockade Road. It was abandoned during King Philip's War. The Sachem of this town was one of the Chief's, along with the Sachem in Wethersfield and East Hartford, who went to Boston to ask the settlers for help against the Pequots and Mohawks. The name given to the Pequots was "destroyers" and to the Mohawks was "man-eaters." Though those are not what the Native American words meant, these interpretations probably frightened the Puritans into looking deeper into the Pequot issue. It may have been used as a successful scare tactic. There was a large Mohawk village set up here, too. No one knows why the New York tribe would set up a village here, but perhaps it was to keep the Connecticut tribes in check or to collect tribute from the tribes. Eventually, this is the tribe that

annihilated the Mattabesetts of Middletown. In 1692, the settlers built a fort here to protect them from the Native Americans. It stood across the street from the present day high school.

Whenever the treasure seeker is looking for artifacts, one research tip is that water changes course often. Where the change occurred, and the new directions may lead the seeker under water, it may be that the treasure was buried initially on dry land before the course change. For example, according to an map of Glastonbury, taken from Chapin's *Glastonbury Centennial*, published in 1853, it showed the former course of the Salmon River through the meadows, joining the Sturgeon River, now known as Roaring Brook, and flowing into the Connecticut River above Nayaug. Today, the Salmon River enters the river at Naubuc.

In South Glastonbury, one can find the ghost town of Cotton Hollow. It can be found in the Nayaug area at the edge of Roaring Brook. There were once several factories, but all that is left are the remains of the mill and foundations of the homes of the workers. There is also the legend in South Glastonbury of the Red Hill People. It is said that this tribe existed centuries before Christ. The sand color on Red Hill is red in color. Not much is known about this ancient tribe. It is thought that it was a clan of the Pequots known as the Red Hill Indians, before the settlers came. The story is that there was a Native American fort here built and manned by this tribe that repelled the Mohawks from entering this area. *Why?* is the question. The Mohawks were generally friendly to the Pequots, but apparently not to this clan. So, perhaps they were not a clan of the Pequots. The story does not end well for this unknown tribe. It has been told that the Mohawks exterminated every member who lived here. Though the tribe had been told that the Mohawks were coming, the Mohawks are said to have waded through Roaring Brook and could not be tracked. This is said to have happened right before the Europeans arrived.

There was a lot of death that occurred here whatever really happened. There is a Native American word that Roaring Brook was sometimes called, Amannantocksuck, meaning "a look-out place at the brook." Perhaps that word brings to mind what could happen if the tribe was not always on the look out for trouble. There are also other extinct tribe villages that once existed here: the Nayaugs, Naubucs, and Wongunks. It was the resort place for the contemporary tribes.

It is interesting to note that Diamond Pond, which is really a small lake in town near where the red hill tribe once existed, is named for the small red crystals found on its banks.

At the junction of Manchester Road and Route 2, there was a large White Oak, which was 20 feet in circumference. It is said that Ashbury, the father of American Methodism, preached under this tree during the Revolutionary era. Soldiers of the War of 1812 used the tree for target practice. Bullets from that era could be found inside at one time. Nipsic Pool can be found on Nipsic Road. It was used for medicinal purposes by the tribes in the area and considered a healing place.

In the Dark Hollow area, white granite, mica, and precious gems have been discovered. This valley supposedly holds gold and silver that are guarded by "the weird sisters," but none of it has ever been found. Are these ghosts or witches? The details are vague, at best. Amethyst and Beryl have been found in the Case Quarry and Simpson Quarry.

The Native American tribe in South Glastonbury were the Quinitikoock or Qunihtitucquot. They were living on the Connecticut River. In 1673, Chief Terramuggus, sold the land to the settlers. He actually sold the same pieces of land more than once. Land was not something that was owned in the Native American culture. Since one did not own land, one could not sell land. It belonged to all, though, many tribes fought battles among themselves before the Europeans arrived. These battles were fought over the right to use the land for hunting, fishing, and living. This area was a Native American battlefield between the New York Mohawks and Pequots and the Mohegans. After the Pequots took over this entire area, the new Pequot Sachem called the town of Nayaug. Nayaug means "noisy water or roaring brook." This would be in the center of South Glastonbury. The entire area is a natural amphitheater so sound is magnified.

This entire region was considered to be a great hunting and fishing place by the Native Americans. Perhaps that is why the woods still seem mysterious today – a feeling that is left by the many visitors over the centuries. In January 1939, the first reported sighting of the Glawackus was in the woods here. This creature has the head of a dog, body of a lion or head of a lion and body of a dog. Footsteps and horrible shrieking was heard. Many animals were being killed mysteriously. Though it sounds silly, it should be noted that a hurricane came through this area in 1938. It is believed that perhaps some animal may have escaped from a Vermont zoo. Perhaps a panther or lion. It was a black creature and very powerful. It almost sounded like a fisher, though they were thought to have been extinct. Perhaps that was an incorrect assumption. There is more to this story in the Salisbury section of this book.

Philips' Cave on Kongscut Mountain in East Glastonbury is not named for King Philip, as most Philip-named places are, though there is a Native American connection. It is named for Stanley Philips who found the site. It was located at the east of Forest Lane. In 1957, it was a major discovery of Native American artifacts, including stone pendants, fish-tail arrow points, and axes. Some of these artifacts were 3,000 to 4,000 years old. This cave is on private property today.

The towns are mysterious. Near the New London Turnpike, there was a seventeen-year locust invasion. In 1818, 1835, and 1852, these pests were born, lived, and died in the same spot. Why did this occur? No one knows, and no one can be sure that it will not happen again. Still not convinced that there is something special about this place? In 1787, a tornado ripped through the Rocky Hill area. It killed a woman and her son, but it also took her wedding dress and left it on the roof of her sister's home in Glastonbury.

GRANBY/SIMSBURY/EAST GRANBY

Simsbury was called Weatogue, which is a Tunxis word meaning "at the wigwams place." This was where the first copper coins were minted in America. This money was called the Higley pennies or coppers minted in 1737 by John or Samuel Higley. These coins are stamped "I am good copper. Value me as you will." or "Connecticut 1737."

Ironically, Higley died at sea with the ship that was carrying this copper back to England. These were three pence pieces. Some of the coins can be seen at the Connecticut Historical Society today.

This town was attacked by King Philip during the War in 1676. It is said that King Philip sat in a large cave on Talcott Mountain in Avon and watched the destruction of the town. See the Avon section of this book for more information. Today, the range is known as the Metacomet Range in his honor. This town was attacked and burned again by Native Americans in 1800.

There is a haunted legend of an old tavern or roadhouse that was built on the crossroad from Hartford to Boston in 1780 called Pettibone's Tavern, formerly the Chart House Restaurant. This was a stop in the Underground Railroad during the Civil War. Parts of the tunnel system are now filled with sand from the flood of 1955. It was where Mr. Pettibone supposedly committed a murder. The victim was his wife who is said to still haunt the area today. Lights flicker and faucets in the bathroom turn on and off. This was where Mrs. Pettibone's bedroom once was. It is said that when the place was first bought by the new owner, they discovered a picture of the former family with a female's head cut out of it.

The Granby copper mine and Newgate Prison, also known as Simsbury Mines, is located about one mile north of Newgate Road. The mine was first opened in 1707, and the coins minted were called "Granby Coppers" in 1709. The copper found here in 1705 was between 12-50 percent copper, but due to the limited knowledge of refining, the mine closed. By 1773, the mines were no longer productive.

After that, it was turned into prison, and remained a prison until 1827. It was a Revolutionary War prison, the first to keep the most serious criminals and the first State Prison in America. The first prisoner was John Hinson who committed burglary in 1773. This place is also said to be haunted. A man was killed here during a cave-in and his face has been seen in the rock. The last man killed here was trying to escape from prison by using a rope. The rope snapped and he died when he impacted the rock floor. Today, the mine and prison are considered a state historic landmark and listed on the

National Register. A stairway was built in 1972, which allows tourists to visit the site.

Shaw's Fort was built by settlers in 1708 as protection from the Native Americans. It was on the Southwick Road and a blockhouse could be found on Salmon Brook Street.

Around $2 million in gold is said to be buried during the Revolutionary War for Washington's army in East Granby in Harford County. It was buried during a Tory and Native American raid in the vicinity of a tavern owned by Captain Bates.

GREENWICH/GROTON

Greenwich was called Patuquapaen, Sicascock, and Monakeqego by the Native Americans. In 1644, Native American battles were fought here. The Native American village of Petuquapaen was located on the west side of Stricklan Brook, north of Mill Pond at Cos Cob. The town was attacked by General Tyron during American Revolution at Round Hill. Byram River Gorge is located north from Pemberwick. This chasm is glacier in origin. There is a legend here that during the Revolution, in February 1779, General Israel Putnam escaped from the British while visiting Knapp's Tavern, built in 1731, by spurring his horse over a cliff. The area has been called Horse Neck ever since. However, it is possible that all Putnam did was ride his horse down the stone steps that formerly led to the church at the top of the hill. The inn site is now part of Putnam College grounds. The hill does not exist presently, but there is a bronze tablet on what used to be called Put's Hill.

The town of Groton in New London County was the site of two forts; both located near the mouth of Thames River. Fort Trumbull was located on the west side of the River and Fort Griswold was found on Groton Heights or Hill at Monument Street and Park Avenue. Both were destroyed by British led by Benedict Arnold on September 6, 1781. This is the only site of a Revolutionary War battle in Connecticut. The eighty-five Patriots who died here were killed after the surrender. A strange legend surrounds the Fort Griswold death of a 15-year-old boy. It is said that one patriot in 1777 allowed his son to substitute for another man during the defense of Fort Griswold for the price of one barrel of cider. The boy died and the records of the era show that the barrel of cider was delivered to the family as promised. Connecticut's first naval expedition was at Fort Griswold in 1776.

Groton was the site of a trading post in 1650. Some of bloodiest battles ever recorded were fought here, before settlers came, between the Pequots and Narragansetts. This was the Pequot hunting grounds. There was a Pequot fort overlooking Noank near Groton on Fort Hill at Weinshauks. The battles were during the era of the Sachem Sassacus.

There is a ghost town here called Gungywamp, which is said to be a Gaelic word, meaning "church of the people." This is about a twenty-acre area that is privately owned. Permission must be gained to explore the area. There are pointed stone remains here and chambers, but no one knows why or who built the site. There are said to be strange magnetic fields here and some say that the visitor gets suddenly depressed when visiting. It was inhabited by the settlers when they first came to Connecticut and there is a chamber that when the sun hits it, the rocks illuminate the entire chamber.

HADDAM/MOODUS/HADDAM NECK/
EAST HADDAM/GUILFORD

This East Haddam Devil's Hopyard State Park is a very unusual place. The woods have many stories about people hearing voices all around them, but no one is there. These stories pre-date the colonial times and even the oral tradition of the Native Americans talk about the voices heard in the woods. The Mohegans and Pequots state that this was the stomping area of Manitou, their great spirit. The Moodus-type noises were caused when Manitou rolled over in his sleep or he was having a stomach ache. It is where the Puritan's said that witches danced with the Devil. They believed that this was the land where the Devil actually lived. The Puritans called this place "The Devil's Hopyard," where Samuel Adams Drake said that "old witches meet on stormy nights to make potions."

Apparently, some witnesses even saw this act transpire. Perhaps this is one place that the dwarf people lived. The entire dwarf people story is told in the Ledyard, Connecticut section of the book. At Chapman Falls, on the Eight Mile River, there is an unusual geologic feature: perfectly round pot holes. The Native Americans said that these were their God's footprints and the Puritans thought that these holes were created by the Devil's tail.

Superstitions ran rampart in Connecticut during the Puritan era, and even into our own century. Many people here carried newborns into their house with gold or silver in their hands, so they would grow up wealthy.

Governor Winthrop is said to have searched for valuable minerals in the northwest part of Haddam. On Route 151, there are the remains of the old Lithia Mine, otherwise known as Swanson Quarry, where many minerals can still be found. In Middle Haddam, Beryl, Garnet, and Tourmaline have been found at the east bank of the Connecticut River at the Gillette Quarry. The last time any blasting occurred here, it yielded $700 worth of Tourmaline. There is also a rare earth element found here, Epidote or Basic Calcium Aluminum Ferric Iron Silicate. The Native American name for Haddam was tomheg, meaning "tomahawk rock." The tribe members would gather stones from the river here to make axes. At the Turkey Hill Mine, Beryl and Tourmaline have been discovered.

Remember: whenever exploring mines or other dangerous areas, always ask for permission from the owners; tell someone where you are going and when you will be back, and be very, very careful. Death has occurred in these places.

There was a settler fort here in 1676 built as protection from the Native Americans. In 1668, the first gristmill was here on the Mill River. This is also where the smugglers met on the Connecticut River in the early 1600s. It is said that the pirates Blackbeard, Stede, Bonnett, and Townley met here at different times. Perhaps this was a good place to bury some loot.

East of Higganum Station there is a dirt road that leads to The Landing. This is the site of early mills and shipyards. There is a Shopboard Rock, which is a boulder with a flat top. The story is that a tailor used the rock for his clients to stand on as he measured them for suits. Seven Falls is a roadside park near Middletown. Directly opposite this park, about fifty feet west of the old highway, is Bible Rock, which is several layers of stone standing on end, and it looks like an open book.

Alexandrite was found at Haddam Neck. Also, Cat's Eye gemstones were discovered. Legend states that this gem can make the wearer invisible. One would think that this would be a very useful jewel to have when hiding any type of treasure! Also a pirate treasure is said to be buried on Haddam Island. It is said to be Kidd's treasure. Claims were reported that pirates were seen burying a treasure in a hill, under a ledge, west of Clarkhurst Road. Lord's Island is another place where pirate treasure is said to exist.

Moodus Reservoir, Native American village, and river are all located in the Middlesex County area, near Mount Tom. It is the region where the Moodus and Salmon Rivers meet, just before merging with the Connecticut River. Mount Tom is a State Park and can be reached by following Route 25. This was the place where the last wild turkey was known to be shot before 1936. Turkeys have since been re-introduced to the wild. There is a yet another legend about a small cave on the north face of Mount Tom. A man tried to kill a school teacher by cutting her throat. He killed himself and died, but she survived. His ghost has been seen here. There is a legend that there is a hole that has no bottom on this mountain. Some divers believe that it may be an entrance to a cave which goes a distance under the river. It is said that many caves in the area can only be explored to a certain point. After that, all matches, flashlights, and torches go out and cannot be refired.

Long Lake, also known as Shaw Lake, is an extinct volcano crater. Even stranger than that, is the answer to the question: Where does the water come from? The lake exists on a mountain top and no one is really sure where the water came from. Perhaps rainfall?

This is the site of the famous or infamous Moodus Sounds. See Newburyport, Massachusetts, for more information about the origin of these sounds. Mount Tom is where the rumblings

of the Earth are the worst. It is said that chimneys would topple, walls would fall, and heavy boulders would move. The sound would seem like volleys of musket fire.

Native American legend tells that the sounds are created by their angry God, who also creates earthquakes. The Native Americans held the greatest powwows here to appease their God. The Wangunk word for Mount Tom is Machimoodus, meaning "place of noises" or "bad noises." This is the chief home of the spirit called Hobbamoko. He would sit on his Sapphire throne and would create the sounds. There is more to the Hobbamoko story. Refer to the part of the story in the Hamden, Connecticut section about Sleeping Giant. Anyway, the rumblings and explosions come from the mountain. (See *Lost Loot, Ghostly New England Treasure Tales* for further explanations of these sounds.)

An early legend from the Puritans is that the noises were caused by encounters between good witches of East Haddam, who practiced white magic and the bad witches of Haddam, who practiced black magic. There is also a bright blue light or Sapphire that would shine from a cave in the center of Mount Tom.

As an interesting side note, there has been aquamarine gemstones found in the area and in Rocky Moodus Cave, pearls were discovered in 1765.

The scientific explanation is that minor earthquakes occur here along the fault that lies in Connecticut. There are usually two reasons for earthquakes, volcanic and tectonic. There is now evidence that the Moodus Sounds occur at the same time as tectonic earthquakes. Many rare elements and minerals are found in earthquake-prone areas. One earthquake zone occurs from Fall River through Bridgewater and Rockland, Massachusetts, into the Bay. Another zone passes from Colchester, north through Willimantic, Connecticut.

This is considered the most active earthquake zone in New England. There was an earthquake in 1791, a 5 on the Ricter Scale. Earthquakes were also documented in 1727, 1792, 1793, 1794, 1805, 1812, 1813, 1840, 1844, 1860, 1862, 1886, 1894, 1897, 1899, 1913,1916, 1917, 1919, 1925, 1927, 1968 and 1982. In 1981, a 3.7 quake occurred here. On May 16, 1791, sounds were heard and felt from this mountain as far away as on the Kennebec River in Maine, in Boston, and New York. There were reports of an earthquake in June in 1638, felt in southern New England and on October 27, 1727, called the great earthquake in Connecticut. Another modern theory explaining the sounds is that perhaps it is the sound of the globe cooling.

Guilford is the site of bloody battle during King Philip's War. Leete's Island, (it is not really an island, but during flood stages, there is water all around the area creating an island), is the site of a battle. In June 1777, the British were repulsed from the area by the Colonists. There is a place called Indian Rock Shelter on the east side of the bay where the tribe members would jump out and surprise enemies. This is near the road leading to Sachem Head; the name comes from the time when a Pequot warrior was shot and killed in the War of 1637 as he tried to swim the harbor. His head was placed in a fork of an oak at Sachem Head.

A silversmith shop was reported to be located ten rods north of the bridge at the "sign of the Golden Kettle." What that actually meant is not recorded.

HAMPTON/EAST HAMPTON/HAMDEN

Blackbeard is said to have buried a treasure in Hampton in a granite wall. In 1938, a man named Cady owned property in the Howard's Valley section called the Jewett Homestead. A stranger came to this home, named Barney Reynolds, and told a strange tale. He said that he was a direct descendant of Captain Edward Teach, also known as Blackbeard. He said that he had a map that told of Blackbeard's treasure buried here. It was under a stone shaped like a horse head, followed a southeast line across the road to a boulder that looked like a dog's head. The map then pointed south, across a brook, to the fish carved on the stone, which looked directly at the treasure site. He would do all the work, if Cady would pay for the equipment to dig. Cady agreed, but all he saw was a pit dug and nothing else. Reynolds disappeared forever. It is possible that Blackbeard anchored off New London, unloaded his ship, and walked north on the Nipmuck

Trail, perhaps to evade pursuers. Cady's home was just off the Nipmuck Trail, a place where many paths intersected. However, if Reynolds found the gold, he certainly did not share it.

Rose Quartz is found at the old Nathan Hall Quarry on Route 14 in East Hampton. There is also a Cobalt mine at the foot of Great Hill near Portland. It lies in the Meshomasic State Forest and has been worked since 1762.

Sleeping Giant State Park in Hamden, also known as Blue Hills or Mount Carmel, is made of five ridges of brownstone, a red-hued sandstone, complete with an abandoned mine and lots of rattlesnakes. The entire area is a geologist treasure trove. Greenstone has been found here. The quarries have actually dramatically reduced the height of the mountain. The largest copper deposit ever found, just one piece, was near Mount Carmel in 1790. It was ninety pounds and was attached to the rock by metal strands. In 1912, quarrying was started on the giant's head. Public outrage at the destruction cause the quarrying to stop in 1933.

The head of Sleeping Giant. Notice the scarring from the mining that was just ended abruptly.

The Native American legend of the mountain is that a large irritable spirit named Hobbomock stamped his foot and caused the abrupt turn of the Connecticut River to the east at Middletown. To stop these types of events from happening, the kind spirit, Keihtan cast a spell for him to sleep forever, thus the sleeping giant. In July 1989, an F-4 tornado spun through town with winds at 200 mph. If this type of phenomena happened here in earlier times, no wonder the Native Americans thought this was a magical, enchanted place.

The Sleeping Giant remains deep in slumber.

Tidal Marsh Peat is a deposit of organic material formed by the rise of the sea level following the melting of an ice sheet. Tree stumps can be found under the peat. On Shepard Avenue, west of York Hill, there are large glacial rocks known as the Brethren Rocks that were dropped here by the ice.

HARTFORD

A brook was created in this city in a strange way. A large rock was found with no water around it. The miners were digging in the stone to fill it with dynamite to blast it into powder, when the auger hit water, it was so powerful that the water came out of the well and ran over the sides. It created a brook with no visible source for over 100 years.

The remains of one of the rivers in Hartford that have been driven underground.

On June 6, 1633, the Dutch erected a fort and trading post here to trade with the Pequot tribe. They actually purchased this area from the Pequots. Native Americans who lived in the region were called the Sicaog; they called this place Matacomacok meaning "bad plantation," perhaps due to the swamps in the area or "bad going, where paths or trails are difficult" or "ineffective refuge." The area was also known as Squotuck, meaning "red river" or "place of red earth." The Sequin tribe lived on the east side of the river, called Hochanum and the Podunks lived on the west side of the river called Suckiaug or Hartford today. Front Street was a Native American trail and the village was actually located at Soldiers Field. Main Street was the trail to their fishing place on the Connecticut River. The village at Warehouse Point was called Nameroke, a Podunk word meaning "fishing place." Pesiponck means "sweating place" and there was a little cave in the hillside, west of Rocky Hill Brook at the corner of Broad and Grand Streets. It is even said that there is a King Philip Cave here. He did actually come from this area originally, but is it possible that he lived in so many places named after him? It may be that King Philip is like Captain Kidd, everything associated with Connecticut Native Americans is automatically named King Philip, just like everything associated with pirates is associated with Captain Kidd.

The first witch in America was hanged here in 1647 or 1649 or 1650 or 1652. In some year, in May, Alyse or Achsah Young was hanged at the Old State House for being a witch. Why the years are different is because she was probably accused in one year and hanged in another. The really sad part to this story is that apparently, the evil practices she is said to have done were found not true, but since she had already confessed, she was hanged anyway. In 1653, Lydia Gilbert was hanged as a witch. The charge? She is said to have caused one man to shoot another. Trinity College is known as Gallows Hill as well as South Green, near the corner of Main and Wethersfield Streets.

The first American woolen mill was built in 1788 by Jeremiah Wadsworth. The new President elect, George Washington, wore cloth from this mill at his inauguration in 1789. Until the late 1800s, the settlers waded through deep red mud in town. Adventurers Green on the east side of Main Street between Arch Street and the Park River was named in 1935 in honor of a party of English adventurers who first came to Hartford. This green is now under the Hartford Public Library. Brook Street is named because at one time it was actually the course of the brook. Charter Oak Avenue is formerly the ancient highway to a meadow and the ferry. The Charter Oak stood near the south side of the street which originally ran southeast of the present line into the meadow. Evidence of the old roadway can still be seen today.

On September 21, 1938, the town was hit by hurricane, as much as New England was, which flooded the power station for the Trolley cars, when the Connecticut River overflowed. Built in 1917, the Travelers Insurance Company tower was the tallest building between Boston and New York until 1983. It stands 527 feet and is made from Rhode Island granite. The South Green was originally a circus ground, until a larger site was created on Barbour Street in the north end of the city. This Barbour Street was the site of the fatal circus tent fire in 1944. The treasure of Elisha Babcock is said to be buried at this spot.

Amethysts were found in the Park River, which used to flow where the Hartford Public Library is today. It is now channeled underground with the Hog River. There is a stone arch or bridge, which crosses the road that used to span the Park River in 1833. This 104-foot arch was the largest arch bridge in the United States. Elias Rathbun was the masonry contractor. The Park River was called a muddy, sluggish river that emptied into the Connecticut River at Dutch Point.

Even in the big city of Hartford, wildlife and a sense of another era can still be found.

Gold Street was named for industry gold beating that occurred here. The industry was started in 1819 by Marcus Bull. The gold leaf in state Capitol dome was created on the Street.

As an interesting side note, a Sioux Warrior killed in Wyoming is said to have all the gold buttons and metal on his clothing beaten by the people from Hartford.

It has been speculated that perhaps there is gold in this area. In 1986, geologists and University of Connecticut students found gold in Meshomasic State Forest around an abandoned mine near Great Hill, about twenty miles southeast of Hartford. The gold found was about 100 times the amount usually found in North American mines. Claims about gold being in the area date back to 1654. The gold is said to be in a canoe-shaped channel that runs north through Massachusetts and into the White Mountains of New Hampshire. This deposit is above an old cobalt deposit that was mined in the 1600s. Why those miners missed the gold is not known. Are the gold and cobalt deposits linked? It is theorized that perhaps during the Avalonia collision with North America, water or other liquids were forced through the cobalt deposit, perhaps dissolving the minerals that were mixed with the gold, and left the gold above. Whatever happened, gold may still be discovered in Connecticut.

In 1765, a silversmith shop was located on King Street, the old name for State Street. Another silversmith shop was found on Morgan Street near the bridge in 1867.

The Old State House was built in 1796 and was the former State Capitol Building. It is said to be haunted by those who were here in the past. The ghosts are said to be the first witch hanged in the colonies and a former museum keeper. Footsteps and voices are the claims here.

HARWINTON/HIGGANUM/HEBRON

In Harwinton on Lead Mine Brook, it was claimed that gold, as well as lead was found in 1657. The settler name for this town comes from the two first owners who came from Hartford and Windsor. If you take the first three letters from each town, add a "ton," and a new town name is created.

Higganum in Middlesex County was the location of a Native American village and reservoir. The Mohegan name for this region was Tomheganompsk, which means "quarry where we get stone for axes." The stones are also known as tomahawk rocks. There should be plenty of Native American artifacts to be discovered.

On the Wells Woods Road in Hebron, in the east part of town, there is a ghost town that was called Wells Woods. All that remain are cellar holes, stone walls, and foundations. Permission must be obtained to visit this area. Entering any abandoned area is risky and caution should be maintained.

There is another well-known ghost town here in Gay City State Park, called Gay City or Factory Hollow. This town is considered haunted. It was a small village at one time located on the Blackledge River, but the people just left and there are ruins in the area. The town was originally settled in 1786 by a religious sect. By the Civil War era, the mills had burned and the town was in decline. There are stories of a murder that took place and of a headless ghost that stalks the town, perhaps looking for the murderer. One strange note to add here is that the river in this ghost town flows uphill! This is a state park, so permission must be gained to search for artifacts.

Notch Hollow is another ghost town that can be found in Bolton Notch. There were twenty-six buildings here in 1913. From the 1700s to the 1900s, this was a granite and flagstone quarry town. It was named due to the thirty-foot trench that the quarrying caused right through town. In 1952, most of the town was destroyed because Route 6 was upgraded. Then, in 1956, a hurricane destroyed the rest of town. Visitors claim that a phantom engine can still be seen and heard. Singing can be heard, as well as the moans of victims from quarry accidents. There is also a murder victim that is looking for justice. A Dutch man was murdered here, but the crime was never solved.

As an interesting side note, Route 6 was considered the second most dangerous road with numerous fatal accidents according to Reader's Digest in 1995.

KENT/KILLINGLY

After King Philip's War, in 1735, a small number of tribe members from the Paugussets, Uncowas, and Pootatuck formed a village along the Housatonic River called Schaghicoke in Kent today, which was about 400 acres at the foot of the mountain.

Molly Fisher Rock can be found here. She was born in 1750, and some called her a witch. On the west side of the road about three miles south of Kent, there is a mountain called Lane's Hill and this is where the rock lies. This rock was dropped here by the glacier and it is made of pure white quartz. It is twelve feet long and nine feet wide, six feet high. It does appear that this rock was used as a fireplace at one time. On the southeast side of the rock are several characters cut deeply into the stone. These are made by man, not nature, but no one knows what they mean or who carved them. Molly Fisher was said to always visit this place to look for Kidd's buried treasure chests. It is said that one has to be absolutely silent, if any sound is made, one will never find the gold. A man did find the treasure once, but spoke a word, and the treasure disappeared forever. Those who visited the area said they smelled brimstone. There is no natural reason for this smell to occur here.

Kent Falls is one of the Marble Valley waterfall sites. Bulls Bridge is also found here. It is one of the few covered bridges left in Connecticut. There is an iron mine and forge in the area. The oak timbers can still be seen under Forge Brook at the entrance to Macedonia Park. The ore was transported up the mountain to the forge by horseback.

There is kind of a ghost town here. It is near the Cobble Brook Farm area. In 1739 there was a settlement at the falls on Cobble Brook, containing a forge, tannery, cider mill, grist mill, fulling mill, saw mill, two churches, school, general store, trading post, butcher shop, blacksmith shop, brick yard, animal pound, burial ground, and parade ground. All are gone today.

Killingly is a Native American battlefield. The Native American name was Aspinock. Skeletons were found from a Narragansett and Nipmuch battle over who would fish lamprey eels that came here at some time.

Treasure Hunting Tip

When searching for Native American artifacts, always research where the tribes would meet or where something unusual is said to have happened. The story below is one area to search.

A Native American legend about the region is about the birth of Loon Island in Alexander Lake. The Native American name for the lake was Lake Mashapaug. The story goes that there was once a mountain called Lake Mashapaug, and that it rose where the lake is today. It was submerged quickly by the Great Spirit as a punishment for those tribe members who were engaged in drunken dances on the summit. Just the top remained and that is the island today. Pines could be seen under the lake for many years. The question arises as to why this particular legend exists. What happened here? Was there once a mountain? Did something catastrophic occur very quickly? Whatever happened, there were once Native Americans living in the area.

KILLINGWORTH/LEDYARD

The Hammonasset tribe lived in Killingworth and Clinton before the settlers arrived. Killingworth is located on the Hammonansett River and is the former site of Nineveh Falls. The Sachem of the era when the Europeans first arrived was called Sebequanash, meaning "man who weeps." At the former site of Nineveh Falls, which did fall on the Hammonasset River, the legend that a ghost of a young Native American girl and warrior haunt this area. In pre-colonial times, a warrior went to war and left his love behind. The word of a great battle came back to the Native American village and it was told to the girl that her love died. She wandered to the cliffs and jumped. Shortly after that, the warrior came back to the village, and when he heard the news, he went to the same cliff and jumped to be with his love.

That is not the only ghostly love story to haunt this town. This second story starts at the North Parker Hill Road Cemetery. The ghosts of a bride and groom have been observed crossing the road here.

A third love ghost story also exists. This story takes place in the Old Inn. Since 1790, many taverns and roadhouses have been here. The ghosts of a man and woman have been observed and a presence felt throughout all the different buildings that have been here at one time or another.

A Native American cave exists about a third mile up the brook on the east bank. It is part of Cockaponset State Forest. It is also the site of an old mill.

There are huge kettle holes to be found in Ledyard. They are dry ice blocks left behind by the glacier that melted. The Mohegan and Pequot tribes are closely related by blood and royal marriage. They lived on the banks of the Thames River in the Ledyard region. The Native American name for river was Mashapequottuck. This is a Mohegan word meaning, "great Pequot river" or "river of the great destroyers of men." In the early 1600s, the Pequot nation was in charge of the area and by the 1630s, tensions started to rise between the settlers and tribe. This tension was helped by the other Native American tribes all through Connecticut, who did not want to live in fear of the Pequots any longer. So, after the Sachems traveled to Boston to request help from the settlers, the Pequot War began. The Mohegans and Narragansetts aligned with the English settlers, and in 1637, war was declared. After the war, the Mohegans came to power, but were no longer aligned with the English, by 1675 and King Philip's War. The results of that war have been told throughout the book. The Pequot village here was called Mushantuxet or Maushantuxet.

There is a Pequot legend about this region. There is a treasure buried in a swamp here and a Native American ghost protects and guards the loot. There is gold and other types of treasures to be found, but the exact swamp location is not clear. It could be Cuppacommock or Chomowauke, which means "owls nest," due to the large number of owls who lived here or took shelter here, and Cuppacommock means "place of refuge or where we hide from enemies." It was here that the last battle of the Pequot War occurred. Perhaps the treasure is in Mast Swamp.

Mast Swamp covered much of eastern Connecticut. The swamp is also known as Pine Swamp or Ledyard's flower garden. Only in this place does a rare flower grow, a Red-Heart Rhododendron. The flower has a dark crimson heart, instead of the usual golden center. This place, in an enclosed grove, was the last refuge of the Pequot when they were hiding from the English after the destruction of their fort in Mystic. Actually, the Pequot tried to hide here after Major Mason destroyed their fort, but they were followed. In late June 1637, just as the flower was blooming, the Pequots were starved and captured here. Most died, never leaving the swamp. On July 13, 1637, the Pequot Sachem, Puttaquapouk was captured and taken to the swamp and killed (shot). It is said that he died lying in the blossoms and he uttered the curse upon the swamp, because of the starvation of his people and on the

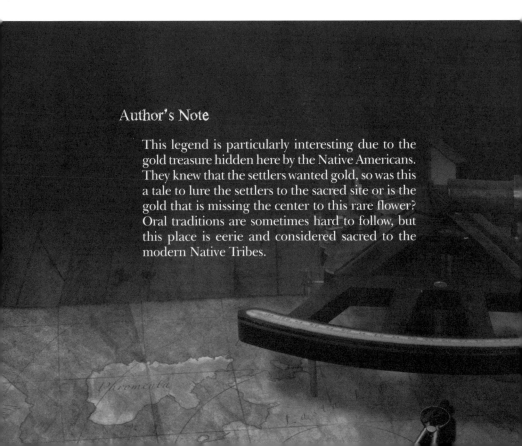

Author's Note

This legend is particularly interesting due to the gold treasure hidden here by the Native Americans. They knew that the settlers wanted gold, so was this a tale to lure the settlers to the sacred site or is the gold that is missing the center to this rare flower? Oral traditions are sometimes hard to follow, but this place is eerie and considered sacred to the modern Native Tribes.

settlers who killed the Pequots. The swamp blossoms lost their golden center and became blood red forever.

Not only do the Native American ghosts guard the lost treasure, but also any personal property that has been left there. It is said that if the visitor sees swamp or will-o'-the-wisp lights, those are the spirits who guard the treasure. Workers at the spring in the swamp are said to have found some of the gold that was said to be here, and perhaps still more was left to be found. The Mohegans are said to have dreamed about Captain Kidd, and that he was to bury gold on the Thames River banks. Tribe members supposedly found that gold, but were scared away by a large black dog or sometimes a pig or sometimes the pirate himself will scare them away from the gold. The location of this loot will only be told to the seeker in a dream, and the only way to retrieve the gold is by driving a stake into the being that chases them away. Perhaps some of the gold that was found on the banks of the Thames was buried in the swamp that the Pequots took refuge in.

There is also a Mohegan legend about a place called Basagwanantaksag, an area south of Shantic Point, called Muddy Cove today. The Native American word means "mud." Just southwest of the Cove is a rocky ledge. The foot of the rock is a deep red color and has the general outline of a human. This rock is called Papoose Rock. It is said that a Mohegan took her child's life and then her own on this rock. The red color is the blood left by her dying here. It is a sad and sacred place, and guarded by their spirits. On Shewville Road, there is a dark, and overgrown area called Dark Hall. A presence is often felt here, too.

There is also a tale of the little people living secretly in the woods. The Mohegans have legends of the "Wooden People," the dwarfs living in the forest. They could be raucous and malevolent if provoked. This legend sounds like the Penobscot tribe legend in Maine.

LITCHFIELD/MADISON

The Native American name for Litchfield was Wimpeting, which means "ruinous help" or "pile of discarded goods."

There was also a village here or at least a rest area. The area was also known as Wiatik, which means "village of wigwams." Another name, Wecquaesgeek, means, "at the end of the march." The tribe that lived here was an important member of the Wappinger confederacy and was almost totally destroyed by the Dutch in 1643, led by Captain Underhill. The principal Native American village was called Keetutenny, which is Mahician meaning "principal town." Gold, Beryl, Garnet, Corundum, and Tourmaline have all been found in the area.

On the Old Mount Tom Trail, there is a strange foundation that when the stairs are climbed, the hiker can hear a moaning sound from the floors below. It is said that this is a high school-aged hiker who died on the trail. This area is considered a mini-tornado alley. The density of tornadic activity is as high in this place as anywhere else in the country.

English silver and gold coins from the late 1700s found on the beach in Madison. These coins were found several miles south of the number 61 Exit off the Connecticut Turnpike. In the 1950s, residents said they saw the remains of an old sailing vessel rotting off shore. Perhaps the coins come from that ship or perhaps from the British battle fought in 1782 on East Wharf toward the south end of East Wharf Road.

MANCHESTER/MARLBOROUGH

Several Podunk villages existed in Manchester. The Cheney Silk mills once created silk here in the nineteenth century. The town is also known as the Five Mile Tract. About thirteen miles east of town, around the Mansfield Depot, there was a manufacturing town called Merrow. Remains of this ghost town include abandoned buildings and ruins. During its heyday, about 250 people lived there.

Marlborough was a resort area for the Native Americans. Pahegansic, means "bear-hill" and Washiack means, "place of paint." Diamond Pond is named for the clear water, not any diamonds. In 1959, in the woods, a skeleton was discovered. This was a Native American who died around 1675. Perhaps during King Philip's War? He was found under Indian

Rock Shelter and was killed by a musket ball. The Native Americans always buried their dead toward the setting sun. It was obviously not a natural death. This is part of the Native American Trail from Hartford to Norwich, but is now on private property. The colonials found arrowheads, scrapers, and spear heads all along this trail. The Native Americans believed that a spirit dwelled here on the western slope of Bader Hill.

MERIDEN/MIDDLETOWN/NEW BRITAIN

Meriden, also known as Merideen, Moridan, and Merredan, is the silver-making center of Connecticut since 1794. The gem, Amethyst has been found here. Though precious minerals have been found in the region, the area has a dark side. The original settlers came from New Haven. The town is really a cold harbor spring of Pilgrims Harbor Brook. What that means is that it is and was used as a shelter from the weather for wayfarers. This place was a refuge for travelers before the 1660s.

The Hanging Hills of town were created by two successive lava flows. At the top of West Peak also known as West Mountain, the visitor can see Long Island Sound to the Massachusetts Hills or Mount Tom. To reach West Peak from the northeast shore of Mirror Lake in Hubbard Park is a 600-foot climb to the first summit. This hike is part of an old Native American trail.

On the West Peak, a peak that rises 1,007 feet in the Hanging Hills, the Black Dog legend starts when the hiker sees a friendly black dog on the trail. Usually it is described as a spaniel-type dog with sad eyes. The dog never leaves paw prints, even in the snow, and is seen barking, but no sound is ever heard. If the dog is seen once, it will bring joy to the hiker's life. However, if the dog is seen again, it will bring sorrow, and if it is seen three times, it will bring death. Many hikers have claimed to have seen the dog; some of the hikers have seen the dog twice. There have also been many hikers who have died by falling in these hills. Black dogs are thought to be guards of a portal to somewhere or guarding where a master died.

This area seems to bring bad luck to some of those who come. Think about the names of some of the places in the area. For example, Misery Brook, Lamentation Mountain, and Black Pond. The hikes here are challenging, but the geology is fascinating. As stated earlier, the Hanging Hills that surround the town were created from ancient lava flows. There is an old Trap Rock quarry that shows the first lava flow very well. There is also an ash bed found on the west side of Mount Lamentation. The material is a greenish color with bodies of ash embedded in it. This was probably formed by explosions when the hot rock came in contact with water or gas. The ash is thought to be volcanic.

The settlers built a fort here during the 1675 King Philip's War. A tavern was built in 1752 on the main road between Hartford and New Haven, located on the corner of Broad and East Main Street called the "Merry Den." It was torn down in 1890. In the northwest part of the road from Meriden to Berlin, there was hardly room for a path, which is why it was called Cat Hole Pass.

There is a chest treasure buried, by Captain Kidd of course, on Kelsey Point in Middletown in Middlesex County. The Native American names for the area are Wesumpsha, which means "path" or "shining or glistening rocks," or Waktiompsk or Wampanoag, meaning "dwelling among the rocks." The Native American village was called Mattabeset or Mattabesick. The Europeans called this place Middletown, because it is halfway between Hartford and Saybrook.

There was a Native American fort on Indian Hill. Native American relics were found near the West River Bridge. The Sachem Sowheag is said to have built a home or even a castle on a hill near here. Near the Sebeth River was a field, north of Middletown, where many Native American artifacts has been found, including arrowheads. That may mean that a battle was fought here at some time.

A ghost lumbering town can be found half-way between Middletown and New London. Lumber was sent to ship builders along the Connecticut River. All that remains are ruins today. There was a shipwreck here. The *City of Hartford*, struck the drawbridge, completely destroying the bridge in 1876. In

The Connecticut River.

the late 1700s, a silversmith shop was located south of the corner of Court and Main Streets. Perhaps it was around the site of a savings bank today. Another silversmith shop was found at the northwest corner of Main Street and Henshaw Lane, now College Street, in 1776.

At the White Rocks Quarry, green Beryl and Tourmaline have been found. Topaz has also been mined in the China Stone Quarry. There is an old Middletown Lead Mine first used in 1661 on a small stream in the area. Lead for bullets were mined here during the Revolution. In Middlefield, which was part of Middletown until 1866, is the site of an abandoned sandstone quarry. About 100 feet back from the road leading to the quarry are dinosaur tracks.

A copper vein was discovered in New Britain. The vein runs north to south for two miles. This town is also the site of an ancient Native American Woodland village that existed here around 1120 A.D. The village covered almost five acres at the meeting of the Farmington and Pequabuck Rivers. The

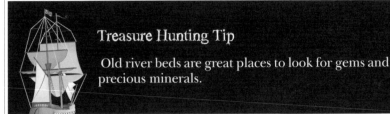

Treasure Hunting Tip

Old river beds are great places to look for gems and precious minerals.

first fort built in the 1600s was to protect the settlers from the Native Americans. The fort no longer exists, but the water well was used until the 1900s.

This town has a great geological history. The Rock and Walnut Hills that surround this area is basalt, a form of lava, also known as traprock. Those hills are actually part of a mountain chain that includes Mount Tom, the Hanging Hills of Meriden and others. The ice age and glacial activity actually changed the river course in New Britain. A distant predecessor of the Farmington River actually made the gap at Cooks Cap, but no river exists now. The debris from the ice age have dammed up that part, as well as the eastern end of Compounce Pond. This stopped the river at both ends, so Lake Compounce is actually the river that has been naturally dammed for about twenty miles. As time went by, the water flowing in Tariffville ended and the water started flowing elsewhere, thus creating the Farmington River. The bottom of the area that used to have water in it, became a sandy plain, eventually becoming the town of New Britain. The gap between Mount Tom and Mount Holyoke was created by the Connecticut River. This entire area was called the Great Swamp by first settlers. The Old Farmington River channel was located in Plainville, before glacial debris closed it up.

MILFORD

This town is located on the banks of the Housatonic River. The Pootatuck tribe who lived here are said to have built a "palace." People came from miles away to see this building.

It was a great Long House, said to be 20 feet long and 100 feet wide. This was obviously a well-used place by the Native Americans. A shell heap was found that covered 21 acres. These shell heaps have been found all over New England and were really the garbage piles for the tribes for thousands of years. The great thing is that these heaps tell us much about the tribes that once lived in our area. The Paugasuck Reservation was located in Milford from 1675 to 1861.

This was a battlefield in 1648 between the Wepawaug, or Milford tribe, and the Mohawk Nation. The Wepawaug defeated the Mohawks in a swamp about one mile east of the ferry site. The victory did not mean that the Wepawaug tribe was safe, however. There was a Native American fort north of the bridge that the Mohawks attacked and destroyed in 1671. The settler fort at West Point on the west side of the harbor built in 1776 was called Fort Trumbull. Liberty Rock is located on the north side of Post Road. This boulder was used to hide the colonials while they were watching the British movements in Long Island Sound.

Charles Island is located off Silver Sands State Beach and has a long haunted treasure-rich history. This thrice cursed, haunted island started as a place of conflict between the settlers and the Native Americans, the Wepaoway or Wepawaug tribe, who lived here first. The tribe believed that this was a sacred place, connected to spirits. A battle occurred with the settlers, but the tribe lost. It is said that the Sachem or Chief named Ansantaway, put a curse on the island, saying, "Any shelter will crumble to the earth and he shall be cursed." It is said that the Native American spirits guard the Island and discourage any treasure seekers. Some legends state that the spirits of the Paugassett tribe, who once lived here as well, beheaded the pirates for burying the treasure in their sacred land. They are also the ones who made the treasure invisible to any who sought it.

Twenty-five years later, Captain Kidd buried his treasure on Charles Island, located off Silver Sands State Beach, under a place called Hog Rock in 1699. It is said that he stopped here, while he was heading toward Boston. Or Kidd may have buried treasure on Stratford Point. The exact spot is vague. Anyway, the story goes that a chest was buried in 1699 and was witnessed by residents. These people said that the chest was buried by pirates and that they knew it was Kidd's crew no less. There have been coins from his era found under the sand, so there may be something to the legend. It is said that in 1850, two men did find a treasure chest, but saw a shrilly, whistling, headless body wrapped in a flaming sheet, plunge toward them from above, so they ran away terrified by a flaming skeleton. They went insane, never to recover from the fright. So many people have searched here that the island has many pits, where no vegetation grows. That is considered the second curse of the island, by the pirate Kidd and his pirate ghosts who protect his treasure.

As an interesting side note, there is documentation that Kidd did visit this area twice, so to dismiss the legend out of hand may be an error on the treasure seekers part.

The third curse was placed here twenty-two years after Kidd's visit. Five sailors buried a Mexican Emperor's stolen treasure in a cave. In 1721, the Emperor cursed the treasure and those who stole it. Legend states that four out of the five sailors had a tragic death and the treasure was never recovered.

At the end of the eighteenth century, a monastery was built on the island. Though the monks dismissed the Native American curse, many mysterious deaths, suicides, and insanity forced them to abandon the monastery. The ruins can still be seen today.

In the 1950s, a restaurant was opened, but a lethal fire ended this enterprise. Hikers report seeing glowing objects, hearing voices, and monks walking among the ruins. The only access to the Island is a causeway that only surfaces at low tide. DO NOT DIG ON THIS ISLAND! This is now a nature preserve, posted with no trespassing signs.

By 2003, the island is uninhabited, but people still see something on the beach going on by fishermen in the surrounding waters. When investigated, there are no sign of the people or of people ever being on the beach.

On Tuxis Island, just offshore of Milford, a large amount of eighteenth century coins were supposedly found by campers in 1903. It is apparent that some sort of treasure can be found, whether a pirate left lost loot or a shipwreck nearby is still giving coins to the lucky seeker.

Marble was mined in Milford in 1800. It is a green swirl marble called "Verde antique." The East Room in the White House fireplace is made with this stone. The mine here may be hidden under a trailer park in town. The mineral Serpentine has also been found in this haunted place.

MONROE/MORRIS/MONTVILLE

On the Boy's Halfway River in Monroe, there is a cave where silver was once searched for in 1820. Exactly why someone felt that silver would be there is unknown, but the search was abandoned with no silver ever found. However, in 1880, there was once again a search for silver in this cave, the reason still unknown, but again, nothing was ever found. The area was once known as Flat Rock and Huntington. However, the treasure seekers should not be discouraged by the lack of silver here; large two-foot to four-foot-long green Beryl crystals have been taken out of the area.

Morris is the town where Bantam Lake lies. This is the largest natural lake in state, covering 1,200 acres. The lake was a favorite camping site of the Pootatuck tribe. There have been numerous finds of arrowheads in the area, suggesting that there were battles fought in the region, perhaps with the Mohawks.

Montville is the town for Native American forts. Fort Hill State Park was the fort of the Sachem Uncas of the Mohegans. Only stones remain today. This town is also the site of another Native American battle. The battle took place in 1634 and the area is now a state park. Fort Shantok, off state 32, was built by the Mohegans in the early 1600s. The Mohegan word means "midway up the river." This battlefield is halfway up the Thames River from New London to Norwich. In 1645, the Narrgansetts were repelled at this spot by the Mohegans. This fort was attacked again by the Narragansetts in 1659, but again were repelled. There is a place under a rock, perhaps a cave, where it is said that Uncas sat awaiting help from the

residents of Saybrook during the 1645 battle the took place here. The war finally ended due to the English settlers coming to Norwich. It is also a Mohegan burial ground today. It is believed that Uncas is buried in this park.

I visited this fascinating park on a hot July afternoon. What is amazing is that there are small stones here that are tombstones everywhere through the park. The wildlife is abundant and its easy to go back in time and "see" how things were in Uncas' era. There were many people around, walking, having a picnic, but it was quiet and very somber. The word I came up with is respectful. There are certain places in the world that have a flavor and feeling when visited. It is truly amazing how this place, sacred to the Mohegans, has a feel of history and reverence surrounding it. There are picnic tables and a playground for children, but they seem out of place. Though the day was cloudy with rain in the air, to me, this place would feel the same even when there is a blue sky. You feel you should speak in hushed tones, and you know there is something special about this little known state park.

More Native American battles were fought in this spot during historic times than any place else in the state. There is a miniature desert found below Trading

Stone markers are found all through the park.

Fort Shantok is a place of peace and reverence. Wildlife abounds throughout the park.

Námatuwangug --- Xantok
Regulations --- Shantok

Babámi yo ki, dá babámi nig kiug bazikinhudud, wigun niga ne wocay nihux.
Toward this earth, and towards those buried in this earth, show therefore
appropriate good behavior.

Babámi yox ukix Mohiksinug dá babámi unaxawang Mohiksinug wigun niga ne
wocay wang nihux.
Toward these Mohegan lands and toward the Mohegan way of life also
accordingly show the proper respect.

Unikámaug Mohiksinug cikunabu mumpax dá pudax.
(In the presence of) Mohegan ceremonies, quietly observe and listen.

Nigani nikama wusuquámin, kwit nayi.
Before photographing a ceremony, ask permission.

Uwunigin Xantok kanun, migwanux---yo uki Mundo; nihux gi ne wocay wigun.
As you experience the beauty of Shantok, remember---this is the land of Mundo
(a sacred place); conduct yourself therefore accordingly.

Respecting the Native American sacred places is mandatory and
expected when visiting these places.

Cove, known as Sandy Desert. It was believed to be a
cursed place by the tribes in the area.

Cutchegun or Corchegan or Cochegan Rock is the largest
glacial rock in Connecticut. It is fifty-foot square and sixty
feet high, weighing 6,000 tons. Uncas used this as a retreat and
hiding place in 1637. In the colonial era, a Mohegan named
Caleb Cochegan lived here, hence the reason for the name.

MYSTIC

The Mystic River was called Siccanemos by the Native
Americans. The name meant "River of the Sachem." There
are islands in the Mystic River called: Mouse, Penny, Sixpenny,
Mason's (the largest), Abigal (where a pirate treasure lies
buried, see the New London section of the book for more
information), Andrews, and Dodge. It is also believed that
Mason Island may hold a buried treasure. This island was
called Chippachaug by the Native Americans. The island

Mystic River in Mystic, Connecticut.

was given to Captain John Mason, but it is thought that privateers may have stashed loot here before it was given away. Hurtleberries grew here once and arrowheads, stone axes, black wampum beads, and clay pipes have all been found. In 1912, two Native American burial sites were uncovered on this island, one south of Wolf Ledge and the other south of Coconke Point.

The town was first called Southertown, but changed to Mystic. Why? Southertown was what Massachusetts called the area when they owned it. After the Pequot War, Connecticut took over this entire area and called this part of the state, Mystic. In 1665, the Connecticut General Court stated, "In memory of that victory God hath pleased to give to his people of Connecticut over the Pequot Indians." It meant that it was believed that this place has mystical qualities. According to the *Oxford Dictionary* of 1607, the meaning of Mystic is "spiritually allegorical or symbolic", or perhaps the name was a corruption from a Native American word, Misstukset, meaning, "a river whose waters are driven in waves by tides or wind." In other words, a great tidal river, which the Mystic River is. Blue Shell Crabs have been found here. This area was first described as jelly-like masses of bogs or thick bushes and plants or black water ponds. Perhaps the name comes from the fact that Native American medicine men came here to perform magic or gather medicinal plants.

Black water pond site in Connecticut.

There was a Pequot fort here during the era of the Sachem Mamoho. It was destroyed by the British in 1637 during the Pequot War. The person who destroyed the fort was Captain John Mason, who was given the island in the Mystic River as a reward. The fort was located on the western side of the river about three miles from the center of town. Over 300 Pequot were killed when the fort was burned by the British, Mohegan, and Narragansett tribes. The fort was a circular area of several acres, surrounded by a twelve-foot palisade and contained over seventy wigwams. It was a surprise attack and everyone in the fort was killed, or murdered in the swamp where the survivors fled.

NEW HARTFORD/BARKHAMSTED LIGHTHOUSE/ NEW FAIRFIELD

Barkhamsted Lighthouse is now a ghost town located in People's State Forest near New Hartford. This small town existed in the 1700s to 1850s. However, this town is no where near water. So the question arises: Why the name? The lights from this town, actually it was just one homestead, served as a navigational beacon in the night for stagecoaches on the way to Hartford. When the stagecoach driver saw these lights, they knew they were only five miles from the city. The story is that James Chaugham, a Narragansett tribe member from Block Island, married Molly Barber from Wethersfield in 1740. Molly was prevented by her parents from marrying her first choice, so she said that she would accept the next marriage offer, and she did. They moved to Barkhamsted. The remains of the site still exist to be seen, off the Jessie Gerard Trail in the state park. Even after the people who lived here died or mysteriously disappeared and no one lived here, travelers still claimed to see a light guiding them through the area. In the 1800s, a gang of robbers is said to have moved in. They were feared by the people in the region, and their campfire lights could be seen from the valley. Suddenly, the lights disappeared, and bodies were found. As strange as it may seem, ghosts were blamed for these deaths. Today, travelers still claim to sometimes see the light guiding them through the darkness.

Another place to visit is the Indian Council Cave on the Tunxis Trail northeast of the Barkhamstead Post Office.

New Hartford, also known as the "daughter of Berlin and grand-daughter of Farminton," is located on the West Branch of the Farmington River. Part of the river that runs through this area is called Satan's Kingdom. Though the name sounds spooky, it is a recreation area with class III rapids. There was a Tunxis tribe village, called Indian Head, and an old abandoned asbestos mine in the area. Perhaps the name is correct. A sulfur spring exists, and arrowheads have been found in the region. The name actually comes from the 1700s, when clergy reported that the gorge was populated by criminals, misfits, and other evil type people. There was a Native American camp site on West Hill Pond, and a settler fort was built on Town Hill.

The Apple trees in New Fairfield, to the east of Wood Creek, were planted by the Native Americans who lived in the village here. It is also the site of a burial ground. The artifacts that have been found are of a rare quality. Some can be seen at the Smithsonian Institution in Washington, D.C.

NEW HAVEN

The East Rock and West Rock in this town are very colorful rocks that when seen by Adrian Block as he explored the Connecticut River were called Rodeberg, meaning "red mountain." The area was settled in 1637. Actually, this town was where the Puritans chose to bury their dead. However, only the wealthy had stones or markers. Those who could not afford stones, were buried wherever, sometimes on top of another. The town is said to have held over 5,000 graves. The grave stones that were around the area were moved to a cemetery in 1812, but the bodies were not moved. That could certainly give a place a dark feeling.

Revolutionary War battles were fought here. Treasure hunters have found colonial items at the waterfront. Captain Kidd's treasure is said to be buried on Thimble Island. In 1924, a New Haven fireman found a gold ring, said to be part of Kidd's lost treasure on the island.

The Native American village once existed on the Quinnipiac River. The name means "where we change our route." This was where the Native Americans would go inland, or north of New Haven Harbor, along the great path, also known as the Boston Post Road. There is more about this great Native American path in Massachusetts section of this book.

There is also a ghost fort to be found. A ghost fort is a fort that no longer exists or its exact location is unknown. It is said that there was a Native American fort and village here, just north of Black Rock Harbor. This fort was known as Black Rock Fort, and it overlooked New Haven Harbor, near Fort Nathan Hale. Forts were needed between 1770 and 1781, this town was ransacked by the British.

Early in the eighteenth century, Mr. Atwater of New Haven, Connecticut, purchased a keg of nails in Boston and found a large quantity of silver money in the bottom. With the money, he had the silversmiths in the area make thirteen silver candle cups and a large baptismal basin and gave them to the church. It is said that during the British invasion of 1779, all this silver was hidden in the chimney of the House of the Deacon, where the Yale Art School stands today. Whether it was ever recovered is not recorded. A silversmith shop was located on the west side of Fleet Street, which ran from State Street to the Wharf. Another shop could be found at the junction of Church and Chapel Streets from 1770-1800. The owner, Richard Cutler, was a Tory in the Revolutionary War era and the spot is still known as Cutler's Corner.

Garnet, as well as marble and serpentine, was mined in New Haven. Also copper coins were minted here called fugio. The mint was located on the south side of Water Street between Franklin and Hamilton Streets. Hamilton Street is now called Townsend Street.

In 1840, a workman named William Thompson found a stone jar under a house being excavated on Elm Street. This jar was filled with doubloons and pieces of eight dated prior to 1768. Records show that the house was built during the Revolution, so perhaps during the raids by the British, these coins were buried for safety and not recovered.

NEW LONDON

The New London area was created by a drowned valley which formed one of the deepest harbors on the Atlantic Coast. The town is located on the mouth of Thames River and was settled in 1646. The Native American name for this place was Nameaug or Nambock, meaning "fishing place." The Thames River is not really a river, but an estuary of Long Island Sound that extends fifteen miles to Norwich.

Other Native American names for the area are Yewtack, meaning "fireplace" or in Mohegan-Pequot, Yotaanit, meaning "fire God." The area was also called Towawog and Pequot, after the defeat of the Pequots in 1637. There is also an ancient Mohegan village site around here called Checapscaddock, meaning "rocky hill."

A small island offshore is called Nayantacawnick, which was recorded by Roger Williams, but the precise spot is not exactly known. The Native American word means "at the place across from the Niantic." Perhaps it is Gull Island or Plum Island, New York?

The Thames River in Connecticut.

A British raid, commanded by Benedict Arnold occurred on September 6, 1781, and the town was burned. The British landed at two points, Groton Point and near the Lighthouse. There were numerous shipwrecks here, some may be from a hurricane that blew through the state on October 19, 1770. There were said to be over twenty ships wrecked during that storm. In 1812, the Merchantman *Osprey* was wrecked on Pleasure Beach and in 1816, the Spanish ship, *Anion* sank near on Goshen Point.

The New London Ledge Lighthouse, stands at the mouth of the Thames River at Avery Point. It was built in 1910 to prevent ships from running into Black Ledge. It is haunted by a previous Lighthouse keeper called Ernie. Ernie has been felt by numerous visitors and previous lighthouse keepers. It is said that he is not a very friendly ghost, at all. The New London Harbor Lighthouse, located on the edge of the city, was the fourth lighthouse built in America. The money to build the lighthouse came from a lottery in 1761.

There is a legend in the area since 1895 about two men who came to Lawrence's Wharf from Vermont. They reported that they were the descendants of a Revolutionary-era witch, who was against the war, named Strickland and they were looking for buried gold. They were hunting for the treasure of the Spanish Galleons, the *St. Joseph* and *St. Helena*. These ships were moored at the docks in 1753-1754 and were plundered there. As a side note, these ships were looked for, as well as their treasure, in the 1700s, so this was not a new story to the residents. The two men told that the Strickland witch possessed a magic pebble, as clear as a crystal, and that she could see any treasure buried at sea or on the land.

Here are the 1753 facts about these ships. Both ships hit a reef outside the harbor. They managed to get into the harbor, and off load. It was at the wharf that the valuable cargo disappeared. No one really records what happened after that. Some say it was thrown into the ocean, so Spain could not get it. Others say that is was stolen by the Connecticut authorities. Still others claim that it was secretly buried by the crew just on shore. The legend goes on to say that iron boxes were found just under the surface of the river. Of

course, black dogs appeared and green-eyed geese drove the treasure under the water again. There the story ends; it is never reported if these two men or others have ever found the two Spanish Galleon's treasure.

A silversmith shop could be found on State Street, somewhere between Number 138 and Bank Street.

There is a story about a haunted preacher house here. The real story is that steel nails in a the house created a strange popping sound as the temperature dropped or a sudden gust of wind occurred. Not all folk tales lead down the path to a ghost or a treasure which is why research is so important.

NEW MILFORD/NEW PRESTON/ NEWFIELD/NEWINGTON

Travel Route 25 and it will bring the treasure hunter to the Housatonic Gorge in New Milford. Another name for the Housatonic River is Native American. The word is Naromiychknowhusnkatankshunk, meaning "the water that comes from the big hills." The falls are called Great Falls or Eel Rocks. This was the place where lampreys and shad were caught in great numbers in a long ago era. It was a favorite camping spot of the Native Americans.

Another Native American legend describes how the narrow river gap on the Housatonic River got the name of Lover's Leap on Pumpkin Hill Road. Lillinonah, (Lake Lillinonah is named for her), was the daughter of the Chief of the Waramaug tribe. She thought her lover had left and went into the rapids in the mountain gap in a canoe. She heard her lover call to her from the banks, but she was doomed.

He leaped into the river, but both died in each others arms. They were buried together on this hill, overlooking the narrow river gap.

There is another story, a bit darker, that in the late 1600s, the Sachem Waramoukeag came to a minister's home in Woodbury to hear about Christianity. In the summer of 1687, the minister's niece came to visit and the two fell in love. They were not allowed to marry. One day, both bodies were found beneath the Bethel Rock. Something happened here to people who may have been in love. Not surprisingly, there is treasure to be found. In the abandoned quarries in the area, gem Garnet, Beryl, Tourmaline, Columbite, and Uraninite have all been mined. There is also a marble quarry in New Preston.

At a place called the Point in Newfield, Native American relics were found, as well as a burial site. It is said that this site was used for generations. Indian Hill is where the Sachem

Sometimes finding a special area to treasure hunt is as easy as following the road signs.

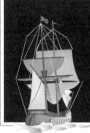

Treasure Hunting Tip

Anytime a place is called Indian, it is usually because the tribes in the area used this spot for a particular reason. It may be a good place to search for relics of that era.

is said to have once lived. He would summon the tribe by blowing on a conch shell. It was thought that this shell had magical powers because the tones could be heard at great distances.

NEWINGTON

This town was also known as East Tier. The region was sold to the Europeans by the Hartford Sachem, Sowheag in 1671. Cedar Mountain is a lava formation created about two million years ago. Somewhere beneath the town are hundreds of dinosaur prints, they just have not been found yet. Why would dinosaur prints be here? Two hundred million years ago, Newington was a flood plain and that means that there must be prints to be found. Prints have been found in Rocky Hill and Holyoke, Massachusetts in exactly the same type of environment.

The Wangunk tribe village must have been located on the shore of Mill Pond toward the center of town. The meadow nearby was called Cow Plain. Relics have been found, but no known village was documented. The types of items found are arrowheads, grinding pestles, and pottery from about 8,000 years ago. There are ancient paths that crossed through. Mill Street, also known as Back Lane or Maple Hill Road or Ted Rod Road, were once trails. An old road actually ran under Cedar Mountain, perhaps joining Deming Avenue. Newington was once said to be part of the underground railroad during the Civil War.

Vexation Woods (there is more about this strange place in the Wethersfield part of this book) is found in the southeastern corner of town. There is a legend here that a woman hanged herself and is buried on top of a hill on the Twenty Rod Highway. It was customary to bury murderers and suicides at the road crossing with a stake through the body to keep them from wandering. Her ghost is said to still haunt the area.

There is a steep and rocky hill in these woods and another legend tells of why the name Vexation was used. Often a team of horses or oxen would try to haul wood up this hill and it would cause vexation. Bottomless pits abound here. There is quicksand in the swamps, and construction crews have found places where no bottom was ever found. Perhaps the name Vexation comes from another legend. In the Red Rock Brook area, there is the story of the appearance of a horse-drawn wagon appearing to be trying to make it up a hill, but it falls into a bottomless pit.

NEWTON/NEWTOWN/NIANTIC

The Sandy Hook area is said to have been mined for gold by the British during the American Revolution, but where that mine may be is unknown. Zoar Lake was created by the building of Stevenson Dam on the Hoosantic River in 1919 in Newtown. This area flooded many dry places where lost treasure or artifacts may be buried. A silversmith shop was located at the head of Newtown Street on the road leading to Brookfield. Rare elements could be found here. There was a documented meteorite landing in 1925.

Niantic, also known as, Nayantick was a battlefield between the Narragansett and Mohegan tribes in August 1657.

NORWICH/NORWALK

Norwich was the heart of Mohegan territory. The Mohegans are said to have originally came from the Hudson River area in New York. The town is located at the junction of the Yantic and Shetucket Rivers, where they merge into the drowned valley known as the Thames River region. The Mohgeans and Narragansetts battled often for this land, after the Pequot War.

The entire area was infested with rattlesnakes in the late 1600s. A legend of the area is that Reverend Gordon Saltonstall used a violin to charm all of the snakes out of the town. The Native American name for this place was Soudahque or Sowduck, which is a variation of Shoutuck or Showtucket. In the Native American language, anytime a syllable of "tick" or "tuck" is used, it means a "stream of water."

The nine square mile area was purchased by the settlers on June 6, 1659. There are actually three rivers that are found here. The Thames River, also called the Pequot or Mohegan River, is the "Great River." The Native American name is unknown, but it is thought to have meant, the great river. The Shetucket River, also known as the Middle River, when compared to the Great River or Thames and the Yantic or Yontahaque River, also known as the Little River, when compared to the Great River or Thames. The Native Americans would erect weirs and pens to catch fish here in April and May. The technique was called "driving the river" and it meant that as the fish migrated upriver, the tribe would pen the fish in shallow water, then plunge into the river with their hands and throw the fish into baskets. There was an abundance of fish, which included, Shad, Alewives, Bass, Mackerel, Eels, Oysters, and Lobster. The fishing was phenomenal and a necessity to the survival of the tribes. It is no wonder when the settlers came and demanded that the Native Americans not use the rivers because they had been purchased that many issues arose. In May 1861, a Sturgeon weighing 125 pounds was caught above Gales Ferry in the Thames River. In February 1729, over 20,000 bass were caught in the Norwich River within a few days just below the Landing.

The story of this place begins in a time before the Pequots came from New York. There were five Sachems or brothers that ruled this land in peace. The Pequots were a sub-tribe of the Iroquois Nation of New York who conquered this peaceful tribe. During the Pequot era, around 1643, the area was claimed by Uncas, whose name means "the bold," a Mohegan chief. The Mohegans were a River Tribe from the East Hartford and East Windsor area. He married into the Royal Pequot family, and was given this village to rule near the Yantic River waterfall. This became the landing site and fishing place of the Mohegans. There have been Native American graves found here; it is said that these are the remains of where Uncas' parents and relatives were buried. Before the marriage, the Pequot ruler, Sassacus, at this time, had defeated Uncas in battle at least five times. Uncas would always go back to the Windsor area after being defeated, though some of the Mohegan tribe would usually remain. Finally, in May 1637, Uncas joined the English to defeat the Pequots. After that, he stayed in Norwich.

The Narragansett tribe did not want the Mohegans here, and often Norwich was their battlefield. The War between these two tribes lasted from 1642 to 1660. Three miles on State 12 north of town in New London County, is also known as Chelsea Plain. The Chelsea Plain is the bed of an ancient lake and the site of the Native American seat of power in the region. Arrowheads and stone pestles, as well as a royal burial ground, are all found here. There is also a perpendicular Cliff on the Yantic River, a waterfall site called Indian Leap, today. The Native American legend is that the Mohegans would often drive enemies, usually the Narragansett tribe, over the cliff to the pointed rocks below. Waweekus Hill, also known as Fort Hill, is the Native American name, meaning "watch place or place of refuge." There is more to Fort Hill in the Ledyard part of this book.

Sachems Head is the site of a Native American grave from a very bloody Native American battle. Norwalk was the actual battle site of "The Battle of the Great Plains," considered one of the bloodiest battles in 1643 between the Mohegans and the Narrgansetts, whose Sachem was called Miantonomoh. Over 2,000 warriors were killed on both sides. The Narrgansetts were caught fording the Shetucket River by the Mohegans. The Narragansett Sachem was captured by the Mohegan, called Tantaquieson or Tantaquidgin. With this capture, the Mohegans ultimately won the battle. Miantonomoh was executed by caving his head in with a hatchet. He was buried at a site called Sachem's Plain or Point. This site was marked, but is now unknown. It was said to be on the west bank of the Shetucket River.

Acadians, driven from their homes in Nova Scotia in the 1700s, came here searching for a new home. During the French and Indian War, the United States captured Nova Scotia and expelled over 7,000 Acadians from there. These people were scattered all through New England, including a site here. This town was also burned by the British during the Revolutionary War. In the War of 1812, a battle was fought here on Lundy's Lane in 1814.

At the junction of 117 and 2A, about five miles SE of the town, there was once a trading center and port town on the Thames River. The ghost town was called Poquetanuck and faded from the area in the 1800s. There are many ruins and buildings at this location. Caution and permission must be obtained when visiting any abandoned area. A Silversmith shop was operated by Joseph Carpenter in 1747 on the old town green. In the ruins of this shop were found engraved copper plates with his business cards imprinted.

Norwalk, in Fairfield County is located on the mouth of Norwalk River. The town was also known as Nayang or Noyank. It is an Algonquin word meaning "point of land." The Native American village named Norwauke was here. The reason for the name Norwalk is because when purchased from the Native Americans, its boundary was to extend northward from the sea one day's walk. Mohawk tribe artifacts have been found west of the harbor on Wilson Point. This was also the site of the settler fort called Old Forte Point.

The town was settled in 1651. Between 1770 and 1781, the British ransacked this town, as part of General Tyron's raids. Sheffeld Island, also known as Smith Island, is the place where numerous colonial artifacts were discovered. This is the site of the Sheffield Island Lighthouse built in 1826. This light was extinguished forever in 1900. Currently it is owned by the Norwalk Seaport Association.

Another Captain Kidd treasure lies waiting to be discovered on Pilot Island. The treasure is said to be in the fissures of a large rock formation connected to the island, but under water at high tide. There is also a pirate treasure buried on Goose Island. After the Civil War, Captain Joseph Merrill found a rich hoard of Spanish coins here. It is said that he

had three dreams telling him exactly where the money was to be found.

OLD LYME/LYME/EAST LYME

Pataganset Lake in East Lyme is known for its unusual aquatic plants. The boundary of Old Lyme and New London was disputed and the settlers used the Trial-By-Ordeal to settle the argument. The strongest man from each group would combat on the disputed land. Whoever won, that town got the area. It was America's first bare-knuckles fist-fight. The fight is said to have lasted over five hours with a lot of betting going on. Finally, Matthew Griswold of Old Lyme knocked out his opponent. Old Lyme claimed the disputed land, and the boundary stands today. Again, magical and enchanted areas where ghosts and treasure are said to lay usually have unique stories to tell.

As an interesting side note, the Native Americans often used this type of combat to settle all types of disputes well before the settlers ever arrived.

The mouth of the Connecticut River is a very dangerous place for ships. The first recorded wreck on Griswold Point was a brig in 1749. In 1801, the schooner, *Avery*, was wrecked here during a squall. During the hurricane of 1815, the Middlesex Gazette reported in the living memory of inhabitants at that time, the highest storm surge occurred here. In 1833, the wooden steam ship, *New England*, exploded. In Old Lyme, Captain Kidd buried a chest of gold under a boulder called Lions Rock on Conanicut Island in the Connecticut River. Moonstone has been discovered about two and a half miles south along the beach toward Long Island Sound. The gem has also been found in Unionville and is sometimes known as Albite or Orthoclase.

Joshua's Rock can be found in Lyme, north of Eight Mile Cove. This is where it is said that a Native American Sachem would hurl weapons at enemies in the canoes below. This spot can only be reached by boat.

ORANGE /PLAINVILLE/POMFRET/PORTLAND

Lambert's Mine in Orange has yielded yellow copper. Plainville is another spot where copper was found. It was another stop on the route of the ill-fated Farmington Canal project. It is named Plainville because of its level topography. It was also known as the Great Plain or the Great Plain of Farmington until the 1800s.

The last wolf in Connecticut was said to have been killed in Pomfret by Israel Putnam. The Native American name for this town was Mashamoquet.

The town was a lawless settlement from the time it was settled in 1686 to 1750. The lost village of Bara-Hack, which is a Welsh word meaning "breaking of bread" is here. It is also known as the village of voices. All that is left of this ghost town are stone foundations. However, it is a true ghost town. There are stories that the visitor always hears voices or humming or children's laughter and the occasional sound of a wagon coming down the road. There are strange sightings in the area too, everything from orbs of light to children sitting in tree branches.

The Portland quarries are why Connecticut has the nickname of the Brownstone State. The Native American names were Wangunk or Wongunk, meaning "bend." There was a Native American village in the area. This town, located in Middlesex County, is the mining site for Beryl, a blue to green to gold color. Also, Garnet, Spodumene, and Tourmaline were found here in small amounts. One of the mines where all these gems and minerals were discovered is called the Strickland Mine or Gotta-Walden Mine. As stated earlier, Connecticut has the nickname the Brownstone State, due to the large amount and fine quality of the Brownstone quarries that were once in this area. About thirty-five different varieties of minerals have been mined from this place. It is the largest mined assortment of minerals found in the state. Some of the noted quarries here are: Andrews Quarry in Meshomasic State Forest, Pelton Quarry on Cox's Road, Brownstone Quarries lie between Route 15 and the River. Many dinosaur footprints were also

found in the north part of the quarry. Many are thought to still exist there and many can still be seen.

Jobs Pond is found on Route 14. It is a series of glacial kettles, the most perfectly formed in the state. These kettles were created when isolated blocks of ice melted, then were buried in glacial sand and gravel. Jobs Pond has no outlet and is fed by distant springs or rain. It can rise and fall very quickly, sometimes up to 15 feet.

REDDING/RIDGEFIELD/RIVERTON/ROCKY HILL

Redding Ridge leads to Poverty Hollow, and then goes south along the Aspetuck River to Aspetuck Falls, where the river falls into a deep gorge. On both sides of Route 58, just below Bethel, is the Putnam Memorial Camp Ground, called the Valley Forge of Connecticut. This is where General Israel Putnam were encamped during the winter of 1778-79. The property is a State Reservation. Revolutionary War artifacts have been found in the area.

There is a Phillips Cave here, but unlike many caves and places named Philip in Connecticut, it has nothing to do with King Philip or the War. It was named for a soldier who lived here, but was killed when caught stealing from town residents. Where those items were buried is not clear.

Ridgefield saw a lot of encampments throughout its history. After burning Danbury, General Tryon's troops marched through here on April 26, 1777. Rochambeau had his headquarters at the Samuel Keeler Tavern. This tavern was built in 1730, and General George Washington is said to have even stopped here. The French troops were encamped here in 1781.

Copper was discovered in Rocky Hill. There is also a Native American Woodland village site on the Connecticut River. It is called the Morgan site, and existed around 1170 A.D. This is on a flood plain and was not used in the winter or early Spring due to flooding. The village was found near a clay source, many ceramic pots were found, as well as pipe bowls and a stone shovel. This site is on Mill Brook, found upsteam of Goffes Brook. Relics can also be found in the fork between Beaver and Goffe Brooks.

This town is the site of dinosaur tracks and Dinosaur State Park. The Puritans considered that slate rock dinosaur tracks were created by the Devil. Edward McCarthy unearthed the sandstone prints in 1966 while working on the new State building. The footprints were created during the Jurassic period about 200 million years ago. The prints are called Eubrontes. It is almost impossible to know exactly what dinosaur made the print, but the creature was three-toed and was closely related to the Dilophosaurus.

In Riverton, gold has been found in the West Branch of the Farmington River.

ROXBURY/SALEM/SALISBURY

Brown Garnet was found at Roxbury Falls in Litchfield County. Roxbury Falls are really rapids where the river flows between high cliffs. Silver Hill, Ore Hill, or Mine Hill on the Shepaug River, meaning "rocky river," is where iron was discovered in 1724. The owners called the mine Silver Hill, hoping that it would one day yield silver. It did yield some silver, but its spathic iron ore was considered to be the richest and possibly the only one to be found in the United States. Ruins of the smelting furnace can be found here. A German con man came to the town to prove that silver existed in the mine, but was caught and run out of town. He left his luggage though, and several bars of 100 percent silver. The ore from this mine was superior in quality and used for making car wheels, musket barrels, anchors, and chains. There are also granite quarries around the region, and it is said that pearls have been found in the Shepaug River.

There is a ravine on the south side of the Shepaug River called Gamaliel's Den, with a history of housing counterfeiters. At Roxbury Station, a large boulder called Pulpit Rock is found. This is where John Eliot is said to have preached to the tribes.

Though this town named Salem does not have the dark history of Salem in Massachusetts, there is a strange story about the area. There is a house that can be found at the bottom of the 487-acre Gardner Lake. In 1899, owners decided to drag their home from one side to another across

the ice. The ice cracked under the heavy weight and became stuck. The house did not completely sink for years; it was visible to tourists for awhile. The house is under fifty feet of water, and in 1959, divers found a piano still in the home. Fisherman had been claiming for years that they could hear a piano play at night. Why would this occur? No one really knows, though the fisherman say it may be a mermaid.

The Native American name for Salisbury was Weeataug, which means "place of the dwelling." Twin Lakes was known to the Native Americans as Wahining, which meant "Laughing Water" and Washinee, which meant "Smiling Water." According to legend, two daughters of a Native American Chief who ruled the tribes between the Housatonic and the Hudson Rivers, lived here. Suitors traveled far to seek the maidens' love, but all were rejected. During a tribal war, a young warrior was captured and brought to the lake to be tortured. The sisters befriended him, loved him and tried to get him released. He refused and on the evening before his execution, the girls went out on the lake and were never seen again.

There is more to the story of these lakes. There are limestone caves in the region. Jack-in-the-Pulpit cave is very difficult to enter. There is a marble opening in this 612-foot cave. The visitor can get lost in here easily. This limestone cave was discovered during the Civil War era by a man looking for his dog, who went in, but never re-appeared. In the Cave of the Bashful Lady found in this area, the Glawackus story (see Glastonbury for more information about this creature) continues here. It is said that members of the Spelunkers Club of New England in 1939 entered the cave and killed this creature. Apparently the creature had sought refuge here. Examination of the beast revealed it was a cross between a bear and a lynx. The creature measured 3 feet and weighed ninety pounds. What happened after that is not reported.

This was a battlefield in 1676 during King Philip's War. It was fought in the northeast corner of town where the Native American trail from Stockbridge to Kent once traveled. The first bridge across the Housatonic River was built here in 1774, called Falls Bridge or Burrall's Bridge. There was also a Moravian mission here in 1750.

The ghost town of Mt. Riga is just north of the area and is 2,000 feet high. This town prospered from the iron industry. There was once a great iron furnace here, but now the cellar holes are covered with dirt and forest growth. This was America's most important furnace in its heyday. Swiss and Russian immigrants worked here before the American Revolution. They mined the brown hematite ore and turned it into iron. This town created iron for the Revolutionary War. Many of the cannons, sabers, and the anchors of the frigate *USS Constitution* were forged here.

In 1802, a mysterious stone bombardment occurred in town. The stone that fell from the sky was called lithobolia. On November 8, 1802, around 10- 11pm, and for four succeeding evenings, stone, wood, charcoal, and a strange mortar never seen before, fell on Mt. Riga. No explanation has ever been given. The name comes from people who lived here. The Swiss called the place Righi and the Russians called it Riga. In 1847, the furnace became silent and the workers walked away from the town, letting nature reclaim the mountain.

However, that is not the end of the story. Those old abandoned places were soon occupied by strange short people. No one knows where they came from, but they spoke a different language, thought to be Hessian deserters, and believed to have supernatural powers. They were called "Raggies." One day, these dwellers also walked away and left Mt. Riga. The place remains uninhabited today.

SAYBROOK/OLD SAYBROOK/SHARON/ SHERMAN/SHELTON

Saybrook was once a huge town. In 1632, this town encompassed 40,000 acres. Many towns were part of this area, including: Lyme, Chester, Westbrook, Esses, Old Saybrook, Old Lyme, Deep River, Clinton, and Killingworth.

In Saybrook in 1632, Govenor Van Twiller of New Netherland purchased this area and nailed a Dutch Coat of Arms to a tree. During the Narragansett and Mohegan War era, there was a Native American village at the place called Trading Cove. This was where the Mohegan tribe and the settlers in Saybrook traded goods. This village was often abandoned during the time it existed due to the constant attacks from the Narragansett Tribe.

Old Saybrook, also known as Sea Brooke, between 1635-1636, was one place that the Pequots kept attacking. The settlers built Gardiner's Fort on Saybrook Point for

The Connecticut River flows through many New England states. It was the lifeblood of Native American people living here.

protection against the tribe. It was not only the Pequots that kept attacking the fort. It was also constantly attacked by the Narragansetts. The Native American village here was called Pasbeshauke in 1614 when Adrian Block visited. This area was a battlefield often. The Dutch attacked here in the 1600s, the Pequot attacked here all through the 1600s, and the British attacked here in 1814.

In 1647, a second fort was built near the mouth of the Connecticut River in Old Saybrook. It was built of wood, like many structures at that time, and was destroyed by fire in the same year. A new fort was built at New Fort Hill. Ruins of this fort can be found. There is a rock here left by the glacier, but with strange carvings on it. No one knows who or why these markings were made.

Sharon was a Native American village found at the foot of Indian, or Poconnuck Mountain on Indian, or Wequadnach Pond in the northwestern part of town. There is also a Native American burial site on the Webotuck River. This was the old factory site of Hotchkiss and Sons, who made rifles, cannons, and bullets.

Platinum has been mined in Sherman. The town was named after Roger Sherman, a signer of the Declaration of Independence.

Shelton was called Quorum by the Native Americans. In 1673, there were two Native American forts here, one was west of the Housatonic River, the other on Fort Hill. There is also a Native American well here, thought by the tribes to be over 100 feet deep. It is part of the gorge on Housatonic River about a mile from the dam on the Shelton side.

SOUTH WINDSOR/SOUTHINGTON

South Windsor is the site of a Native American fort called Wapping. Along the Connecticut River between the Scantic and Podunk Rivers, is a Native American camping ground and burial site of the Podunk tribe. Many relics have been found here. This is considered one of the most notable campsites in the state. Northeast of the Native American village is an active sand dune on Route 15. It is one of the largest in the state.

Southington was also known as Pant-Horn. Why such an unusual name? Because a teamster used to drive cattle through the area. It was very difficult terrain and the cattle became exhausted. The teamster is claimed to have said, "My cattle were so wearied out, that they panted clear to the end of their horns."

Lake Compounce, first opened in 1846, is the first United States amusement park and the oldest running amusement park in the world. It was named after a seventeenth century Tunxis chief, who sold the land to the settlers. The Native American word, Compounce is thought to mean, "other side falls." The ghost of the former owner, Chief Compounce, is said to roam here. It is said that he committed suicide by drowning in the lake, the day before the land changed hands. Another story is that he was crossing the lake to have some fun in the tavern there, but he could not find a canoe. So, he used a copper kettle, but a large wave tipped the kettle and he drowned. However he died, since that time, every building on the land has experienced some sort of haunting. It should be noted, however, that other deaths have occurred here as well. A child died from injuries while in the lake; a worker was killed underneath a motor ride; and another was decapitated by a roller coaster. The Star Light Ball Room is where most of the hauntings have occurred. It is even said that the settler who bought the land from Coupounce is said to have fallen from a ladder and died.

Sometime in 1940, the body of a crashed trolley car was pushed into the lake in the park, where it is supposedly still there today. The crash occurred on February 21, 1921, when the car lost brakes coming down Southington Mountain. The train was almost cut in half by the maple trees it went through. The car was left on the site where it crashed. The old trolley bed is on the ridge where the King's Highway once was.

A cache of perfect jasper arrowheads were discovered in 1882. It was actually considered a very lonely place by the Native Americans. There was an old trail found here and relics from long ago eras were discovered including arrowheads and pottery. There are abandoned encampments and a burial ground. This was the ancient source of the Quinnipac

River and at one time white and gold fish lived here, they are now extinct.

There is a cave here called Papoose Cave on the western shore of the lake. It is considered a boulder cave, formed by a slab that tumbled off the hill, landing on rocks that hold it up. The ceiling has a reddish tint. It is also haunted by Chief Compounce. There is a lost mine for blue copper somewhere between Southington and New Britain. A silversmith shop was located in the Plantsville area.

STAFFORD/STAFFORD SPRINGS/SPRAGUE

Diamond Ledge is found in Stafford. The ledge is found on the bank of a ravine. It has a vein of quartz crystals, which gives the ledge the name. According to Native American legend, the sulphured mineral water in Stafford Springs had curative properties. It became a resort after the Revolutionary War. The town of Sprague was a ghost town for awhile. A flood destroyed the town in 1876 and a fire destroyed the town in 1887.

STAMFORD/STERLING/STRATFORD

Stamford was also known as Rippowams, meaning a river that forms a double harbor in Long Island Sound, or Tequams. The rip effect, called Rippowam, from the Connecticut River creates a double harbor in Long Island Sound. In 1644, the Dutch destroyed and slaughtered the Native American village here. A witch was executed here in 1651. Goody Bassett was hanged at Gallows Brook, the site is south of the railroad.

The Revolutionary War Stamford Fort remains can be found on the Westover Road. Due to the Rippowam effect, there have been many shipwrecks here. In 1915, the steamer, *Isabel,* was shipwrecked at Shippan Point. The gorge of Mianus River is in the northwest corner of the town. Bear Rock Cave, with a large glacial boulder standing right at the ledge, can be found here.

Pink Granite has been quarried in Sterling since the 1800s. Stratford is another site of a battle in the Pequot War. There was also a meteorite landing here in 1974.

STONINGTON/NORTH STONINGTON

The first settlement in Stonington was in Wequetequock Cove in the 1600s. The town was named in 1666, supposedly "in memory of the number of stones we had to pick out of the fields before we could plow." The first hurricane in this area was reported in diaries and came in August 1675. The Native American name was Pawcatuck and Mistack. The Narragansetts were here in 1649.

On April 9, 1676, during King Philip's War, Canonchet, who was the son of Miantonomo and sided with King Philip, was captured on the Pawcatuck River and sentenced to die. He is said to have said, "I like it well that I should die before my heart is softened and I say things unworthy of myself." He was then taken here and executed by the Native Americans, who sided with the English.

There is a pirate treasure on Abigal's Island in the mouth of the Mystic River near Lambert's Cove in Stonington Harbor. Again this treasure is said to be buried by Captain Kidd. The story is that in 1699, Captain John Hallam, a Stonington resident at Wamphasset Point, is said to have stored goods stolen by Kidd and harbored two of his crew members in Stonington.

The town was attacked by the British in the American Revolution. In August 1775, the British frigate, *Rose*, bombarded the town. The fort on this river in the War of 1812 was called Fort Rachel.

North Stonington was also known as Milltown in 1650. There is a 500-foot mound here called Lantern Hill where a pure quartz rock was mined. Why is this spot called Lantern Hill? Because the sun shining on the white quartz crystals created a "lantern" to guide sailors coming into port. The Pequot believed that the Devil was met when traveling on the road to Lantern Hill. The area was called Mashentuxet by the Native Americans.

Pearls have been found midway between Long Pond and the Lake of Isles in the headwaters of the Mystic River.

This entire Lantern Hill region is part of the Appalachian Orogeny. The Orogeny was a collision between Africa and North America that created the Appalachian Mountains and many of the precious metals, gems, and minerals that one may find in the earth today.

TERRYVILLE/THOMPSON/THOMASTON /TOLLAND/TORRINGTON

Jack's Cave, in Terryville was once inhabited by three Native Americans in the 1830s. The cave, named for leader, opens into a rock chamber. Thompson was the site of a Native American fort called Quinetusset. In Thomaston, copper was mined. In Tolland, the gem Garnet was discovered.

The Torrington settlers came from Windsor in 1732. It was a difficult journey, taking about two weeks.

There is a story that in pre-Revolutionary times near Wolcottville, there was a mine and the valuable items mined were sent by ship to New York, but the vessel wrecked before reaching its destination. The details of exactly what was mined are sparse, but to send the ore to New York, it must have been something of great value. It is believed to have been a high grade of copper. However, there is another suggestion of what may have been sent. In the early 1600s, two men, John Stanley and John Andrews explored Connecticut and returned to Massachusetts with black lead or graphite from a place called "Matetucke." Legends abound that there must be a huge block of pure lead somewhere near here. In 1657, William Lewis and Samuel Steele bought the mining rights to a mountain named "Matetucke" and the eight miles surrounding it from the Chiefs, Kepaquamp, Querimus, and Matanage. This location is still vague, but the area does include Lead Mine Brook in Harwinton.

The hills of Torrington are a continuation of the Hoosac Range of the Green Mountain of Vermont. It is believed that there must be rich minerals still to be found here. There is a tradition that the English found a copper mine around

Occident Hill, now known as Chestnut Hill, in the southwest section of town before the Revolution. Stealite, or soapstone, has also been found here. The person who originally discovered it was lost at sea before revealing the location. Green Quartz has been found, as well as Nickel, about half a mile west of the Torrington Green. Silver has been found north of Wolcottville at the foot of Horse Mountain. White granite is found in Plymouth. Garnet was mined north of Nickel Mine Brook. Gold has also been found in Nickel Mine Brook. Deep red feldspar has been discovered occurring in large boulders by Dr. E.D. Hudson toward the Still River directly west of the old Torrington Meeting House. Other minerals that have been found in the hills, include, Jasper, Chalcedony, Sardonyx, Amethyst, jet black Tourmaline, Epidote, and white, grass green, and rose Quartz.

The Fort, once located near Lyman Place and Klug Hill Road, on a southwest hillside, was built to discourage tribes from the north and west from attacking this area. It was actually the Iroquois and Mohawks from Schnectady and Albany, New York who were the most dangerous. Bonfires were made when the Mohawks came to Connecticut to warn other tribes and settlers that trouble was on the way. It was so difficult to travel, that distance communication between the tribes was basically by smoke signals and fire.

In 1747, the Torrington Pines was a swamp where the east and west branches of the Naugatuck River met. Here great pine grew to amazing height and width. The swamp is huge and is also known as Spruce Swamp and Great Mast Swamp. Tradition states that these pine were so straight that the trees could be used as masts for His Majesty's ships. However, it was not easy to move the pine logs down the Naugatuck River, so they were not used as masts, but instead for homes built in the area. In 1851, the Burrville dam gave way, killing one child. There were major floods all through the town's history. In 1948, severe floods washed away the North Elm Bridge. In 1955, forty campers disappeared during floods. On August 29, 1955, over eight feet of water covered the town and hundreds died.

TRUMBULL/UNCASVILLE

Yellow copper was mined in Trumbull. The first Topaz ever found in the United States was here. Native American relics were found in the region, mainly arrowheads, which may mean a battle was fought in the area.

In Uncasville, at the Mohegan Church, a "Devil's Footprint" is found. This is a large hoof print found in a stone by the church. The same large hoof print can be found on the Mashantucket Reservation. The town is named in honor of the famous Mohegan, Sachem Uncas.

VOLUNTOWN/WALLINGFORD

In 1700, Voluntown became a town and received its name because it was given to the men who volunteered to fight in King Philip's War. One of the first names of the town was Volunteer's Town. There is an area that has never been farmed and where no one lives called Hell Hollow. It is said that whimpering cries are heard here, and there is a legend that may support the story. A Narragansett warrior and family were fleeing from the British during King Philip's War. The soldiers caught up with the family and killed them all, except the wife. She escaped to this area, but could not control her grief at the death of her children and husband. Her cries gave her hiding place away to the soldiers, who found her and killed her. There are abandoned cellars in the area. People tried to live there, but the cries quickly drove them away.

Amethyst has been found at the Traprock Quarry in Wallingford. Copper has also been found here, however, the mines were usually flooded and unworkable. The copper mine was called the Golden Parlour Mine. In 1736, Timothy Royce located the mine near the red rocks in the north part of town. He was really looking for gold, hence the name of the mine, but found copper instead. He said that he did find gold, but that all the employees who were working in the mine took it.

WASHINGTON/WATERBURY

Marble quarries were worked in Washington around 1915. The Silver Street connector, located in Waterbury, is a 1940s name for a section of the expressway that is now I-84. Silversmith shops were once here. The Native American name for the area, Mattatuck, means "badly wooded region" or "place without trees." It was named Waterbury for its "abundant waters." It is believed that it was named badly wooded region due to the constant flooding. The town is known as the "Brass Capitol of the Nation." Nearly fifty percent of the brass for the country has come through Waterbury.

WATERTOWN/CLINTON

John Oldham reported that about 160 miles from the Massachusetts Bay, the Native Americans were mining black lead, probably somewhere in the Watertown, Connecticut area.

This is also the site of Leatherman's Cave located on the Mattituck Trail. This cave was inhabited by the Leatherman, said to be Jules Borglay, named because he dressed in sixty pounds of leather. He would endlessly walk a 365-mile loop between the Connecticut and Hudson Rivers. It is said that he walked over 360 times between 1858 and 1889, only resting in caves along the way. He died in the Saw Mill Woods Cave in Sing Sing, New York. It is said that he haunts all the caves where he stayed. This cave is found about two miles southeast of Black Rock State Park on Route 6. It is also said that he buried over $50,000 in one of his resting caves.

In March, 1779, the American Frigate, *Defense*, a pay ship for General Washington's army, sank four miles off Goshen Reef, now known as Bartlett's Reef, near Waterford, with over $200,000 in gold and silver.

Another of Captain Kidd's treasure may be buried under a large rock in Clinton on Coburn's Island, near Hammonasset Beach. A Leatherman cave can also be found here about one mile and a half west of the railroad station between Nod Road and the tracks.

WALLINGFORD/WESTPORT

Wallingford is the site of a Native American burial ground. Artifacts have been found here, which include Kaolin Pipes, arrow points, and hide scrapers.

Green Farms was an early colonial settlement that no longer exists found in Westport in Fairfield County. The Green Farms area was called Machamux, meaning "paradise," by the Native Americans. There is a stone here called Machamux Boulder where petroglyphs record the history of this place. During its heyday, there were about 200 buildings here. The settlement was totally destroyed on July 9, 1779, by the British, in a raiding force led by Governor William Tyron. He was on his way to burn and destroy Danbury, and landed at Compo Beach. There were two skirmishes here; one just south of Compo Road, there is a marker on the spot, and the other at the Hawthorne Inn, also can be found with a marker. Tar Rock on the Compo Road was used as a signal place during the Revolutionary War. They would have tar on the rock and light it on fire. The smoke and fire would be used as a signal.

WETHERSFIELD/GRISWOLDVILLE

Wethersfield was also known as Adventurers Land or The Great Plain. The settlers found this place to be open land with plenty of Indian corn planted.

Wethersfield Cove was created when the Connecticut River changed its course in the 1600s.

What the treasure seeker needs to remember is that the course of the Connecticut River, and really all rivers at one time or another, changed in the late seventeenth century due to what is called the Great Flood. The shifted river deepened in the east, and the great bend that was here with an island in the middle, called

Wright's Island or Manhannook, is now completely underwater. The area became Wethersfield Cove. Manhannook is a Native American word of this region, meaning "the island place" or "great laughing place" or "place of great merry making." Apparently, it was considered a fun place to be. The river was wide and deep enough on both sides of the island, so a ship could navigate on both sides. Where Warehouse Cove is now were once streets where people and warehouses existed. There is a street that is now basically under this Cove called Fort Street. Wethersfield Cove was created with this flooding, and The Great Meadow in the area was re-shaped. Wright's

There are roads that once traveled on dry land under the water in Wethersfield Cove.

Island was about one mile long and covered 200 acres. People lived there during early eras. The Connecticut River always changes course, but no one really knows why. To live on the river means that one must live with the changes.

The old Connecticut River path entered its northern border about fifty yards east of the present main road between Hartford and Wethersfield, flowed south until it reached the bank where the State Prison is, then curved sharply flowing south. It continued northeast, turning twice to flow south. The land formed by the turns is sometimes called the Gulf. The river resembled the letter "S" or a hook, which is where the Native American term, Hoccanum, what they named the meadow here, came from. Then it flowed south, passing Naubuck, South Glastonbury, and Rocky Hill. Another island disappeared during the great flood called Pennywise. This island was found in the river just over the Wethersfield line in Hartford. Other names for this island

Could there still be a valuable buried treasure somewhere in this vicinity?

were Long, Cole's or Standish's Island. It is now a long narrow knoll in Hartford's South Meadow. The Wethersfield and Glastonbury line was the course of the river and it forever changed during that Spring flood.

When the river flooded it created the Great Swamp, most of which has dried up now, but when the flood first occurred, it created a lake that ran north from the Hartford Hospital area to near the Churchville Road in Griswoldville in the south. Jordan Lane became a ferry site because a ferry was needed due to the deep water at this time. The first Connecticut-made ship, the *Tryall*, was launched from Wethersfield in 1649.

It should come as no surprise that Captains Kidd's treasure is said to be buried in the Cove or on a landing called Tyron's Landing. People who look for the treasure in this place claim to hear horrible noises, created by the ghost of a sailor killed by Kidd to guard his treasure. This is also a battleground.

In April 1637, there was a massacre here by the Pequots. This was a Pequot hunting grounds, and they did not want the settlers here. During the Wethersfield massacre, six men, three women, and two girls were killed. This event basically convinced the settlers that something needed to be done with the attacks by the Pequots. Essentially, this was the start of the Pequot War. The Podunk tribe lived here, but lived in constant fear of the Pequots. They could not help the settlers with this problem. It is considered a very haunted place.

It the site of Native American burial ground and was known as Pyquag, meaning "public games or dancing place." The tribe that lived here were known as the Mattabesick or Mattabesetts. That name means "Black Hill." The first Chief known to the settlers was called Sowheag or Sauheak, meaning "Hard-stone or cold-stone." He was the son of Manittowese or Mantowese, meaning "little God." The first Puritan settled here in 1635. Prior to 1640, there was a fort here, east of the State Prison, which is now an apartment house site on North Main Street.

During witch trials era, in 1648, Mary Johnson was hanged here after her confession of "familiarity with the Devil." And in 1651, John Carrington and his wife were charged with witchcraft and hanged. In 1670, Katherine Harrison was

Ducks at Wethersfield Cove still come. As haunted as this town is, nature still comes to visit.

convicted of practicing witchcraft and asked to leave town, which she wisely did.

It would be very possible to find rare space minerals here. There have been two documented meteorite landings, one in 1971, and the other in 1982. There is a boulder that marks the site of a ferry site that crossed the Connecticut River from 1674-1762 at the junction of Marsh, Ferry, and Broad Streets. Rare artifacts from long ago are also found here. Dinosaur prints have also been discovered in town.

In the vicinity of Mill Pond, there was a place called Warrineagues or Whilneagues or Wollaneag. It is said that something once terrified the people living here. It was described as a creature, shaped like a human, but had horns and was able to inhale and exhale fire. This monster was said to be able to walk on water. The story is a lesson to those who would not investigate a story further and go hunting an unknown creature. It was really the owner of the land, who dressed up to scare any trespassers.

Treasure Hunting Tip

Beware of monster stories. Always be sure to research as much as possible to get the entire story before beginning the search.

Griswoldville was once a part of Wethersfield. The town was also known as Two Stone. These are the west hills at the edge of Vexation Woods. Why the name Vexation Woods? The truth is that the settlers were terrified to go into the woods because of the constant Pequot raids in 1637. Why call the area Two Stone is more of a mystery. This is not a rocky place, but perhaps two stones were uncovered here? There is more on the woods story in the Newington section of this book. The path through this area was probably High Street. It was also the old stagecoach route to New Haven. This is the site of a factory and industry in Mill Woods Park, however most of the remains are on private property. That means NO TRESPASSING ALLOWED!

WILTON/WINDHAM

In April 1777, Wilton was invaded by the British, who were on their way to burn Danbury. The residents hid their silver and gold all around the area.

Windham experienced some bizarre and bad times in June 1754. First a bloody axe was found on the town green in April. It was believed that it was a warning from the Native Americans that they were planning to attack. Suddenly, one evening in 1754, ear-splitting noises were heard coming from the darkness and from everywhere. Everyone was sure that the attack was there. However, no Native Americans ever arrived. Scouts were sent out, and they found nothing. By dawn, the sounds had stopped, but the residents found thousands of dead frogs lying in the hardening mud of the dried up marshes. It was thought that the sound were the thousands of frogs battling for the few wet spots that were left in the marsh. The more interesting question is what caused the marsh to dry up in one night? No explanation was ever found.

Residents had to bury their treasures before leaving to escape a raid by the French in 1758. The town was burnt to the ground and many of the treasures are still buried.

The Native American name for the area was Queghommatch, which is a Nipmuck word, meaning "shaking or trembling mountain." There was also an ancient village on the Fenton River in this area called Nahwesetunk, which is a Mohegan word meaning "small fish stream."

There is a spot called Mukyaweesug, which in Mohegan means "little boys." This was the name for the leprechaun-like dwarfs who lived here. This name has been translated to whippoorwills. There is also a place called Muggs Holes, which in Mohegan, means "storage bins." This could be old dry spring basins that the Native Americans used for storing potatoes and turnips. Perhaps these were also the hiding places for the wee people? There are many Algonquin tribe stories about small people who lived in the woods. The Penobscot tribe in Maine have a similar story. Either it is a mass hallucination, or someone different lived in New England woods during the Native American era.

WINDSOR

Windsor was also known as Matianuck and Dorchester. It is thought that perhaps the Vikings sailed up the Connecticut River as far as Windsor in the year 1000, but no landing site was recorded. However, bronze Viking implements and utensils were found near the Enfield Rapids and in Plymouth Meadow on the Farmington River. Perhaps there was a battle between the Native Americans and the Vikings. When the settlers first arrived, these two places seemed taboo to the tribes. Why? Perhaps memories of a battle with strange people from over the dark sea remained. No one really knows.

The Native American village here was called Poquonnuc and the first Sachem was known was Sehat or Sheat. This was one of the Sachems that asked the English for help in a war against the Pequots in 1631. This request and the constant attacks by the Pequot on settlers who were living in Connecticut were the main reasons that the Massachusetts settlers declared war against the Pequot and eventually settled in Connecticut.

Forts were built here in 1637 along the present day Palisado Avenue. In 1699, there was an old stone fort located about one mile north of the Congregational Meeting house on the east side of the highway. There was a Native American trail between Plymouth Meadow in Windsor and Hartford. It was said to be the first public highway used by the settlers.

There is a body of water here called "Devil's Pond." In the Spring of 1758, it was reported by the inhabitants that unseen demons began to growl and scream from the pond in the middle of the night, waking everyone. However, it was not demons that were making the sound, it was mating bullfrogs. However, the name of the pond stayed the same. The modern reader must remember that this was a strange, completely unknown region to the settlers. They were terrified and had no support from where they came. Everything was scary and they had no where to turn to ask questions or find answers. They had to supply their own theories as to why events occurred.

This is the site of a battle in the Pequot War. It was also a trading post, but the settlers were driven out by Pequots. However, it may be that Native Americans were living in this area well before the Pequots came. In 1973, Native American artifacts were found from the 1600 B.C. era.

Yet another Captain Kidd buried treasure may be found on an island called Clarks or Clarkes Island. The story is that Kidd is thought to have traveled the Connecticut River and left two chests on his last trip to Boston while visiting his friend Whiskir Clarke or Whisking Clark. The chests were said to be left on Clarke Island and have never been found.

One of Kidd's ships, a sloop called, *San Antonio*, came ashore with a huge chest bulging with gold. Witnesses say that it was a dark, foggy night when the pirates buried the treasure here. The man who drew the short straw is said to have been killed to guard the site forever. A phantom pirate ship is said to roam the Connecticut River, believers claim that it is the *San Antonio*. It is also thought that Kidd will finally rest in peace, if his treasure is found.

WINSTED/WOODBURY/WOODSTOCK

Winsted abounds with tales and legends of witchcraft, owls that speak, and mysterious "wildmen" who roam the woods, attacking people. The wildmen are said to be about six feet tall, weighing about 200 pounds. They are covered with blond or brown hair. It sounds a lot like a "bigfoot" sighting and that is what many people say, but these creatures are different. These sightings have been documented since the 1800s. The difference between "bigfoot" sightings and "wildmen" sightings is that the hair is thin on the wildmen and thick on the bigfoot. The creature is said to make yelps and whooping sounds, and has been seen in dark locations, including the area's Lovers' Lane.

Castle Rock in Woodbury was the fort of the Native American Sachem, Pomperaug on the Pomperaug River. Squaw Rock is named for a cliff where a Native American either fell or jumped off to her death. It must be a female if the name is squaw.

Various minerals have been found here. A yellow copper mine was discovered here in 1731. Minerals that have been mined from town are, purple Quartz, Garnet, and Opal. A mine was opened in 1750, looking for silver.

Crystal Lake, a 250-acre Woodstock lake is named because of its sparkling water. Many Native American relics have been found and there is a burial site at the north part of the lake. Fort Hill, also known as Plaine Hill is located on Route 191

and built by settlers due to constant Native American attacks. There is another rock here called "Eliot Rock" where John Eliot preached to the tribes in the area in 1674. There were several villages of the "Praying Indians" in this area. One site may be near Hatchet Pond. Many Native American artifacts have been found here. It is also thought to be the site of a burial ground. Perhaps this was the site of the unknown Native American village, Mayanexit, meaning "where the road lies."

Conclusion

So we end this journey at where the road lies, though that place is really unknown. The haunted treasure hunt appears to end, but we know that is just an illusion. What must be evident to the reader by now, is that this entire region was heavily used by the Native Americans and settlers since the country first started.

The land in southern New England is no stranger to traumatic events and when these events occur, a place tends to become marked with the

The story begins with the setting sun and the early explorers searching for gold by following the sun. It would appear that they did indeed find a treasure in the land that they discovered.

occurrence. No wonder there are numerous enchanted, magical places here. The haunted treasure hunts can really start anywhere, and with the finding of one small object.

I know a story of a person who found a jar filled with gold in his home, but the objects were gold teeth. Now, the answer to the question of why were these items collected is a great place to start a treasure hunt.

Happy hunting! Yo Ho!

Bibliography

BOOKS

Abbott, Katharine M., *Old Paths & Legends of New England*, G.P. Putnam's & Sons, New York, NY, 1904

Allen, Joseph C., *Tales & Trails of Martha's Vineyard*, Little, Brown & Co., Boston, MA, 1938

Allis, Marguerite, *Connecticut River*, G.P. Putnam & Sons, New York, NY, 1939

Anderson, Virginia B., *Maritime Mystic*, Marine Historical Association, Mystic, CT, 1962

Andrews, Gregory E., & Ransom, David F., Structures & Styles – *Guided Tours of Hartford Architecture*, Connecticut Historical Society of Connecticut Architecture Foundation, Hartford, CT, 1988

Augusta, Anna & Chapin Charles, V., *A History of Rhode Island Ferries 1640-1923*, The Oxford Press, Providence, RI, 1925

Ayres, Harral, *Great Trail of New England*, Meador Publishing Co., Boston, MA 1940

Bailey, Bess and Merrill, *The Formative Years – Torrington*, Torrington Historical Society, Torrington, CT, 1975

Bailey, Bess and Merrill, *The Growth Years – Torrington*, Torrington Historical Society, Torrington, CT, 1976

Bailey, Bess and Merrill, *The Annealing Years – Torrington*, Torrington Historical Society, Torrington, CT, 1979

Baxter, Elizabeth Sweetser, *The Centennial History of Newington*, Finlay Brothers, Hartford, CT, 1971

Bearse, Ray, *Massachusetts – A Guide to the Pilgrim*, State American Guide Series, Houghton, Mifflin & Co., Boston, MA, 1971

Becker, Thomas W., *The Coin Makers*, Doubleday & Co., Garden City, NY, 1970

Bell, Michael, *The Face of Connecticut, People, Geology, and the Land, State Geological & Natural History Survey of Connecticut*, Hartford, CT, 1985

Billings, Marland P., *Cooperative Geologic Project – Bulletin No. 5 – Pegmatites of Massachusetts*, Massachusetts Department of Public Works, Boston, MA, 1941

Blackington, Alton H., *More Yankee Yarns*, Dodd, Mead & Co., New York, NY, 1956

Bragdon, Kathleen J., *Native People of Southern New England – 1500-1650*, University of Oklahoma Press, Norman, OK, 1996

Brenna, John T., *Ghosts of Newport*, Haunted America, Charleston, SC, 2007

Brewer, Ebenezer Cobbam, *Brewer's Dictionary of Phrase & Fable*, Harper & Brothers, New York, NY, 1953

Brown, Mary, L. T., *Gems for the Taking*, The Macmillan Co., New York, NY, 1981

Cahill, Robert Ellis, *Lighthouse Mysteries of the North Atlantic*, Old Saltbox, ME, 1998

Cahill, Robert Ellis, *Strange Superstitions*, Old Saltbox, ME, 1990

Cahill, Robert Ellis, *New England's Marvelous Monsters*, Chandler-Smith Publishing House, Peabody, MA, 1983

Cahill, Robert Ellis, *New England's Visitors from Outer Space*, Chandler-Smith Publishing House, Peabody, MA 1986

Campbell, Susan & Heald Bill, *Connecticut Curiosities*, Morris Book Publishing, Guilford, CT, 2007

Campisi, Jack, *The Mashpee Indians, Tribe on Trial*, Syracuse University Press, Syracuse, NY, 1991

Carlisle, Norman & Michelsohn, David, *The Complete Guide to Treasure Hunting*, Henry Regency Co., Chicago, IL, 1910

Caulkins, Francis Manwaring, *History of Norwich, Connecticut*, Pequot Press, Chester, CT, 1976

Chapin, Alonzo, Reverend D. D., *Glastonbury for Two Hundred Years*, St. Luke's Episcopal Church, South Glastonbury, CT, 1976

Choundas, George, *The Pirate Primer*, Writers Digest Books, Cincinnati, OH, 2007

Close, F. Perry, *History of Hartford Streets*, The Connecticut Historical Society, Hartford, CT, 1969

Clouette, Bruce & Roth, Matthew, *Bristol Connecticut: A Bicentennial History*, Phoenix Publishing, Canaan, NH, 1984

Connecticut Trolley Museum, *Hartford County Trolleys*, Arcadia Publishing, Charleston, SC, 2005

Cordingly, David, *Under the Black Flag*, Random House, New York, NY, 1995

Cordingly, David, *Illustrated History of Pirates – Terror on the High Seas from the Caribbean to the South China Sea*, Turner Publishing, Atlanta, GA, 1996

Crawford, Mary Caroline, *St. Botolph's Town*, LC Page & Co., Boston, MA, 1908

Crofut, Florence S. Marcy, *Guide of the History and Historic Sites of Connecticut, Volume 1 & 2*, Yale University Press, New Haven, CT, 1938

Curley, Robert Patrick, *Off the Beaten Path – Rhode Island*, Insiders Guide, Guilford, CT, 2005

Curtis, Florence Hollister, *Glastonbury*, Women's Club of Glastonbury, Glastonbury, CT, 1928

Curtis, George Munson, *Early Silver of Connecticut & Its Makers*, International Silver Co., Meriden, CT, 1913

D'Amoto, David A., *Warwick's 350-Year Heritage, A Pictorial History*, The Donning Company, Virginia Beach, VA, 1992

D'Amoto, David A., *Warwick, A City at the Crossroads*, Arcadia Publishing, Charleston, SC, 2001

DeForest, John W., *History of the Indians of Connecticut*, Archon Book, Hamden, CT, 1964

Dodges, The, *Puritan Path from Naumkeag to Piscatqua*, Newberry Press Inc., Newbury, MA, 1963

Drake, Samuel Adams, *Old Boston Taverns and Tavern Clubs*, W.A. Butterfield, Boston, MA, 1917

Eckert, Allan W., *Earth Treasures – Volume 1 – The Northeastern Quadrant*, Perennial Library Harper & Row, New York, NY, 1987

Faraum, Alexander, *Rhode Island Historical Tracts No. 2 Visits of the Northmen to Rhode Island*, Sidney S. Rider, Providence, RI, 1877

Faude, Wilson H. & Friedland, Joan W., *Connecticut Firsts*, The Globe Pequot Press, Chester, CT, 1978

Francis, Scott, *Monster Spotters*, HOW Books, Cincinnati, OH, 2007

Fox, Frances Wells, *Wethersfield and her Daughters from 1634-1934*, The Case, Lockwood & Brainard Co., Hartford, CT, 1934

Foye, Wilbur G. Ph.D., *The Geology of Eastern Connecticut*, State Geological & Natural History Survey Public Document No. 49, Bulletin No. 74, Hartford, CT, 1949

Fox, G. & Company, *Highways & Byways of Connecticut*, G. Fox & Co., Hartford, CT, 1947

Gelba, Peter, *Massachusetts Mineral & Fossil Localities*, Krueger Enterprises, Cambridge, MA, 1978

Gellerman, Bruce & Sherman, Erik, *Massachusetts Curiosities*, The Globe Pequot Press, Guilford, CT, 2005

Haley, John Williams, *The Old Stone Bank – History of Rhode Island, Vol. #III*, Providence Institution for Savings, Providence, RI, 1939

Harris, William W., *The Battle of Groton Heights*, New London, CT, 1870

Hauptman, Lawrence M., & Wherry, James D., *The Pequots in Southern New England*, University of Oklahoma Press, Norman, OK, 1990

Haynes, William, *The Stonington Chronology 1649-1949*, Pequot Press, Stonington, CT, 1949

Hicks, Judith A., *A Mystic River Anthology*, The Dutch Island Press, Wickford, RI, 1988

Horner, Dave, Shipwreck – *A Saga of Sea Tragedy & Sunken Treasure*, Sheridan House, Inc., Dobbs Ferry, NY, 1999

Horner, Dave, *The Treasure Galleons*, Dodd, Mead & Co., New York, NY, 1971

Houghby, Charles C., *Antiquities of the New England Indians*, Peabody Museum of American Archaeology & Ethnology, Harvard Press, Cambridge, MA 1935

Howard, Daniel, *A New History of Old Windsor, CT*, Journal Press, Windsor Locks, CT, 1935

Howard, Nora, *Stories of Wethersfield*, White Publishing, Wethersfield, CT, 1997

Hubbard, William Reverend, *The History of the Indian Wars in New England – Vol.#1 & 2*, Heritage Books Inc., Bowie, MD, 1990

Huden, John C., *Indian Place Names of New England*, Museum of the American Indian Heye Foundation, New York, NY, 1962

Jameson, W. C., *Buried Treasures of New England*, August House, Inc., 1998

Johnston, Alexander, *American Commonwealths – Connecticut*, The Cambridge Press, Cambridge, MA, 1888

Karr, Ronald Dale, *Indian New England – 1524-1674 – A Compendium of Eyewitness Accounts of Native American Life*, Branch Line Press, Pepperell, MA, 1999

Kittredge, Henry C., *Mooncussers of Cape Cod*, Houghton, Mifflin Co., Boston, MA, 1937

Krappe, Alexander Haggerty, *The Science of Folklore*, Barnes & Noble, Inc., New York, NY, 1929

Kunz, George Frederick, *Gems & Precious Stones of North America*, Dover Publishing, New York, NY, 1968

Lane, Kris, E., *Pillaging the Empire – Piracy in the Americas – 1500-1570*, M. E. Sharpe, Armonk, NY, 1998

Lithgow, R. A. Douglas, *Nantucket – A History*, G. P. Putnams & Sons, New York, NY, 1914

Litteermance, Edgar, *The Connecticut Guide – What to See and Where to Find it*, Emergency Relief Commission, Hartford, CT, 1935

Lodi, Edward, *Ghosts from King Philip's War*, Rock Village Publishing, Middleborough, MA, 2006

Magasich-Airola, Jorge & de Beer, Jean-Marc, *America Magica*, Anthem Press, London, England, 2006

Marx, Robert F., *Buried Treasure You Can Find*, Ram Publishing, Dallas, TX, 1999

Means, Philip Ainsworth, *Newport Tower*, Henry Holt & Co., New York, NY, 1942

McCormick, Samuel Jarvis, *General History of Connecticut*, Books for Libraries Press, Freeport, NY, 1877

McLoughlin, William G., *Rhode Island: A History*, W.W. Norton & Co., New York, NY, 1978

McNulty, Marjorie Grant, *Glastonbury from Settlement to Suburb*, The Historical Society of Glastonbury, Glastonbury, CT, 1995

Members of the Federal Writers Project of the Works Progress Administration for Massachusetts, *The Berkshire Hills*, Ovell, Sloan & Pearce, New York, NY, 1939

Metz, Rudolf, *Precious Stones & Other Crystals*, Viking Press, New York, NY, 1964

Mooney, Robert F. & Sigourney, Andre R., *The Nantucket Way – Untold Legends and Lore of Americas Most Intriguing Island*, Doubleday & Co., Garden City, NY, 1980

Mooney, Robert F., *Tales of Nantucket*, Wesco Publishing, Nantucket Island, MA, 1990

Monagan, Charles, *Connecticut Icons*, Insiders Guide, Guilford, CT, 2007

Morgan, Forrest, *Connecticut, as a Colony and as a State or One of the Original Thirteen – Vol. #1*, The Publishing Society of Connecticut, Hartford, CT, 1904

Munro, Wilfred Harold, *Tales of an Old Seaport*, Princeton University Press, Princeton, NJ, 1917

O'Brien, Robert, *The Encyclopedia of New England*, Facts on File Publications, New York, NY, 1985

O'Donnell, Liam, *Pirate Treasure Stolen Riches*, Capstone Press, Mankato, MN, 2007

Oppel, Frank, *Tales of Old New England*, Castle Division of Book Sales, Secaucus, NJ, 1986

Oppel, Frank, *Tales of The New England Coast*, Castle Division of Book Sales, Secaucus, NJ, 1985

Orcutt, Samuel, Reverend, *History of Torrington Connecticut*, J. Munsell Printer, Albany, NY, 1878

Packard, Winthrop, *Old Plymouth Trails*, Winthrop Packard Inc., Boston, MA, 1920

Page, Michael & Ingpen, Robert, *Encyclopedia of Things that Never Were*, Dragon's World, Middlesex, England, 1985

Palfrey, John Gorham, *History of New England*, Little, Brown & Co., Boston, MA, 1882

Peck, Epaphroditus, *History of Bristol Connecticut*, Unigraphic Inc., Evansville, IN, 1932

Penfield, Thomas, *Lost Treasure Tales*, Grosset & Dunlap, 1954

Perry, Clay, *New England's Buried Treasure – The American Cave Series*, Stephen Daye Press, New York, NY, 1946

Peters, Samuel, *General History of Connecticut*, London, England, 1781

Peterson, Edward, Rev., *History of Rhode Island*, John S. Taylor, New York, NY, 1853

Philips, David E., *Legendary Connecticut*, Spoonwood Press, Hartford, CT, 1984

Preston, Howard Willis, *Rhode Island Historic Background*, Remington Press, Providence, RI, 1936

Pohl, Frederick J., *Atlantic Crossings Before Columbus*, W. W. Norton & Co., New York, NY, 1961

Polly, Jane, *American Folklore & Legend*, Readers Digest Association, New York, NY, 1978

Pratt, Enoch, Rev., *Comprehensive History of Eastham, Wellfleet & Orleans*, W. S. Fisher, Yarmouth, MA, 1844

Prince, J. Pyneley & Speck, Frank G., *American Language Reprints – Vol. #9 – Mohegan-Pequot*, Evolution Publishing, Southampton, PA, 1904

Quinn, William P., *Shipwrecks Around New England*, Lower Cape Publishing, Co., Orleans, MA, 1979

Radford, E. and M.A., *The Encyclopedia of Superstitions*, Barnes & Noble Books, New York, NY, 1948

Reeseberg, Harry E., *Fell's Complete Guide to Buried Treasure, Land & Sea*, Frederick Fell, Inc., New York, NY, 1970

Revai, Cheri, *Haunted Connecticut – Ghost & Strange Phenomena of the Constitution State*, Stackpole Books, Mechanicsburg, PA, 2006

Reynard, Elizabeth, *The Narrow Land: Folk Chronicles of Old Cape Cod*, Houghton, Mifflin & Co., Boston, MA, 1934

Reynolds, Mike D., *Falling Stars – A Guide to Meteors & Meteorites*, Stackpole Books, Mechanicsburg, PA, 2001

Rich, Shebriah, *Truro – Cape Cod*, D. Lothrop & Co., Boston, MA, 1833

Roads, Samuel, Jr., *History & Traditions of Marblehead*, Houghton, Osgood & Co., Boston, MA, 1880

Roberts, George S., *Historic Towns of the Connecticut River Valley*, Robson & Adee, Schenectady, NY, 1906

Rogers, Barbara Radcliffe & Rogers, Stillman D., *The Rhode Island Guide*, Fulcrum Publishing, Golden, CO, 1998

Rogers, Barbara Radcliffe & Rogers, Stillman D., *Off the Beaten Path – Massachusetts*, Globe Pequot Press, Guilford, CT, 1992

Russell, Howard S., *Indian New England Before the Mayflower*, University Press of New England, Havover, NH, 1980

Schairer, John Frank, Ph.D., *The Minerals of Connecticut*, State Of Connecticut, Hartford, CT, 1931

Sellers, Helen Earle, *Connecticut town Origins – Their Names, Boundaries, Early Histories & First Families*, The Pequot Press, Chester, CT, 1942

Sherman, Steve, *Country Roads of Connecticut & Rhode Island*, Country Roads Press, Castine, ME, 1994

Sheedy, Jack & Coogan, Jim, *Cape Cod Companion*, Harvest Home Books, Hyannis, MA, 1999

Simmons, William, S., *Spirit of the New England Tribes – Indian History & Folklore – 1620 – 1984*, University Press of New England, Hanover, NH, 1986

Skinner, Charles M., *Myths & Legends of our own Land Vol. #1*, J.B. Lippincott & Co., Philadelphia, PA, 1896

Smitten, Susan, *Ghost Stories of New England*, Ghost House Books, Edmonton, AB, Canada, 2003

Snow, Edward Rowe, *Mysterious Tales of the New England Coast*, Dodd, Mead & Co., New York, NY, 1962

Snow, Edward Rowe, *Astounding Tales of the Sea*, Dodd, Mead & Co., New York, NY, 1965

Snow, Edward Rowe, *Tales of Sea & Shore*, Dodd, Mead & Co., New York, NY, 1934

Snow, Edward Rowe, *Pirates, Shipwrecks & Historic Chronicles*, Dodd, Mead & Co., New York, NY, 1981

Snow, Edward Rowe, *Sea Disasters & Inland Catastrophes*, Dodd, Mead & Co., New York, NY, 1980

Snow, Edward Rowe, *The Islands of Boston Harbor*, Dodd, Mead & Co., New York, NY, 1971

Somerset Publishers, *Encyclopedia of Connecticut, A volume of Encyclopedia of United States*, Somerset Publishers Inc., New York, NY, 1994

Steinbery, Sheila & McGuigan, Cathleen, *Rhode Island: A Historical Guide*, Rhode Island Bicentennial Foundation, Providence, RI, 1976

Stiles, Henry R., A.M.MD., *The History of Ancient Wethersfield – Vol. #1*, The Grafton Press, New York, NY., 1904

Strahler, Arthur N., *A Geologist's View of Cape Cod*, The American Museum of Natural History, Garden City, NY, 1966

Storm, Rory, *Monster Hunt*, Metro Books, New York, NY, 2008

Swift, Charles F., *History of Old Yarmouth, 1794-1876*, Historical Society of Old Yarmouth, Yarmouthport, MA, 1975

Taft, Lewis A., *Profile of Old New England – Yankee Legends, Tales, &* *Folklore*, Dodd, Mead & Co., New York, NY, 1965

Thompson, Courtney, *Massachusetts Lighthouses: A Pictorial Guide*, Cap Nap Publications, Mount Desert, ME, 1998

Thomson, William O., *Coastal Ghosts & Lighthouse Lore*, "Scapes Me, Kennebunk, ME, 2001

Todd, Charles Burr, *In Olde Connecticut*, The Grafton Press, New York, NY, 1906

Tomlinson, R.G., *Witchcraft Trials of Connecticut*, The Bond Press, Hartford, CT, 1978

Tryon, Lillian Hart, *The Story of New Britain*, Esther Stanley Chapter D. A. R. Finlay Bros. Inc., Hartford, CT, 1925

Vaughan, Alden, T., *New England Frontier – Puritans & Indians – 1620-1675*, University of Oklahoma Press, Norman, OK, 1965

Verrill, A. Hyatt, *Heart of Old New England*, Dodd, Mead, & Co., New York, NY, 1936

Vuilleumier, Marion, *From the Vikings to Vonnegut: A Cape Cod Reader*, B & W Hutchinson, Co., Orleans, MA, 1983

White, Glenn E., *Folk Tales of Connecticut*, The Journal Press, Meriden, CT, 1977

Wieder, Lois M., *The Wethersfield Story*, The Pequot Press, Stonington, CT, 1966

Wiencek, Henry, *The Smithsonian Guide to Historic America – Southern New England*, Steward, Tabori & Chang, New York, NY, 1989

Wilson, J. Howard, A.M. Ph.D, *The Glacial History of Nantucket & Cape Cod*, The Columbia University Press, New York, NY, 1906

Willoughby, Charles C., *Antiquities of the New England Indians*, Peabody Museum of American Archaeology & Ethnology, Cambridge, MA, 1935

Workers of the Federal Writer's Project of the Works Progress Administration for the State of Connecticut, *Connecticut: A Guide to its Roads, Lore, & People*, Houghton, Mifflin & Co., Boston, MA, 1938

Wright, George E., *Crossing the Connecticut*, The Smith-Linsley Co., Hartford, CT, 1908

Zwicker, Roxie J., *Haunted Pubs of New England*, Haunted America, Charleston, SC, 2007

NEWSPAPER ARTICLES

Hartford Courant, 1/1/89 – Bill Ryan – column – "Connecticut Crossroads"

New York Times, 10/8/1895 – "Legend in the New London area"

New York Times, 7/8/86, Amy Wallace, "Gold Lures Geologists to Connecticut"

WEBSITES

www.astronomypictureoftheday.com
www.aquaquest.com
www.beavertaillight.org
www.bio.umass.edu
www.cumberlandlibrary.com
www.freepages.history.rootsweb.com
www.flw.org
www.geol.binghamton.edu
www.georgehail.org
www.gungywamp.com
www.lighthouses.cc
www.meteorites.com
www.middletownri.com
www.narraganset-tribe.org
www.newenglandsite.com
www.newportchamber.com
www.novaspace.com
www.old-lymeconservtrust.org
www.overnspark.com
www.patriciahughes.net
www.piratemuseum.com
www.quarriesandbeyond.org
http://query.nytimes.com
www.shgresources.com/gems/found
www.skyweb.net
www.solarviews.com
http://theshadowlands.net
www.tiverton.org
www.treasure-adventure.com

REPRINTS

Bristol Connecticut – In Olden Times, City Printing Co., Hartford, CT 1907

Bristol's Mines & Quarries, George R. Perry, from the files of Bristol, Connecticut Public Library

Copper Mining in Connecticut, E. M. Hulbert, Taken from the Connecticut Quarterly, Vol. #III – January – December, 1897, from the files of Bristol, Connecticut Public Library

Guide to Historically Famous Lighthouses in the United States, United States Coastguard, U.S. Government Printing Office, Washington, D.C., 1939

Memoirs of the Connecticut Academy of Arts & Sciences, Vol. 1 No. 1, 1810 – Weston Meteorite

War Minerals Report – WWII – 1943, United States Department of the Interior Bureau of Mines, Report of the Bureau of Mines to Hon. Harold L. Ickes, Secretary of the Interior, From files found at the Bristol, Connecticut Public Library

Warwick Rhode Island Statewide Historical Preservation Report – K-W-1, Rhode Island Historical Society

Index

RHODE ISLAND

Barrington, 32
Block Island, 8, 26, 27, 29
Bristol, 22, 30, 32
Central Falls, 32, 35
Charlestown, 33
Coventry, 33, 35
Coweset, 20
Cumberland, 34
East Greenwich, 35, 36
Exeter, 35
Greene, 35
Jamestown, 36, 37
Kingstown or Kingston, 44
Lincoln, 34
Little Compton, 19
Middletown,24, 38
Mount Hope, 30, 31, 45, 53, 125

Newport, 14, 22, 24, 37, 38, 39, 40, 41, 42, 43, 54
North Kingston, 44, 46
Pawtucket, 46
Portsmouth, 24, 46, 47
Potterville, 50
Providence, 21, 47, 48, 50
Scituate, 50
Smithfield, 52
South Kingston, 44
Tiverton, 51
Wakefield, 52
Warwick, 53, 54, 55
Warren, 22, 30, 52, 53
Watch Hill, 26, 29
West Gloucester, 25
Westerly, 21, 52, 53, 144
Wickford, 53, 55

MASSACHUSETTS

Adams, 65
Alford, 129
Andover, 56
Arlington, 67
Asuchnet, 67
Becket, 106
Bedford, 67, 68
Berkley, 69
Bernardston, 67
Beverly, 68, 95
Blue Hills, 69
Bolton, 79
Boston, 7, 57, 61, 63, 68, 69, 70, 71, 75, 76, 77, 78, 79, 89, 117, 175, 234
Bourne, 82

Bridgewater, 67
Brockton, 79
Brookline, 70
Byfield, 80
Cambridge, 69
Cape Ann, 94, 95, 97
Cape Cod, 80, 81, 82, 83, 84, 87, 96, 113
Carlisle, 88
Chatham, 84
Chelsea, 88
Cheshire, 88
Chester, 79
Chesterfield, 79
Cohasset, 89
Conway, 63

Concord, 63
Dalton, 88
Dartmouth, 91
Deerfield, 91, 100
Dighton, 49, 91, 92
Dover, 79
Dracut, 92, 93
Easton, 92, 93
Easthampton, 123
Essex, 61
Fall River, 19, 92, 93
Fitchburg, 61, 64, 79
Florida, 93
Framingham, 61
Freetown, 92
Gloucester, 94, 96, 97, 98
Goshen, 61, 63
Gosnold, 94
Grafton, 61, 92
Granville, 92
Great Barrington, 98
Greenfield, 122
Groton, 100
Hadley, 100
Harvard, 106
Hatfield, 100
Hingham, 90, 101
Holliston, 101
Holyoke, 101
Hopkinton, 61
Hubbardston,101
Huntington, 101
Hyannis, 87
Ipswich, 74, 102. 103
Lakeville, 101
Lancaster, 101
Lanesborough, 103
Lee, 105, 106
Lenox, 130
Leominster, 106
Leyden, 106
Littleton, 106
Lowell, 61
Ludlow, 109

Lynn, 14, 106, 108
Marblehead, 108
Marlborough, 109
Marshfield, 109
Martha's Vineyard, 9, 57, 110, 111, 113
Mashpee, 59, 86
Maynard, 116
Medfield, 115
Mendon, 56, 115
Methuen, 115
Middleborough, 116
Mills, 116
Montaque, 116
Mount Washington, 117, 118
Nahant, 102
Nantucket Island, 9, 57, 96, 113, 118, 158
Natick, 122
New Ashford, 121
New Bedford, 121
New Marlborough, 121
New Salem, 122
Newton, 70, 122
Newburyport, 61, 97, 122, 173
Northfield, 122
North Adams, 65
North Reading, 64
North Chelmsford, 131
Northhampton, 61, 123
Norton, 123
Orleans, 84, 87
Peabody, 123
Pelham, 63
Pembroke, 123
Pittsfield,103, 104
Plymouth, 32, 45, 123, 124
Provincetown, 83, 84
Quincy, 123
Raynham, 124, 125, 152
Rehoboth, 124
Revere, 126
Risingdale, 63
Rockland, 126

Rockport, 94, 96, 97, 98
Royalston, 126
Rutland, 128
Sandwich, 87, 127
Salem, 14, 35, 40, 126, 127
Salisbury, 74, 102
Scituate, 127
Sheffield, 128
Shelburne, 63
Shirley, 127
Shutesbury, 56
Somerset, 62
South Deerfield, 91
South Egremont, 127
Southfield, 127
South Hadley, 100
South Mashpee, 129, 130
Springfield, 65, 128
Stockbridge, 99, 129, 130
Stow, 124
Sudbury, 61
Sunderland, 100, 124
Swansea, 124
Taunton, 125, 129, 130
Tiverton, 40

Turner Falls, 116, 130, 131
Tyngsborough, 131
Upton, 132
Uxbridge, 132
Wales, 132
Ware, 132, 133
Watertown, 61
Webster, 56
Wellfleet, 85
West Andover, 56
West Chesterfield, 132, 133
West Lanesborough, 103
West Stockbridge, 129
West Tisbury, 133
Westborough, 133
Westhampton, 65
Westfield, 134
Westford, 60
Westwood, 134
Williamtown, 66
Wilmington, 134
Winthrop, 74, 75, 134
Woburn, 61
Worcester, 57, 134
Yarmouthport, 83

CONNECTICUT

Avon, 138, 145
Barkhamsted Lighthouse, 200
Beacon Falls, 145
Berlin, 138, 142, 146
Bloomfield, 142
Bolton, 146
Box Mountain, 146
Branford, 146, 147
Bridgeport, 148
Bristol, 136, 137, 142, 148, 149, 150
Brookfield, 152
Brooklyn, 142
Canaan, 137, 145

Canton, 152
Cheshire, 136, 137, 153
Clinton, 184, 226
Cornwall Bridge, 153
Cromwell, 154
Cos Cob, 154
Danbury, 137, 154
Danielson, 156
Darien, 156
Derby, 137, 156, 157
Dudleytown, 153
East Granby, 136, 168, 169
East Haddam, 171, 174
East Hampton, 137, 157, 175,

176
East Hartford, 119, 138, 139,
140, 142, 157, 158, 165, 209
East Haven, 157, 159
East Litchfield, 137
East Lyme, 212
East Windsor, 139, 142, 209
Enfield, 133, 157, 159
Essex, 160
Fairfield, 162
Farmington, 138, 163
Franklin, 163, 164
Gaylordsville, 136
Glastonbury, 137, 142, 164,
166
Granby, 137, 142, 164, 169
Greenwich, 170
Griswoldville, 227, 230, 232
Groton, 49, 170, 171
Guilford, 140, 171
Haddam, 137, 171, 172, 175
Haddam Neck, 171, 173
Hadlyme, 160
Hampton, 175
Hamden, 174, 175, 176, 177
Hartford, 40, 135, 136, 142,
162, 177, 180, 181, 189, 229,
230
Harwinton, 181
Higganum, 181
Hebron, 181, 182
Kent, 136, 137, 182, 183
Killingly, 182, 183
Killingworth, 184
Ledyard, 172, 184, 185
Litchfield, 187
Lyme, 212
Madison, 140, 187
Manchester, 142, 188
Marlborough, 188
Meriden, 137, 138, 189
Middletown, 137, 166, 173,
189, 190, 191
Milford, 140, 192, 193, 194,

195
Monroe, 137, 195
Montville, 195
Moodus, 171, 173
Morris, 195
Mystic, 139, 197, 199
New Britain, 142, 189, 191,
192, 221
New Fairfield, 200, 201
New Hartford, 200, 201
New Haven, 16, 136, 140, 201,
202
New London, 49, 139, 141,
190, 203, 204
New Milford, 137, 205
New Preston, 205, 206
Newfield, 205, 206
Newington, 205, 207
Newton, 208
Newtown, 208
Niantic, 208
North Branford, 146
North Cromwell, 154
North Guilford, 138
North Stonington, 137, 222
Norwich, 139, 189, 208
Norwalk, 208, 211
Nott Island, 160, 161
Old Lyme, 212
Old Saybrook, 136, 217, 219
Orange, 137, 213
Plainville, 142, 213
Pomfret, 213
Portland, 137, 213
Redding, 214
Ridgefield, 137, 213
Riverton, 214, 215
Rocky Hill, 138, 142, 168, 214,
229
Roxbury, 137, 215
Salem, 215
Salisbury, 137, 168, 215, 216
Saybrook, 217
Seldon Island, 160, 161

Sharon, 137, 217
Sherman, 217, 219
Shelton, 217, 219
Simsbury, 137, 145, 168
South Glastonbury, 164, 166,
167, 229
South Windsor, 219
Somers, 142
Southington, 142, 219, 220,
221
Sprague, 221
Stafford, 221
Stafford Springs, 221
Stamford, 221
Sterling, 221, 222
Stratford, 221, 222
Stonington, 21, 28, 141, 222
Suffield, 91, 142
Terryville, 223
Thompson, 142, 223
Thomaston, 223

Tolland, 138, 223
Torrington, 223, 224
Trumbull, 137, 225
Uncasville, 40, 225
Union, 138
Voluntown, 225
Wallingford, 225, 227
Washington, 226
Waterbury, 226
Watertown, 71, 227
Westport, 227
Wethersfield, 138, 165, 207,
227, 229, 230, 232
Wilimantic, 137, 174
Wilton, 232
Windham, 232
Windsor, 135, 142, 233
Windsor Locks, 142
Winsted, 235
Woodbury, 137, 235
Woodstock, 61, 235